FORGOTTEN FILMS TO REMEMBER

FORGOTTEN FILMS TO REMEMBER

And a Brief History of Fifty Years of the American Talking Picture

by

John Springer

The Citadel Press   Secaucus, N.J.

Published by Citadel Press
A division of Lyle Stuart Inc.
120 Enterprise Ave., Secaucus, N.J. 07094
In Canada: General Publishing Co. Limited
Don Mills, Ontario
Manufactured in the United States of America by
Halliday Lithograph, West Hanover, Mass.

Designed by Lester Glassner

Library of Congress Cataloging in Publication Data
Springer, John Shipman, [date]
    Forgotten films to remember.

    1.   Moving-pictures—United States—Catalogs.
2.   Moving-pictures—Plots, themes, etc.
I.   Title.
PN1998.S697   791.43′0973   80-11048
ISBN 0-8065-0797-7   2   3   4   5   6

Introduction

You won't find *Citizen Kane* in this book, or *Gone With the Wind* or even *Jaws*—1 or 2.

There is a body of film that doesn't show up on "Best Movies of All Time" lists, is almost never theatrically revived and would be seen on television, if at all, only in the tiny hours of the morning. Some, notable in their day, have completely disappeared. Even Danny Selznick, who owns prints of almost all pictures produced by his father, David O., could not turn up a print of *The Animal Kingdom,* one of the most important films in her career, for a Myrna Loy retrospective. (*The Animal Kingdom* may have been destroyed when it was sold to Warners to protect its ridiculously inferior remake.) Lubitsch's *The Smiling Lieutenant* seems to exist only in one print at the Museum of Modern Art—a print with Danish subtitles turned up in a European search.

So some important pictures are forgotten because they apparently have been lost to posterity. But most of them have vanished in the mists of memory because they never won film classic or box-office bonanza reputations. Yet each of these had its value in its own day—an extraordinary performance perhaps, an interesting piece of direction, a fresh story line. Or maybe it was just a good movie, something that worked for what it was.

These are the movies that don't turn up in histories but do occasionally surface in the memories of buffs who saw them—forgotten films, yes, but movies worth a special niche of their own.

(Only talking films in the English language are covered.)

Acknowledgments

Almost all of the pictures in this book are from The John Springer Collection of the Bettmann Archive. Mary Corliss of the Museum of Modern Art, New York, supplied eleven stills that I preferred to those from Springer/ Bettmann. Thanks also to Douglas Whitney for replacing, from his own collection, a *Child of Manhattan* still that had disappeared from Bettmann. And, of course, thanks to all the studios and magazines—you know who you are—who contributed to the Springer Collection in the first place.

J.S.

Chapter One

The Movie Years of 1928–29

October 6, 1927. Jolson sings—and the screen begins to talk, babbling a bit at first but quickly growing more coherent.

The first all-talking picture, *Lights of New York,* is released in 1928, and by the end of 1929 silent pictures are virtually extinct.

The star situation changes. John Gilbert speaks for the first time in a highly romantic moment—and audiences hoot. Other silent stars, such as Shearer, Barthelmess, Novarro, Colman, and Bancroft, pass their talkie test successfully while Harold Lloyd, Clara Bow, Colleen Moore, and others get by, too. Some waning names, like Bessie Love, Warner Baxter, Gloria Swanson, Bebe Daniels, get a new lease on life with well-received talkie appearances.

Nancy Carroll, Janet Gaynor, Buddy Rogers, and Gary Cooper head the younger set who talk and score. But some of the pioneer talkie players of 1928 have just about faded from the screen by the end of 1929—May McAvoy, Betty Bronson, and the Costello sisters among them. Of established stars, only Garbo, Chaplin, Jannings, and Chaney continue to remain aloof from the new medium.

The star of *Steamboat Willie* doesn't get as much publicity as most newcomers of the period. But Mickey Mouse—and all the denizens of Disneyland to come—will prove more durable than almost any other movie name.

The Broadway invasion begins as players with a solid reputation are lured to Hollywood, along with others—bit players from second-rate stock companies, broken-down vaudevillians, anyone who has ever stepped on a platform. Some of the invaders—Harding, Chatterton, March, Colbert, Arliss and more—are to stay. Others, like Fanny Brice, Beatrice Lillie, Eddie Dowling, Jack Benny, Paul Muni, and Irene Bordoni, decide Hollywood is not for them—at least not for the moment—and scuttle back to Broadway.

The Broadway influence shows in movies produced almost as photographed stage plays without regard for cinema technique. But with Rouben Mamoulian *(Applause)* and King Vidor *(Hallelujah)* leading the way, other directors learn to use the movie camera once again.

Among the movies of 1929 that attract attention, besides those by Mamoulian and Vidor, are *Broadway Melody, In Old Arizona,* George Arliss's *Disraeli,* Jeanne Eagels' *The Letter,* Ruth Chatterton's *Madame X,* the Lubitsch–Chevalier *Love Parade,* those all-star revues, *The Show of Shows* and *The Hollywood Revue, Alibi* and, of course, *The Cocoanuts,* which introduced the Marx brothers.

There are others which may have faded in the memory but deserve attention again—the forgotten films to remember of 1929.

Anny Ondra, Charles Paton, and Sara Allgood are visited by Donald Calthrop in Alfred Hitchcock's *Blackmail*.

Detective Philo Vance (William Powell) investigates the murder of a showgirl (Louise Brooks) in *The Canary Murder Case*.

Believe it or not, it's Claudette Colbert B.B. (Before Bangs—she grew more youthful with the years) and Walter Huston pre-*Dodsworth* in *The Lady Lies*.

Youthful Mary Brian meets the older generation (Kay Francis, sympathetic Fredric March) in *The Marriage Playground*.

Forgotten Films of 1929

Blackmail. Alfred Hitchcock's first talking picture (and the first all-talker made in England) is primarily interesting today as an example of the master's early work. The cast of actors unfamiliar to American audiences included several (Sara Allgood, Cyril Ritchard, and Donald Calthrop) who would become more widely known. Based on a play by Charles Bennett.

Louise Brooks in feathers was enough to make *The Canary Murder Case* memorable even though you didn't hear her own throbby voice. (She has confessed that she refused to return to dub her dialogue because she was having too much fun as an international playgirl. Thus she alienated Hollywood bigwigs and scuttled her own career in the process. Margaret Livingston spoke her lines.) It was William Powell's first inning as S. S. Van Dine's suave detective, Philo Vance. Directed by Mal St. Clair. Script by Florence Ryerson and Alfred S. LeVino.

Broadway Melody was the first but, for early movie backstage musicals, let's give the nod to *The Dance of Life.* Based on Broadway's hit, *Burlesque,* its yarn about the small-time team who split up—he goes into the Follies and gets a swelled head while she waits loyally in the sticks—was already shopworn. But Nancy Carroll was so warm and tender and Hal Skelly, repeating his stage Skid role, so convincing that the movie worked as well as the play. Carroll, incidentally, replaced the stage Bonnie, who had no "name." She was Barbara Stanwyck. Directed by John Cromwell and A. Edward Sutherland. Benjamin Glazer adapted the George Manker Watters/Arthur Hopkins play.

It was no surprise that John Barrymore had no traumas about turning to talking pictures. His first, *General Crack,* was a floridly romantic adventure with a peppery youngster, Armida, standing out as his faithless gypsy bride. Directed by Alan Crosland. J. Grubb Alexander, Walter Anthony screenplay.

The Lady Lies dealt intelligently with a mature love story (Walter Huston and Claudette Colbert), complicated by his children, especially an unlikable son, well played by a likable Tom Brown. Hobart Henley directed John Meehan's script.

The Marriage Playground based on Edith Wharton's novel, *The Children,* treated the problems of a number of children of frequently divorced parents. Philippe de Lacey, Anita Louise, and Little Mitzi (later known as Mitzi Green) were among the younger cast members, along with a teenage sister, Mary Brian. Fredric March

"You wouldn't kid, me, would you, mister?" "I would
if I could, sister. I would if I could." Hal Skelly and
Nancy Carroll in burlesque patter in *The Dance of Life*.

John Barrymore, in his first talkie, with his gypsy bride, Armida, in *General Crack*.

Ann Harding and Fredric March before they are *Paris Bound* for divorce.

George Bancroft in custody, Richard Arlen on our side of the bars in *Thunderbolt*.

played the link between them and such frivolous old-sters as Lilyan Tashman and Kay Francis. Lothar Mendes directed. Screenplay by J. Walter Ruben.

Ann Harding was born to play Philip Barry heroines with their shining integrity and rueful wit. *Paris Bound* was her first and Fredric March was a good romantic match for her. E.H. Griffith directed Horace Jackson's script.

Before she became the movies' most syrupy sweet old thing, Beryl Mercer had a couple of roles in which she was much more fun. In *Three Live Ghosts,* she was greedy Mrs. Gubbins, the Cockney mum, whose "re-ported dead in action" soldier son (Charles McNaugh-ton) turns up alive as she is spending his insurance money. With Robert Montgomery, Joan Bennett, Claud Allister, Hilda Vaughn. Thornton Freeland directed the Max Marcin script.

In his pre-Dietrich era, Josef von Sternberg directed a bellowing, roistering George Bancroft in a prison melo-drama, *Thunderbolt.* Jules Furthman and Herman J. Mankiewicz wrote the screenplay. Fay Wray and Richard Arlen provided young love.

Frank Lloyd, usually known for more epic things, made a surprisingly touching little film in *Young Nowheres.* Richard Barthelmess did his Tol'able David part. He played an elevator boy and Marian Nixon a hotel cham-bermaid in a backstairs romance. They kept you caring about the characters even though they were almost too naive even for that day. I. A. R. Wylie's story was adapted by Bradley King Wray.

Other Fogotten 1929 Films Worthy of Note

Broadway lost a lot of its punch in transit to the screen. . . . Ronald Colman made a smooth transition to talkies in *Bulldog Drummond.* . . . Nancy Carroll and Buddy Rogers teamed happily in *Close Harmony* and *Illusion.* Nancy, without Buddy but with Helen Kane, Jack Oakie, and Stuart Erwin, sparkled in a football musical, *Sweetie.* . . . Walter Huston was a believable news-paperman in *Gentlemen of the Press.* . . . Ethel Waters's singing of "Am I Blue?" was the high spot of *On With the Show* and the DeSylva, Brown, and Henderson score (not the Gaynor/Farrell singing of it) of *Sunny Side Up.* . . . Jean Arthur gave hints she was more than just an ingenue as the nasty sister of Clara Bow in *Saturday Night Kid* and the killer in *The Greene Mur-*

Charles Mac-Naughton and Beryl Mercer at left, Claude Allister at right, Robert Montgomery and Joan Bennett between unidentified hands up and moustached gents, along with other players (which is what you write when you haven't a clue to the identity of the "other players" in *Three Live Ghosts.*

Richard Barthelmess and Marian Nixon tentatively explore romance in *Young Nowheres.*

Two lesser "forgotten films" of 1929 — (above) Ronald Colman as *Bulldog Drummond* is menaced by Montagu Love, Tetsu Komai, Lawrence Grant, Lilyan Tashman; (left) Thomas E. Jackson repeated his stage role in the filmization of *Broadway* with Evelyn Brent.

der Case. . . . *The Taming of the Shrew* is remembered —but more for its immortal credit line (Play by William Shakespeare; Additional Dialogue by Sam Taylor) than for performances of Mary Pickford and Douglas Fairbanks. . . . Courtroom dramas were very popular in early talkie days, with *The Trial of Mary Dugan* (Norma Shearer, Raymond Hackett) as the best example. . . . Paul Muni in his debut in *The Valiant* . . . Harold Lloyd's first talkie, *Welcome Danger,* was more of what he had done more successfully in silents. . . .

Chapter Two

The Movie Year of 1930

'Everybody's talking in the movies in 1930, even Garbo and Chaney. Everyone, that is, except Chaplin. And even he is preparing a movie with sound.

Such early triumphs in talkies as those of Jolson, Bessie Love, Bebe Daniels, and others are shaded by the mediocrity of their follow-up pictures and they fade rapidly. Nor is it a happy year for John Gilbert, or for Clara Bow, Mary Pickford, Buddy Rogers, Douglas Fairbanks, Norma Talmadge, Pola Negri, Vilma Banky, to name just a few. Emil Jannings has returned to Germany but sends over a good movie, *The Blue Angel*, with a husky-voiced *Fräulein*, Marlene Dietrich, in the feminine lead.

Other comparatively new faces are those of Robert Montgomery, Leslie Howard, Spencer Tracy, Edward G. Robinson, Barbara Stanwyck, Humphrey Bogart, Ginger Rogers, Jean Harlow. The brilliant Jeanne Eagels is dead, but the song-and-dance honey, Nancy Carroll, makes the dramatic most of an inherited Eagels assignment. Marie Dressler and Wallace Beery come into their own.

With every other picture a musical, usually in the original crude Technicolor, it's not long before music, color, or the combination, is box-office poison. Sophisticated comedy drama is in vogue, though, and any number of war pictures follow the glory of *All Quiet*.

Besides *All Quiet on the Western Front* and *The Blue Angel,* these are among the best remembered movies of 1930: Garbo's *Anna Christie*, Ann Harding's *Holiday*, Nancy Carroll in *The Devil's Holiday* and in *Laughter* with Fredric March. March also in *The Royal Family of Broadway,* Howard Hughes's *Hell's Angels,* Lubitsch's *Monte Carlo* while Gary and Marlene appear in von Sternberg's *Morocco*, Dressler and Berry in *Min and Bill.* There's Griffith's *Abraham Lincoln,* Chaney's *Unholy Three, The Big House, Journey's End, The Dawn Patrol, Outward Bound,* and those Marx Brothers in *Animal Crackers.* And there were these others to remember. . . .

Forgotten Films of 1930

Lew Ayres played the movies' first babyfaced gangster in Archie Mayo's *Doorway to Hell.* Playing a lesser hoodlum was someone who wouldn't be "lesser" for long—Jimmy Cagney. Screenplay by George Rosener.

They're both criminals, but Lew Ayres is behind the bars with Jimmy Cagney outside, accompanied by the law, Robert Elliott, in *Doorway to Hell.*

Ruth Chatterton on
stand with Clive Brook
in *The Laughing Lady*.

Fredric March was
leading man for Ruth
Chatterton in *Sarah and
Son*.

Loretta Young meets
the unexpected dinner
guest, John Barrymore,
in *The Man from
Blankley's*.

14

Ruth Chatterton was a big star of the early 1930s but, outside of *Dodsworth* and *Madame X,* her movies have passed into limbo. Two worthy of note are *The Laughing Lady,* from an Alfred Sutro play, in which she played a society matron given to nervous giggling at embarrassing moments, and *Sarah and Son,* a better-than-average mother-love drama by Zoe Akins. Victor Schertzinger and Dorothy Arzner, respectively, directed. Bartlett Cormack and Alfred Richman wrote the screenplay.

Absolutely unseen since its initial release is one of John Barrymore's legendary comedy performances. As *The Man From Blankley's,* he played a droll lush arriving at the wrong party and being mistaken for a "rented guest." Alfred E. Green directed Harvey Thew's screenplay, with Loretta Young, Emily Fitzroy, and Albert Gran.

John Ford was at his best directing movies about the male of the species. An early example was *Men Without Women* which put the crew of a submarine in peril. Kenneth MacKenna and youthful Frank Albertson had principal roles and, if you looked fast, you could glimpse a youthful John Wayne. Screenplay by Dudley Nichols.

Marion Davies, Elliott Nugent, William Holden (no, not that one), and Donald Ogden Stewart in *Not So Dumb.*

The famous George S. Kaufman-Marc Connelly play, *Dulcy,* was the basis for King Vidor's *Not So Dumb.* It was the third (after *The Patsy, Show People*) of Marion Davies's films with Vidor. Each time he brought out comic talents that normally didn't show up in Davies's performances, even though she was hardly a Lynn Fontanne (who had created the role on stage.) Humorist Donald Ogden Stewart stood out in support. Script by Wanda Tuchock and Edwin Justus Mayer.

Stuart Erwin is listening. To his right are Kenneth MacKenna, Warren Hymer, Walter McGrail, J. Farrell Macdonald, and others—*Men Without Women* and trapped in a sunken submarine.

Gary Cooper meets his counterfeit mother, Beryl Mercer, in *Seven Days Leave*.

Regis Toomey discovers that his gambler brother, William Powell, is cheating in *Street of Chance*. Toomey is flanked by Stanley Fields and Irving Bacon.

J. M. Barrie's unashamedly sentimental playlet, *The Old Lady Shows Her Medals,* formed the basis for a delightful little movie, *Seven Days Leave.* Beryl Mercer was so winning as the little London charwoman inventing a soldier son and Gary Cooper such a fine figure as the reluctant "invention" that the picture was an absolute joy. Richard Wallace directed the script by Dan Totheroh and John Farrow.

Vaguely based on the life of Arnold Rothstein was *Street of Chance* with William Powell as the gentleman gambler sacrificing himself to keep young brother Regis Toomey on the straight and narrow. Kay Francis and Jean Arthur were the respective ladies in their lives. John Cromwell directed. Oliver H. P. Garrett's story was adapted by Howard Estabrook and Lenore Coffee.

After *The Big House* revealed the seamy side of prison life according to Hollywood, along came John Ford's *Up the River,* which played it for laughs. Playing the lead in a notable movie debut was Spencer Tracy, with Humphrey Bogart also in his initial screen role in a straighter secondary part. Screenplay by Maurine Watkins.

Norman Foster really didn't have the charisma to carry off the title role in the filmization of Katharine Brush's *Young Man of Manhattan* but the picture was a lively look at New York's newspaper and speakeasy worlds with Claudette Colbert playing the young man's long-suffering movie critic wife. A cute flapper, Ginger Rogers, attracted attention with her "Cigarette me" catch phrase. Monta Bell directed Robert Presnell's screenplay.

Other Forgotten 1930 Pictures to Note

The Devil to Pay was mild fare but Ronald Colman, Loretta Young, Myrna Loy, Florence Britton were pleasant. . . . *The Divorcee* (Norma Shearer, Robert Montgomery, Chester Morris) was considered daring for its day. . . . The Gay 90s were pleasantly reincarnated in Marion Davies's *Florodora Girl.* . . . Nancy Carroll again lived up to a movie title in *Honey* with some amusing people (Mitzi Green, ZaSu Pitts, Jobyna Howland, Lillian Roth, Skeets Gallagher) also present. . . . Two Molnar plays came to the screen—*Liliom,* scuttled by the inadequacy of Charles Farrell in the title role, and *The Swan* turned into *One Romantic Night,* a placid movie with Lillian Gish. . . . Will Rogers fit well into the title role of *Lightnin'.* . . . John Barrymore was a strong Ahab but, as always, what makes *Moby Dick* a great novel eluded the moviemakers. . . . Probably the best of early movie operettas (*The Desert Song* was certainly the worst) were *The Vagabond King* and *Rogue Song* with, respectively, Dennis King and Jeanette MacDonald, Lawrence Tibbett, and Laurel and Hardy.

Three movie debuts: Claire Luce is greeted by Spencer Tracy in *Up the River;* the handsome juvenile at the desk is Humphrey Bogart.

Norman Foster, as the *Young Man of Manhattan*, meets flapper tease Ginger Rogers. His uninterested pipe-smoking buddy is Charles Ruggles.

17

Chapter Three

The Movie Year of 1931

Practically nobody even remembers silent movies in 1931. Only Chaplin's *City Lights* and Murnau's *Tabu,* of important films, are nontalkies. But they, of course, are completely synchronized, sound and music being very necessary to their production.

Movies move again. In 1931 the old camera freedom is back, even when the source is the restricted single set of the theatre. Musicals and color are out. The vogue for chatty, sophisticated comedy dramas has waned. The war cycle of 1930 is over. But, in their place, are the gangland followers of *Little Caesar* and the horror cycle is underway. Newspaper yarns are popular, too.

Comebacks are made by Richard Dix, Adolphe Menjou, and Lionel Barrymore. But many of the big hits are scored by players new to the screen or previously unimportant—Clark Gable, for example, and Sylvia Sidney, Irene Dunne, Miriam Hopkins, Sally Eilers, James Dunn, Jackie Cooper, Aline MacMahon, Wynne Gibson, Mae Clarke, James Cagney, Helen Hayes, the Lunts, Tallulah Bankhead all have their first real screen splash—with varying success.

It is a bad year for Garbo (*Susan Lenox, Inspiration*) and other stars who do themselves little good are Constance Bennett, Nancy Carroll, Gloria Swanson, Clara Bow, Pola Negri, Ramon Novarro, Janet Gaynor, Buddy Rogers, and even Marie Dressler (with *Emma*).

Let's list these as notable 1931 movies—in no special order: *City Lights*; *Tabu*; *Cimarron*; *Dracula*; *Frankenstein*; *The Public Enemy*; *Little Caesar*; Mamoulian's *City Streets*; von Sternberg's *American Tragedy*; and Vidor's *Street Scene* (these last three introducing a glowing Sylvia Sidney). Then there are the Lunts' *Guardsman*; the Marx brothers' *Monkey Business*; Helen Hayes's *Sin of Madelon Claudet*; *The Champ*; *Arrowsmith*; *Trader Horn*; *The Front Page*; *Skippy*; *Bad Girl*; *A Free Soul*; and *Private Lives*.

Forgotten Films of 1931

Jimmy Cagney and Joan Blondell made a lively pair of con artists in *Blonde Crazy*. No moralistic, sordid *Public Enemy* finish for Jimmy this time. It was racy and funny all the way. Roy Del Ruth directed. Written by Kubec Glasman and John Bright. With Noel Francis, Louis Calhern, Guy Kibbee, and Raymond Milland.

Howard Hawks made a strong movie out of Martin Flavin's play, *The Criminal Code,* aided impressively by the performance of Walter Huston. He played a district attorney who becomes the warden of a prison, populated by men he has sent up. Constance Cummings and Phillips Holmes had the love interest such as it was and Boris Karloff skulked about as a squealer.

Ann Harding and Leslie Howard played so well together in *Devotion* that you could almost forgive their material which seemed like lending library romance from another era. (It was based on Pamela Wynne's *A Little Flat in the Temple.*) Robert Milton directed and a first-rate supporting cast included Robert Williams, O. P. Heggie, Dudley Digges, Louise Closser Hale, Allison Skipworth, Doris Lloyd, and Tempe Piggott.

Marlene Dietrich coolly facing a firing squad is the most indelible impression remaining from *Dishonored*. It would have been a routine spy yarn if the spy were not Marlene and if she were not directed in style by Josef von Sternberg. With Lew Cody, Victor McLaglen, Warner Oland, Barry Norton, and everybody's favorite, Gustav von Seyffertitz.

Leslie Howard, Ann Harding, and O. P Heggie dine in *Devotion*.

Prison warden Walter Huston and his daughter Constance Cummings in *The Criminal Code*. Yes, he's receiving word of an escape.

Jimmy Cagney takes in the sights in *Blonde Crazy*.

Lew Cody thinks Marlene Dietrich is a peasant lass, but she's really an international spy, in *Dishonored.*

Mitzi Green was a marvelously madcap moppet and Jackie Searle the supremely snotty little boy. They were teamed enjoyably in two 1931 comedies—*Finn and Hattie* (from a Donald Ogden Stewart book) and *Newly Rich* (title changed after release to *Forbidden Adventure*), based on a book by, of all people, Sinclair Lewis. Both were stretched beyond their farcical limits but each had its fun—the first in its depiction of Americans in Europe, the second in amusing takeoffs of Hollywood child stars. Such adults as Edna May Oliver, ZaSu Pitts, Lilyan Tashman, Leon Errol, and Louise Fazenda helped. Norman Taurog and Norman McLeod directed the first, Taurog alone the second.

Mervyn Le Roy brought Louis Weitzenkorn's exposé of tabloid journalism, *Five Star Final,* to the screen as an intense, if somewhat theatrical melodrama about the yellow press. There was a good role for Edward G. Robinson as an editor willing to destroy anyone to boost circulation. Aline MacMahon had a gem of a characterization in the supporting cast which also included Frances Starr and Boris Karloff.

Kay Francis and Lilyan Tashman played *Girls About Town,* probably the raciest pair of gold diggers around up to the time that Marilyn Monroe and Jane Russell became Lorelei Lee and her friend Dorothy. George Cukor's directorial style was already very much in evidence. With Joel McCrea and Eugene Pallette. By Zöe Akins.

Owing not a little to Hemingway and *The Sun Also Rises, The Last Flight* followed the escapades of four former war aviators in postwar Europe. The four—well played by David Manners, Richard Barthelmess, Elliott Nugent, John Mack Brown—are joined by one of the original movie screwball girls (her slogan is "I'll take vanilla") brightly played by Helen Chandler. John Monk Saunders wrote and William Dieterle directed.

Mitzi Green and Jackie Searle were an early talkie kid team in movies like *Forbidden Adventure* and (above) *Finn and Hattie,* in which Leon Errol and Zasu Pitts had the title roles.

20

Edward G. Robinson, the hard-boiled yellow journalist, and Aline MacMahon, his sympathetic secretary, in *Five Star Final*.

Kay Francis and Lilyan Tashman are *Girls About Town*; Eugene Pallette, Alan Dinehart, and Joel McCrea are some of the men in town.

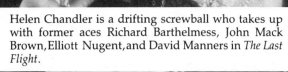

Pity Robert Williams, caught between Loretta Young and Jean Harlow in *Platinum Blonde*.

Helen Chandler is a drifting screwball who takes up with former aces Richard Barthelmess, John Mack Brown, Elliott Nugent, and David Manners in *The Last Flight*.

Platinum Blonde as a title referred, of course, to Jean Harlow but it was far from a Harlow movie. She was an unlikely choice for a society girl, a role in which Loretta Young, playing a reporter, might have been better cast. What counted was Frank Capra's direction and the performance of Robert Williams, just hitting his stride as a Mitchumesque leading man in this last performance before his sudden death. Screenplay by Robert Riskin.

The Smiling Lieutenant is the Lubitsch-Chevalier film that can't be seen any more (unless you can arrange a screening of a Danish-subtitled print at New York's Museum of Modern Art). It's one of their most charming, with Lubitsch touches slyly parodying conventional Viennese operetta. Miriam Hopkins sparkled as a dowdy princess turning into a glamour girl. With Claudette Colbert, George Barbier, and Charles Ruggles. Adapted by Ernest Vajoda and Samson Raphaelson from *The Waltz Dream.*

With another actress, *Stolen Heaven* with its improbable tale of love and money transforming two misfits into socially acceptable types would have been hopelessly maudlin. But Nancy Carroll, as the streetwalker-Cinderella, gave it a special affecting quality. Phillips Holmes and Louis Calhern were around, too. George Abbott directed and adapted Dana Burnett's original story.

Miriam Hopkins gave another of her incisive performances as a tough nightclub singer in *Twenty-Four Hours,* a good screen version of a Louis Bromfield novel. Clive Brook, Kay Francis and a new beauty, Adrienne Ames, represented the upper crust; Miss Hopkins and Regis Toomey much lower on the social scale. Marion Gering directed Louis Weitzenkorn's script.

The Vivien Leigh version was glossier but James Whale's 1931 filmization of Robert E. Sherwood's play, *Waterloo Bridge,* was less compromising in its wartime love story of a young soldier and a prostitute. Mae Clarke and Kent Douglass played these roles and there was a tiny part played by a newcomer named Bette Davis.

It's more than checkers for Miriam Hopkins and Maurice Chevalier in *The Smiling Lieutenant.*

Streetwalker Nancy Carroll shelters thief Phillips Holmes in *Stolen Heaven.*

Miriam Hopkins and Regis Toomey in *Twenty-four Hours.*

Mae Clarke and Kent Douglass (he later changed his screen name to Douglass Montgomery) had the Leigh-Taylor roles in the first version of *Waterloo Bridge.*

Myrna Loy, the seductive wife of Leslie Howard—he also had a wifely mistress—in *The Animal Kingdom*.

The brothers Barrymore—John as the thief, *Arsene Lupin*, and Lionel as his nemesis, the law.

Chapter Four

The Movie Year of 1932

In 1932 the movies still rely to a great extent on books and plays but there are good originals, too. The screen is occupied with contemporary affairs—politics, prohibition, banking, the ever-popular gangland and, of course, depression. Today's headline is frequently tomorrow's movie. *Back Street* ushers in a series of movies about unhappy mistresses and their troubled love lives—and sex, in all of its aspects, is swinging.

Katharine Hepburn, Paul Muni, Mae West, and Lee Tracy are the big new faces of the year. Muni and Tracy had tried before unsuccessfully but this time they click. Also beginning to look good are Cary Grant, Constance Cummings, Charles Laughton, Bing Crosby, Ann Dvorak, Dorothy Wilson, George Raft, and Myrna, Loy, the latter just beginning to emerge from "the Orient."

On the other hand, Clara Bow's comeback Fizzles. . . . Tallulah Bankhead gives up on movies—or vice versa. . . . It is an unimpressive year for Ruth Chatterton, Nancy Carroll, Richard Barthelmess, Janet Gaynor and Charles Farrell, Sally Eilers and James Dunn, Marion Davies. Ronald Colman, Ramon Novarro, Richard Dix. Joan Crawford, Constance Bennett, Ann Harding, Kay Francis have their ups and downs. But Irene Dunne, Sylvia Sidney, James Cagney, Edward G. Robinson do just fine. . . . Barbara Stanwyck is coming along . . . and an ingenue, named Bette Davis, begins to look good in some minor leads. . . . Jean Harlow finds her niche. . . .

Some movies of the year—in no particular order—would be Fredric March's *Dr. Jekyll and Mr. Hyde*; the Dietrich-von Sternberg *Shanghai Express*; the all-star *Grand Hotel*; Mamoulian's *Love Me Tonight*; Lubitsch's *Trouble in Paradise*; Muni's *Scarface* and *I Am a Fugitive*; the Barrymore-Hepburn *Bill of Divorcement*; W. C. Fields and company in *The Million Dollar Legs*; the Marx brothers' *Horsefeathers*; and Tod Browning's *Freaks*. To add a few more, how about *Tarzan the Ape Man*; the Helen Hayes-Gary Cooper *Farewell to Arms*; the William Powell-Kay Francis *One Way Passage*; the Norma Shearer-Fredric March *Smilin' Through*; a Dietrich camp classic, *Blonde Venus*; DeMille's *Sign of the Cross*; Harlow's *Red Dust* (with Gable) and *Red Headed Woman*; Constance Bennett's *What Price Hollywood?*; and the all-star gimmick, *If I Had a Million*. And there were those others—not as quickly remembered but worth a reminder.

Forgotten Films of 1932

Frank Capra presented a graphic picture of a run on a bank in *American Madness*. Walter Huston, as always, was impressive as the bank president in this best topical movie of the year. Pat O'Brien, Constance Cummings, and Kay Johnson also appeared. Written by Robert Riskin.

The Animal Kingdom, Philip Barry's mannered but witty comedy of a man, his wife, and his mistress, was transferred with taste to the screen by Edward H. Griffith, who also directed Barry's *Paris Bound* and *Holiday*. Ann Harding played the wifely mistress in her usual Barry style and Leslie Howard, William Gargan, and Ilka Chase capably recreated roles they had originated on stage. But it was Myrna Loy, heretofore more usually a Eurasian vamp, who was the revelation as the society wife with the instincts of a high-priced courtesan. Remade (badly) in 1946, all prints of the original were, it is said, destroyed to prevent competition. Horace Jackson adapted the Barry play.

Constance Cummings comforts Walter Huston after the run on the bank in *American Madness*.

Nobody could play cat-and-mouse better than John and Lionel Barrymore, at the top of their form in *Arsène Lupin.* The old detective story still had some surprises. It was a much more felicitous outing for the brothers than was *Rasputin and the Empress* of the same year which had John just walking through while Lionel masticated the scenery. Jack Conway directed.

Richard Barthelmess couldn't have been drearier in the dreary *Cabin in the Cotton* but you can't ignore it when you remember Bette Davis's Southern belle bitch who has now passed into the repertoire of camp impersonators. ("Ah'd love t' kiss ya but Ah just washed mah hair.") Michael Curtiz directed Paul Green's script.

Bette Davis, as the sexpot Southern belle, tries her thing on poor white trash Richard Barthelmess in *Cabin in the Cotton.*

David Manners was so handsome that he usually served as mere decoration—to make leading ladies look their best. In *Crooner* he had a role of his own—as a mediocre singer who discovers a megaphone and micro- phone, makes it big, and gets a swelled head. Ann Dvorak and Ken Murray helped but this one was really Manners's movie. Rian James's novel was adapted by Charles Kenyon; Lloyd Bacon directed.

David Manners leads the band, which includes William Janney on trumpet and Eddie Nugent on drums, in *Crooner.*

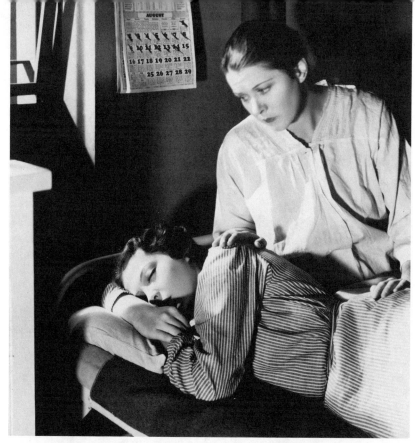

Sylvia Sidney
with Fritzi Ridg-
way in *Ladies of the
Big House*.

Cary Grant, Fre-
dric March and
Sylvia Sidney in
*Merrily We Go to
Hell*.

Lee Tracy's rat-a-tat personality had shown up well in the Winchell takeoff of *Blessed Event*. He was even more at home in the role of a preposterous press agent in *The Half Naked Truth,* speedily directed by Gregory LaCava and with Lupe Velez on her best hot pepper behavior. With Eugene Pallette and Frank Morgan. Story by Ben Markson and H. R. Swanson.

Sylvia Sidney had several 1932 movies including three that were admired at the time but have been overlooked since. She was an unhappy girl unjustly sent to prison in *Ladies of the Big House;* a gay young modern (with Fredric March a bright leading man) in *Merrily We Go to Hell;* and the tragic, flowerlike Cho Cho San in a songless *Madame Butterfly.* All were played with the special radiance that belonged only to Sidney. Gene Raymond and Cary Grant were other leading men. Dorothy Arzner directed *Merrily,* Marion Gering the other two. Scripts respectively by Louis Weitzenkorn, Edwin Justice Mayer, and Josephine Lovett.

Frank Morgan, Lupe Velez, and Lee Tracy in *The Half Naked Truth*.

Nobody could play a tough dame like Wynne Gibson but she could move you, too. She did both in *Lady and Gent* with George Bancroft as the second half of the title (and John Wayne as a clean-cut kid turned punch-drunk pug). Stephen Roberts directed, Grover Jones and William Slavens McNutt scripted. Gibson also did her damndest to redeem *The Strange Case of Clara Deane* but its soppy soaper plot defeated her.

Lovers Courageous was a thin little romance but it had great charm, particularly in the performances of its title players, Robert Montgomery and Madge Evans, with a top supporting cast (Roland Young, Reginald Owen, Beryl Mercer, Frederick Kerr, Jackie Searle). Jack Conway directed Frederick Lonsdale's script.

There was a little more slapstick and a little less heart in *Make Me a Star* but the old *Merton of the Movies* plot still worked for Stuart Erwin and Joan Blondell with help from people like Ben Turpin, ZaSu Pitts, Ruth Donnelly, and Sam Hardy. Directed by William Beaudine. From the George S. Kaufman–Marc Connelly play. Adapted by Arthur Kober, Walter DeLeon, and Sam Mintz.

Ernest Lubitsch had another Maurice Chevalier–Jeanette MacDonald romp with *One Hour With You* but his most notable 1932 film was something quite different. *The Man I Killed* (title later changed to *Broken Lullaby*) was strong antiwar drama with fine performances by Lionel Barrymore and Nancy Carroll, although Philips Holmes, in the pivotal role, rather overdid the hysteria. Samson Raphaelson, Ernest Vajda, and Reginald Berkeley adapted the Maurice Rostand play.

One of the best adventure–horror pictures was *The Most Dangerous Game,* directed by Ernest B. Schoedsack and Irving Pichel from Richard Connell's story. Leslie Banks played the mad Count Zaroff, sick of big game hunting and turning his talents to the "most dangerous game—man" in the person of Joel McCrea, with Fay Wray also menaced.

Harold Lloyd had his most amusing talkie adventures in *Movie Crazy,* as a Merton-like would-be movie star. Constance Cummings was his very attractive leading lady. Directed by Clyde Bruckman; screenplay by Vincent Lawrence.

Louise Carter, Sylvia Sidney, and uncredited child in *Madame Butterfly.*

Rowdy romancers George Bancroft and Wynne Gibson in *Lady and Gent.*

Robert Montgomery and Madge Evans portraying *Lovers Courageous.*

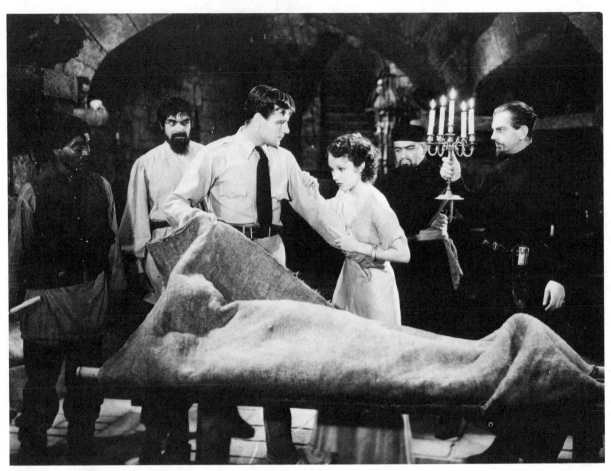

Evil Leslie Banks (right) has Joel McCrea and Fay Wray
in his power in *The Most Dangerous Game*.

Nancy Carroll is horrified at Phillips Holmes's confession in Ernst Lubitsch's *The Man I Killed* (also known as
Broken Lullaby).

Harold Lloyd meets Constance Cummings, made up as Spanish movie star, in *Movie Crazy*.

Stuart Erwin gets a cowboy-movie role, with Ben Turpin and extras, in *Make Me a Star*.

SHERIFF

ASH PAID

1382-62

Louis Bromfield's *Single Night* was expanded to *Night After Night* for the movies with George Raft in one of his best roles as a speakeasy operator surrounded by such as Constance Cummings, Wynne Gibson, Alison Skipworth, and a new gal who scored the minute she was stopped by the hatcheck girl as she sauntered into the club. "Goodness, what beautiful diamonds." "Goodness had nothing to do with it, honey." Who else? Our Mae, of course. Archie Mayo directed Vincent Lawrence's script.

James Whale, who made *Frankenstein,* brought us *The Old Dark House,* inhabited by such grotesques as Boris Karloff, Ernest Thesiger, and Eva Moore, who menaced people like Gloria Stuart, Charles Laughton, Melvyn Douglas, Raymond Massey. Benn W. Levy adapted the J. B. Priestly story.

The George S. Kaufman-Moss Hart hit *Once in a Lifetime* looked pretty stagy as brought to the screen under the direction of Russell Mack with a Seton I. Miller script. But a lot of the barbs were still on target and a top cast, headed by the queen of straight-faced wisecrackers, Aline MacMahon and including Jack Oakie, Russell Hopton, ZaSu Pitts, Gregory Ratoff, Louise Fazenda, Onslow Stevens, Jobyna Howland, Sidney Fox, kept it funny.

The saga of Haw Tabor and Baby Doe (with their names changed) made effective drama in *Silver Dollar* with Edward G. Robinson and Bebe Daniels as the Colorado rowdy who rises to importance and his lady love. Aline MacMahon again made a special contribution as the outgrown wife. Alfred E. Green directed the screenplay by Carl Erickson and Harvey Thew.

You couldn't really believe a minute of it, particularly Douglas Fairbanks, Jr., playing a role that must have been meant for Cagney. But *Union Depot* was a rattle-bang comedy melodrama, directed by Alfred E. Green who didn't let things slow down. Fairbanks did his damndest and Joan Blondell was saucy. And there were

Louella-like columnist Louise Fazenda introduces her "finds"—ex-vaudevillians Aline MacMahon, Jack Oakie, and Russell Hopton—to studio head Gregory Ratoff in *Once in a Lifetime.*

Alison Skipworth, George Raft and Mae West, *Night After Night*.

George Raft subdues Wynne Gibson while Constance Cummings cowers, in *Night After Night*.

Boris Karloff is subdued by Melvyn Douglas and Charles Laughton, while Raymond Massey, Lilian Bond, Gloria Stuart, and Eva Moore register varying expressions of concern, in *The Old Dark House*.

David Landau is the Law; Douglas Fairbanks, Jr., a small-time hoodlum; and Joan Blondell the girl who will wait, in *Union Depot*.

Aline MacMahon and Edward G. Robinson (with still another unbilled child) in their earlier, happier days, in *Silver Dollar*.

plenty of good bits in the *Grand Hotel* format. Kenyon Nicholson and Walter DeLeon adapted the Gene Fowler, Joe Laurie, Jr. play.

Some Other 1932 Forgotten Films to Note

Karen Morley, as a particularly vicious shrew, was notable in a William Haines drama about broadcasting, *Are You Listening?.* . . Pirandello's *As You Desire Me* provided an interesting role for Garbo, platinum-topped and world weary. . . . *The Dark Horse* was a noisy but funny political lampoon with Guy Kibbee in the title role and Warren William, Bette Davis, Sam Hardy and others as connivers. . . . Douglas Fairbanks, Jr., played a Lindbergh type in a spirited little thing about the perils of celebrity, *It's Tough to Be Famous*. . . . *Life Begins*, a harrowing drama of the maternity wards, was enough to scare off prospective mothers but it had good roles for people like Aline MacMahon, Dorothy Peterson, Loretta Young, Glenda Farrell. . . . John Barrymore played a couple of flamboyant lawyers but a Barrymore imitator, Warren William, had the best of the genre in *The Mouthpiece* with Aline MacMahon again stealing the show in support. . . . An excellent cast—most notably Adrianne Allen—played *The Night of June 13* about the effects of small town gossip. . . . Charles Laughton repeated a stage role in an interesting murder drama, *Payment Deferred,* with Dorothy Peterson effective as his wife. . . . Fredric March gave his usual bright performance—two performances in fact, in a dual role—in an amusing *Strangers in Love*. . . . *This is the Night* was Lubitsch-style comedy without the master's touch but with a delightfully droll Roland Young and some other experts (Lili Damita, Charlie Ruggles, Thelma Todd, Cary Grant). . . . Capra's *Mr. Smith* wouldn't go to Washington for years but Lee Tracy was lively as a not-so-innocent discovering political skulduggery in a similar *Washington Merry-Go Round*. . . . Another Tracy—Spencer—got involved in a couple of issues—police graft (in *Disorderly Conduct*) and juvenile delinquency (in *Young America*). Yes, they were issues back in 1932, too.

Chapter Five

The Movie Year of 1933

Many contradictions exist in 1933. Two box office hits are scored by the sweet and wholesome *Little Women* and by Mae West, who is not quite in that category. Movie monsters have almost had it—or that's what you would think—but then along comes *King Kong*. Backstage musicals return to favor with the tuneful *42nd Street* and costume dramas are in again, too. The gangster cycle is dying down but domestic dramas are popular. There are rumblings from the pulpits but sex continues to ride high.

Astaire and Rogers start whirling together, with Dick Powell and Ruby Keeler teaming up, too. Margaret Sullavan, Franchot Tone, Diana Wynyard, Heather Angel, Merle Oberon, Claude Rains, Robert Donat, Wendy Barrie, John Beal, Peter Lorre—and King Kong—are some of the new faces but it's primarily a year for the old reliables.

England makes its first bid for attention internationally with *The Private Life of Henry VIII* and there are Hollywood-made "British" films like Noel Coward's *Cavalcade* and *Berkeley Square* with Leslie Howard. Some of the better pictures of a very full year (in alphabetical order) would include Jean Harlow's *Blonde Bombshell;* John Barrymore's *Consellor at Law;* Crawford's *Dancing Lady;* the Lubitsch version of Noel Coward's *Design For Living* (Fredric March, Gary Cooper, Miriam Hopkins); George Cukor's *Dinner at 8* with a screen full of stars; the Marx brothers' *Duck Soup;* Fredric March and Cary Grant in *The Eagle and the Hawk;* Paul Robeson's *Emperor Jones; Flying Down to Rio* which introduced the team of Fred and Ginger; two other big ones in the return of musicals—*Footlight Parade, Gold Diggers of 1933,* by Busby Berkeley; Mae West's *I'm No Angel,* following closely on *She Done Him Wrong;* James Whale's *The Invisible Man* (Claude Rains); Laughton's *Island of Lost Souls;* Capra's *Lady For a Day;* Spencer Tracy and Loretta Young in Borzage's *A Man's Castle;* Katharine Hepburn's *Morning Glory;* the great Garbo in *Queen Christina;* Will Rogers and Janet Gaynor in *State Fair; Tarzan and His Mate;* the John Barrymore-Myrna Loy *Topaze;* Marie Dressler as *Tugboat Annie;* and William Wellman's *Wild Boys of the Road.* All of these are remembered—most of them worth the memory—but there were others worth a thought, too, even though they may have faded over the years.

Intense young John Beal is in love with the wife (Helen Hayes) of his uncle (Robert Montgomery) in *Another Language.*

Forgotten Films to Remember of 1933

Rose Franken's play, *Another Language,* about the clash of a young wife with her husband's horrendous family, transferred well to the screen especially in the subplot about the infatuation with the wife (Helen Hayes) of her husband's rebellious young nephew. John Beal had sensitivity in that role. Also particularly notable: Louise Closser Hale as the stifling matriarch and Margaret Hamilton as the humorous sister-in-law. Edward H. Griffith directed; screenplay by Herman J. Mankiewicz, Gertrude Russell, and Donald Ogden Stewart.

Who better than Nancy Carroll for the title role in *Child of Manhattan?* The Preston Sturges play dealt with a girl from Miss Carroll's own widely publicized real-life background. The round-faced redhead was pretty and convincing and there were people around like Jane Darwell as her mother and Betty Grable around as her sister. Unfortunately the men in her life were played by that great stick, John Boles, and by Buck Jones, pretty ill at ease away from the sagebrush. Directed by Eddie Buzzell; screenplay by Gertrude Purcell.

With Marie Dressler cast as the family servant, the screen version of Sidney Howard's *The Late Christopher Bean* (retitled *Christopher Bean,* and later *Her Sweetheart* for the screen) leaned more toward slapstick than when Pauline Lord played it on stage. Still it passed as a vehicle for Miss Dressler (her last) and

Nancy Carroll, the dime-a-dance *Child of Manhattan,* has some explaining to do to her mother, Jane Darwell, and sister, a teenage Betty Grable who hasn't yet discovered the virtues of softer makeup.

Greedy Lionel Barrymore and Beulah Bondi try to take away valuable paintings left to their maid, Marie Dressler, in *Christopher Bean*. Jean Hersholt, Helen Shipman, Russell Hardie, and Helen Mack are present too.

Frank Morgan is about to present Nancy Carroll with the title's *Kiss Before the Mirror*.

Lionel Atwill lies unconscious in the fire that destroys his life work and is responsible for *The Mystery of the Wax Museum.*

there were good performances by Lionel Barrymore and Beulah Bondi in the role she had created on Broadway. Sam Wood directed.

The movies of James Whale were always offbeat—from *Frankenstein* to something as special as *The Kiss Before the Mirror,* which had the quality of an import. But we weren't used to European cinema in 1933. Nancy Carroll might have seemed an odd choice for a continental adulterous wife but she fitted in well with more likely cast members such as Frank Morgan, Paul Lukas, and Gloria Stuart. William Anthony McGuire adapted the Ladislaus Fodor play.

The Mystery of the Wax Museum gave us some shudders in its goings on about the proprietor of a waxworks (Lionel Atwill) who is maddened in the fire that destroys his creation. He sets about to replace the original figures with wax-covered humans who resembled them. Fay Wray did her usual screaming as yet another horror victim. Michael Curtiz directed the screenplay by Don Mullaly and Carl Erickson.

A snippet of Gable, a touch or two of Helen Hayes, look-ins by Myrna Loy, Robert Montgomery, William Gargan. It all may have mattered on the marquee but the stars (except for John Barrymore) brought little to *Night Flight.* The film, adapted by Oliver H. P. Garrett, from the novel by Antoine de Saint-Exupery, was engrossing in its pictorial catalogue of dangers in the air. Clarence Brown directed.

Although it used the title of the book, *Only Yesterday* had very little to do with Frederick Lewis Allen's history of the 1920s. Like most of John M. Stahl's movies, it was a "woman's picture" and a pretty basically implausible one at that. But it introduced to the screen a luminous new actress—Margaret Sullavan. Enough said. Screenplay by Arthur Richman, George O'Neill, and William Hurlbut.

Give special thanks to W. S. Van Dyke for recognizing the potential of Myrna Loy as a girl who had a way with a witty line and was a svelte and individual leading lady to boot. *The Thin Man* was the epitome of this discovery, of course, but, before that, came two particularly entertaining comedy melodramas, *Penthouse* and *The Prizefighter and the Lady.* Incidentally, in the latter, Max Baer turned out to be a better movie actor than most thespian athletes. Frances Goodrich and Albert Hackett scripted the first; John Lee Mahan, Jr., John Meehan, and Frances Marion wrote *Prizefighter.*

Helen Hayes gets bad news about her aviator husband from John Barrymore in *Night Flight.*

John Boles meets radiant Margaret Sullavan, and it was our introduction to her too, in *Only Yesterday*.

(ABOVE)
Myrna Loy in the pre-vamp, *Thin Man* era of her career—in *Penthouse*, with Warner Baxter . . .

(LEFT)
. . . and with Max Baer and Walter Huston in *The Prizefighter and the Lady*.

John Ford, who had saluted motherhood in almost maudlin terms (in *Mother Machree,* and *Four Sons*) did it again in *Pilgrimage.* But, as played by Henrietta Crosman, this mother was a harsh, embittered farm woman. Ford managed to get his sentimental innings but the transformation of the woman into a proud Gold-Star Mother was accomplished most believably by Miss Crosman. A long neglected Ford film, written by I. A. R. Wylie, Philip Klein, Barry Connors, and Dudley Nichols.

There are those who feel that the seeds of much that was innovative in *Citizen Kane* can be found in the Preston Sturges (writer)/William K. Howard (director) collaboration, *The Power and the Glory.* An ambitious handling of the story of a life of a tycoon from his early beginnings as seen through the eyes of a lifelong friend, the picture may have been ahead of its time. It caused absolutely no stir. Spencer Tracy was the tycoon, Colleen Moore and Ralph Morgan his wife and friend.

In spite of the leering title, *Professional Sweetheart* was an innocent little piece which took off on the world of radio and sponsors. Ginger Rogers was pretty and perky in the title role and more than held her own in the comedy league with pros like Gregory Ratoff, ZaSu Pitts, Franklin Pangborne, Frank McHugh, Allen Jenkins, and Edgar Kennedy. William Seiter directed the Maurine Watkins script.

Ginger Rogers has fun with such leading men as Frank McHugh, Franklin Pangborne, and Gregory Ratoff in *Professional Sweetheart.*

So many of John Barrymore's talking picture roles are no longer available to us. The Archduke Rudolph von Hapsburg in *Reunion in Vienna* is a case in point. Undaunted by the shadow of Alfred Lunt who played it in the original Robert E. Sherwood play, Barrymore gave one of his most uninhibited performances. Diana Wynyard, in the Lynn Fontanne role, may have been a little placid but the rest of the cast, particularly Frank Morgan, gave thoroughly polished performances under the direction of Sidney Franklin. Ernest Vajda and Claudine West adapted.

Another stage success came to the screen in John Cromwell's filmization of Sidney Howard's *The Silver Cord,* which Cromwell had also directed in the theatre. Laura Hope Crews, too, repeated her devastating Broadway portrait of the sweetly poisonous mama. Irene Dunne, Joel McCrea, Eric Linden and, particularly, Frances Dee were well cast as the victims of smothering mother love and the women who fight it. Jane Murfin scripted.

Diana Wynyard and John Barrymore as the former lovers who have a *Reunion in Vienna.*

As Spencer Tracy ages in *The Power and the Glory*, he acquires a faithless wife (Helen Vinson).

Henrietta Crosman resents Marian Nixon, the girl with whom her son (Norman Foster) is in love, in *Pilgrimage*.

43

Irene Dunne and Frances Dee confront tyrannical mother-in-law Laura Hope Crews in *The Silver Cord.*

Warrior Elissa Landi greets Queen Marjorie Rambeau, as Maude Eburne and other Amazons look on, in *The Warrior's Husband.*

The first of the screwball comedies was *Three Cornered Moon* about one of those madcap families who later became a staple of 1930s entertainment in plays and films like *My Man Godfrey* and *You Can't Take It With You.* Claudette Colbert may have been a little too down to earth to be properly loony as the daughter but Mary Boland was as happily scatterbrained as you could wish as Mrs. Rimplegar. Tom Brown, Wallace Ford, William Bakewell and Lyda Roberti were other likely members of the household. Elliott Nugent directed the S. K. Lauren, Ray Harris screen adaptation of Gertrude Tonkonogy's play.

If *The Warrior's Husband* didn't really live up to its comedy promise, its tale of the Amazons and their effeminate men provided an enjoyable screen romp. Best of all, it gave Elissa Landi a chance to shake the roles of ladies with problems and emerge as something of a glamour girl. David Manners was properly handsome and masculine as the Grecian visitor who introduces real manhood to the Amazon ladies. Majorie Rambeau was robust as the Amazon queen, Ernest Truex and Ferdinand Gottschalk amusing as puny Amazon men. Walter Lang directed. Julian Thompson's play was adapted by Walter Lang, Ralph Spence, and Sonya Levien.

Ann Harding played some of her typical roles (exemplified by the title of one of them, *Gallant Lady*) in 1933 movies. (Two others were *Double Harness* and *Right to Romance.*) Best was *When Ladies Meet,* a movie version of Rachel Crothers's play, with Miss Harding, at her most charming, meeting her unsuspected rival. Myrna Loy did a lot for that part, Alice Brady prattled in the background, Robert Montgomery and Frank Morgan held up the male end. Harry Beaumont directed the John Meehan-Leon Gordon screenplay.

Woman Accused was a movie based on a gimmick novel (separate chapters written by ten popular magazine hacks). But the movie starred Nancy Carroll and she was particularly telling in her frantic attempts to cover up a murder. Cary Grant played opposite her but this was the period when he was still not much more than just another pretty face among leading men. Paul Sloane directed. Bayard Veiller adapted.

Other Forgotten 1933 Pictures to Note

Nobody could play golden-hearted broads better than Wynne Gibson and that, in spite of Charles Farrell, is why *Aggie Appleby, Maker of Men* is listed. The intelligent ingenue, Betty Furness, was also present. . . . Paramount's all-star *Alice in Wonderland* was hardly a

(ABOVE)
Lyda Roberti is the maid in the household of the
screwball Rimplegars (Tom Brown, Claudette Colbert,
Mary Boland, William Bakewell, and Wallace Ford) in
Three Cornered Moon.

Ann Harding and Myrna Loy are the titular pair in
When Ladies Meet. Robert Montgomery, Alice Brady,
and Martin Burton are also meeting.

A shipboard courtroom game becomes the real thing as John Halliday grills Nancy Carroll, but she has Cary Grant to back her up in *The Woman Accused.*

definitive version but it was diverting to try to discover which of its stars (Gary Cooper, Cary Grant, or W. C. Fields, among others) were behind the masks. . . . Barbara Stanwyck played both a very bad girl (in *Baby Face*) and a very good one in Capra's *Bitter Tea of General Yen.* . . . Bad was better for Barbara with Nils Asther taking laurels in *Yen.* . . . Alice Brady and Frank Morgan were good enough in *Broadway to Hollywood* that you could get through the cliché-filled story line. . . . *College Humor* had cute coeds, a passable football yarn, and Bing Crosby as a crooning professor with songs like "Learn to Croon" and "Down the Old Ox Road." *Convention City* was frantic farce but the cast (Joan Blondell, Mary Astor, Adolphe Menjou, Hugh Herbert, Guy Kibbee, Frank McHugh, Ruth Donnelly, Dick Powell, and Patricia Ellis) made it work. . . . Dorothea Wieck, of *Maedchen in Uniform,* made her American debut in *Cradle Song,* a quiet but sometimes moving drama of a nun who becomes mother to an adopted child. . . . Joe E. Brown made *Elmer the*

Great more caricature than characterization (Walter Huston had originated the stage part) but it was still one of the better Brown vehicles. . . . W. S. Van Dyke's *Eskimo* had a story line (unlike Flaherty's *Nanook*)—and a pretty melodramatic one—but there were extraordinary scenes of life in the frozen North. . . . Marion Davies was always at her best in light things like *Going Hollywood* but better than that was Bing Crosby singing a good Brown/Freed score ("Temptation," among others). . . . *Grand Slam* was an amusing sendup of the contract bridge craze with Ferdinand Gottschalk standing out in a good cast (Paul Lukas, Loretta Young, Helen Vinson, and Glenda Farrell). . . . *Hell Below* didn't break any new ground in its study of men trapped in a submarine but the cast (Robert Montgomery, Walter Huston, Robert Young, Madge Evans and, unexpectedly touching, Jimmy Durante) made it worth watching. . . . Kay Francis suffered through the generations in *The House on 56th Street* but Kay's suffering was always high style. . . . *Hold Your Man* was regulation Gable/Harlow rowdy romance. . . . Jimmy Cagney was at his scrappiest in *Lady Killer,* which took him from back alleys to Hollywood stardom, with Mae Clarke taking the punishment, and in another typical Cagney, *Hard to Handle.* . . . Lee Tracy had one of his patented roles—this time as an ambulance chaser—in *The Nuisance* helped a great deal by an excellent cast (Frank Morgan, Charles Butterworth and that most elegant ingenue of the era, Madge Evans). . . . Gary Cooper's version of *One Sunday Afternoon* was somewhat pokey (James Cagney's remake a few years later was the real thing) but Cooper and his charming leading lady, Frances Fuller, had their points. . . . Until the 1950s—with Merman's *Gypsy* and Sylvia Sidney in a Chayefsky TV play—Alice Brady was the definitive *Stage Mother* with Maureen O'Sullivan very lovely as the actress daughter. . . . Miriam Hopkins was always interesting and she had two widely varying 1933 films—a rather grotesque version of William Faulkner's *Sanctuary* called *The Story of Temple Drake* and a Phil (*State Fair*) Stong drama of rustic gossip *The Strangers Return.* . . . There wasn't anything very new in *Twenty Thousand Years in Sing Sing* except that Spencer Tracy always gave something special to even the most hackneyed part. . . . Rowland V. Lee's *Zoo in Budapest* had the look of a Murnau film but the story about one of those free spirits and a little orphan girl (Gene Raymond and Loretta Young, if you can believe it) was juvenile. . . . Although *The World Changes* was a pretty ponderous piece about many generations in the life of a man, its extraordinary cast (Paul Muni, Aline MacMahon, Margaret Lindsay, Jean Muir, Guy Kibbee, Patricia Ellis, Anna Q. Nilsson among others with Mary Astor particularly effective as a hysteric) redeemed it. . . .

Lester Glassner, this book's designer, is such a Stanwyck buff that he insisted on picturing a couple of Barbara's "also rans". (Above) Stanwyck with Margaret Lindsay, Donald Cook in *Baby Face*; (Below) with Nils Asther in *The Bitter Tea of General Yen*.

Chapter Six

The Movie Year of 1934

The movies get their ears slapped back when, in 1934, the Legion of Decency is formed and proves to be much more powerful than anybody would have thought. So much so that the industry does some self-regulation of movie morals with the Motion Picture Production Code.

Plenty of big pictures are being produced but news is made by a couple of sleepers—*It Happened One Night* and *The Thin Man,* both made without any particular pretensions and with stars thought to be well past their peak. The stars—Gable, Powell, Colbert, and Loy—move right up to another peak and stay there for a long, long time.

Opera is popularized for movie audiences—at least occasional arias—with Grace Moore's *One Night of Love.* Goldwyn spends a fortune to promote Anna Sten but she doesn't give Garbo or Marlene a single worried moment. Bigger movie debut news is made by a curly-topped moppet, Shirley Temple. Some others who make their first real movie dent are people like Claude Rains, Margo, Jean Muir, Anne Shirley, Francis Lederer, Jack Benny and, from England, Madeleine Carroll, Robert Donat, Jessie Matthews, Elisabeth Bergner. A couple of ingenues—Bette Davis and Carole Lombard—finally get roles to head them on their starry way.

Some of the better pictures of the year are in alphabetical order: the Hecht-MacArthur *Crime Without Passion*; Astaire and Rogers in *The Gay Divorcee*; John Ford's *The Lost Patrol*; Robert Flaherty's *Man of Aran*; Arliss's *House of Rothschild*; the Lubitsch/Chevalier/MacDonald *Merry Widow*; the Leslie Howard-Bette Davis *Of Human Bondage*; *Our Daily Bread* (ignored at the time but now considered one of King Vidor's masterpieces); and Howard Hawks's *Twentieth Century* with Barrymore and Lombard. Others good, popular, or both would include Shearer's *Barretts of Wimpole Street*; Bergner's *Catherine the Great*; Donat's *Count of Monte Cristo*; Fredric March's *Death Takes a Holiday*; Colbert's *Imitation of Life*; *Little Miss Marker*; Gable/Powell/Loy's *Manhattan Melodrama*; and Wallace Beery's *Viva Villa.* And there were the others—as good but not as well remembered.

Forgotten Films to Remember of 1934

Edwin Justus Mayer's play, *The Firebrand,* was brought to the screen as a bright tongue-in-cheek swashbuckler (here titled *Affairs of Cellini*), directed with wit by Gregory LaCava and with an extremely capable cast having a marvelous time in medieval Florence. Fredric March played Cellini as a kind of combination of Douglas Fairbanks and Groucho Marx, Constance Bennett was a beauteously bitchy duchess and there were amusing bits by Vince Barnett, Louis Calhern and, especially, Fay Wray as a greedy virgin. But the principal joy was Frank Morgan in his bumbling characterization of the fatuous Duke. Bess Meredith wrote the screenplay.

Fredric March introduces the bumbling Duke, Frank Morgan, to virginal Fay Wray in *Affairs of Cellini.*

Clarence Muse harmonizes with Walter Connolly, Myrna Loy, and Warner Baxter—but rides on the outside of the car—in *Broadway Bill*.

Why *Anne of Green Gables* has won such little renown as a movie version of a near-classic novel about an adolescent girl is one of those Hollywood mysteries. The fault is probably that of RKO who found absolutely nothing of any value to follow up the beguiling performance given by Anne Shirley in the title role. Since Miss Shirley then never became a real star, the picture is forgotten. (How it would be replayed if, say, Hepburn had done the part!) But it was a lovely movie and so were the performances of Miss Shirley, Helen Westley, O. P. Heggie, and that most likable juvenile of the era, Tom Brown. Directed by George Nicholls, Jr. Sam Mintz scripted.

The Battle (also released as *Thunder in the East*) was an English language remake of a French film with Charles Boyer repeating his distinguished performance as the Japanese noble who sacrifices his wife and eventually his own life to the demands of his country. The pre-Hollywood (and preartificial) Merle Oberon was touching as the wife. With John Loder. Directed by Nicolas Farkas; screenplay by Robert Stevenson.

School days with Tom Brown and Anne Shirley in *Anne of Green Gables*.

Charles Boyer and Merle Oberon in *The Battle* (also titled *Thunder in the East*).

Jean Muir as the adolescent daughter whose existence is hidden by her vain actress mother, Veree Teasedale, in *Desirable*.

Kay Johnson tries to find out what's wrong with Dorothy Wilson in *Eight Girls in a Boat*.

Broadway Bill is the Frank Capra film that is never revived. (Perhaps it was shelved or destroyed to protect the inferior 1950 remake.) But it was an amiable movie about a man who forsakes his conventional life for the racetrack world he loves. Warner Baxter, usually a pretty stuffy actor, wasn't here and Myrna Loy had all the warmth you would want in a leading lady. There was a usually good Capra supporting cast including Walter Connolly, Helen Vinson, Lynne Overman, Raymond Walburn, Douglass Dumbrille, Clarence Muse, Margaret Hamilton, and Frankie Darro. Screenplay by Robert Riskin.

Jean Muir, in a glowing portrayal of the coltish, adolescent daughter of a popular actress who wants to keep the existence of an offspring hidden, had her only really worthy screen role in *Desirable.* Otherwise Warners used her abominably with only a few other parts (*As the Earth Turns, Dr. Monica,* and the loanout, *Orchids to You*) to hint at her quality. Verree Teasedale played one of her best roles, the mother, with her own special sophistication. Archie Mayo directed the screenplay of Mary McCall, Jr.

Dorothy Wilson, an underrated young actress, had one of the few roles that made any demands on her in *Eight Girls in a Boat.* The movie dealt, simply and without sensationalism, with the pregnancy of a school girl but it was Miss Wilson's performance that made it worthy of note. Richard Wallace directed the screenplay by Lewis Foster and Casey Robinson.

W. S. Van Dyke who had a knack for such things turned an ordinary little melodrama, *Hide-Out,* into a very nice little entertainment. It was helped no end by Robert Montgomery's breezy performance as a big city hoodlum who finds a better life when he hides out on a farm. Since Maureen O'Sullivan was the farm girl, you could understand. Screenplay by Frances Goodrich and Albert Hackett.

I Was A Spy was a quiet but gripping drama, based on the memoirs of real-life agent Marthe McKenna. A worthy cast (Herbert Marshall, Conrad Veidt, Edmund Gwenn, Martita Hunt, Sir Gerald Du Maurier, Nigel Bruce, Donald Calthrop) supported the star. She was a fine actress and certainly one of the great beauties of the world, still virtually unknown outside of England. But Madeleine Carroll did not remain unknown long. Victor Saville directed. Screenplay by W. P. Lipscomb and Ian Hay.

When Will Rogers and John Ford got together, you knew you could expect the folksiest movie of the year. *Judge Priest* was that in spades but it was also one of the best for Will Rogers. Dudley Nichols and Lamar Trotti adapted the Irvin S. Cobb stories with equal amounts of Rogers-style comedy and sentiment. Stepin Fetchit played the kind of role that was popular then but has since made his name a dirty word.

The British sent us *Little Friend,* a terribly touching study of the effect of marital discord on an unhappy, only partially comprehending, child. Nova Pilbeam was heartbreaking in this role, perhaps the best screen child performance in memory. Margaret Kennedy and Christopher Isherwood wrote the script, Berthold Viertel directed.

Little Man, What Now?, the harsh Hans Fallada novel of postwar Germany, was prettied up a lot by Frank Borzage, always in his element with stories of young love. Douglass Montgomery was the boy and there were Catherine Doucet, Alan Hale, Christian Rub, De Witt Jennings, and Alan Mowbray. But, of course, it was the poignant appeal of Margaret Sullavan that made it all work. William Anthony McGuire wrote the script.

Sir James M. Barrie's *The Little Minister,* once a stage vehicle for Maude Adams, came to the screen as something for Katharine Hepburn. It was very sentimental and quaint in the Barrie style but it had a lot of Barrie

Herbert Marshall had been here before, but *I Was a Spy* introduced Americans to beautiful Madeleine Carroll.

Gangster Robert Montgomery discovers the country life and farm girl Maureen O'Sullivan in *Hideout.*

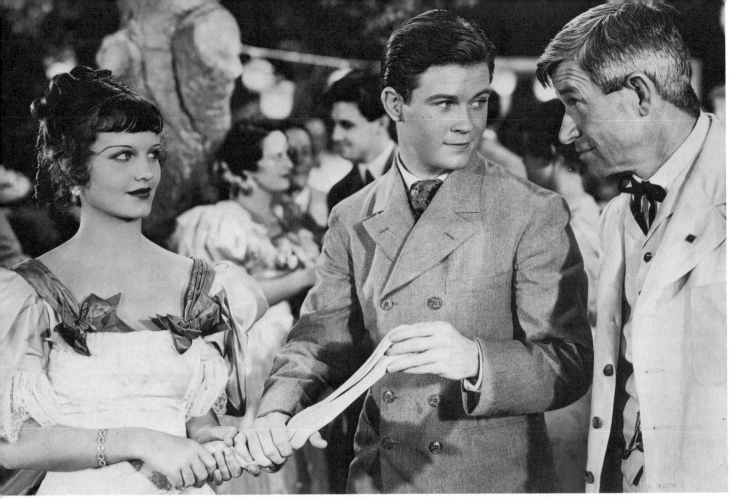

Rochelle Hudson and Tom Brown are the taffy-pulling sweethearts with Will Rogers in the title role of *Judge Priest*.

Douglass Montgomery and Margaret Sullavan as the unhappy young lovers in *Little Man, What Now?*

charm, too. And Hepburn, inclined to be coy, remained fun to watch. But it was John Beal, in the title role, who really wrapped up honors, supported ably by Donald Crisp, Alan Hale, Beryl Mercer, Dorothy Stickney, and others among the Hollywood British contingent who could be believably Scottish. Richard Wallace directed the script adapted by Jane Murfin, Sarah Y. Mason, and Victor Herman.

One of the first pictures to deal with kidnapping was *Miss Fane's Baby is Stolen,* a second and last American movie for Dorothea Wieck, who had been acclaimed in *Maedchen in Uniform.* Miss Wieck as a movie star, frantic when her child is kidnapped, was capable and there was notable work by Alice Brady and the estimable Baby LeRoy. Alexander Hall directed the Adela Rogers St. John script.

Ferenc Molnar's novel *The Paul Street Boys* provided the basis for a movie (*No Greater Glory*) which was something of a junior *All Quiet on the Western Front.* Director Frank Borzage was never happier than when he was turning on the tears and this youthful antiwar preachment gave him plenty of opportunity. The boys (Jimmy Butler, Jackie Searl, Bruce Line, Frankie Darro) were good, particularly George Breakston as the smallest and saddest of all. Script by Jo Swerling.

Catherine the Great, a relatively straightforward British picture with Elisabeth Bergner, Flora Robson, and Douglas Fairbanks, Jr., came to American screens early in 1934. Later in the year, Josef von Sternberg brought out his version, *The Scarlet Empress.* Seldom has von Sternberg been more excessive than in his pageant of madness, passion, and intrigue in the barbaric Russian court. There may have been little depth in the characterization of Marlene Dietrich but she has seldom been more lovingly photographed against sables, gargoyles, and all manner of bizarre furnishings. There were also Louise Dresser, as the Empress Elizabeth, and Sam Jaffe, virtually running berserk as the mad Peter. Screenplay by Manuel Komroff.

Miriam Hopkins, as a chorus girl who has witnessed a gangland killing, escapes to Princeton where she masquerades as the most unlikely boy in the world. Bing Crosby and Eddie Nugent are the college roommates who hide her out—Bing taking time off every so often to croon songs like "Love in Bloom" to Kitty Carlisle, the dean's daughter. This was *She Loves Me Not,* based on an Edward Hope novel and Howard Lindsay play, and a thoroughly entertaining movie as directed by Elliott Nugent and scripted by Benjamin Glazer.

Nova Pilbeam as the child of divorce in *Little Friend,* with Matheson Lang and Lydia Sherwood.

John Beal played the title role and Katherine Hepburn masqueraded as a gypsy in *The Little Minister.*

Alice Brady, Dorothea Wieck, and Baby LeRoy in *Miss Fane's Baby Is Stolen*.

George Breakston with parents Lois Wilson and Ralph Morgan in *No Greater Glory*.

In the middle is Miriam Hopkins; Eddie Nugent and Bing Crosby hold her up in *She Loves Me Not*.

Stan and Ollie elude their wives (Dorothy Christy and the ever-popular Mae Busch) to get to a rowdy convention. *Sons of the Desert* was the best of the Laurel and Hardy feature comedies but, except for some loyal fans who annually convene, it's a forgotten movie. Charley Chase helped make it one of their funniest. Frank Craven and Byron Morgan wrote and William A. Seiter directed.

No, Edward Everett Horton was not in the movie version of Benn Levy's *Springtime for Henry.* Maybe that's what was wrong. Otto Kruger played the title role without any comic style. But the picture still was amusing, mostly because of Nancy Carroll as the flirtatious wife and Heather Angel as an unexpectedly dangerous mousy secretary. Frank Tuttle directed and, with Keene Thompson, wrote the screenplay.

Sylvia Sidney, dressed to the teeth and being happily romantic, had one of her rare excursions into comedy in *Thirty Day Princess* which had no slums, no social problems. She was a joy and so was the movie in which she impersonated both an out-of-work actress and the princess for whom the actress takes over. Cary Grant was the leading man and a princess can't find a Prince Charming more tall, dark, and handsome. Marion Gering directed. Clarence Budington Kelland's story was adapted by several writers, including Preston Sturges.

Just about the most charming role for the charming Helen Hayes was that of Maggie Wylie, who, they told us, had no charm. It was Sir James M. Barrie's early feminist tract (behind every successful man is the bright little woman), *What Every Woman Knows.* Brian Aherne was particularly good as the humorless John Shand but so were Lucile Watson, Dudley Digges, Donald Crisp, the very attractive Madge Evans—as was the entire cast. And Gregory LaCava directed with his usual brightness. Screenplay by Monckton Hoffe.

Always excepting his masterpiece, *The Bank Dick,* W. C. Fields had his very best movie year in 1934. Certainly there is nothing "forgotten" about such of his pictures of the year as *It's a Gift, The Old Fashioned Way,* and his miraculous Mr. Micawber of *David Copperfield* (released just a few days after the 1935 New Year). Other actors predominated (although W. C. was far from submerged) in *Mrs. Wiggs of the Cabbage Patch* and *Six of a Kind.* It was *You're Telling Me,* unaccountably almost unknown today, which to our mind was *the* Fields movie of this big Fields year. This one got him into all kinds of his usual—and some unexpected—trouble and finally paired him with a princess (Adrienne Ames, so you know she was a pretty princess) who got him out of his jams. Erle Kenton directed J. P. McEvoy's screenplay.

Marlene Dietrich as *The Scarlet Empress,* with John Lodge, one day to be Governor of Connecticut and Ambassador to Spain.

Stan and Ollie in a classic, *Sons of the Desert,* with Charley Chase, a staple of shorts, in one of his very rare feature-film appearances.

Sylvia Sidney not only got to dress up, but she also got Cary Grant in *Thirty Day Princess.*

55

Brian Aherne meets Scottish spinster Helen Hayes, who thinks she has no charm, in *What Every Woman Knows*, with Dudley Digges and David Torrence.

Heather Angel, Nigel Bruce, Nancy Carroll, and Otto Kruger in *Springtime for Henry*.

Other Forgotten 1934 Films Worth Noting

Age of Innocence, genteel Edith Wharton adaptation but notable for atmosphere, Irene Dunne, and Helen Westley. . . . *Babbitt* dramatized Sinclair Lewis' famed novel without much insight but Guy Kibbee was well cast, Minna Gombell notable, and Aline MacMahon always sympathetic. (MacMahon was also the only reason for remembering such other 1934 movies as *Heat Lightning, Side Streets, Big Hearted Herbert* (this also with Kibbee.) . . . *Bolero* for the George Raft/Carole Lombard dance treatment of the Ravel . . . *Carolina,* screen version of Paul Green's *The House of Connelly* with good role for Janet Gaynor, strong performance by Henrietta Crosman . . . *The Constant Nymph,* the Margaret Kennedy play with Brian Aherne and Victoria Hooper . . . *Evergreen,* for joyous Jessie Matthews and her dancing . . . *Fog Over Frisco* gave us a hint of things to come with Bette Davis sinking her teeth into the role of a psychopathic rich girl. . . . *Forsaking All Others* was an MGM exercise in using a successful director (W. S. Van Dyke) and a number of stars (Crawford, Gable, Robert Montgomery, Charles Butterworth, Billie Burke, and Rosalind Russell) to make something that would please an audience who would then leave the theatre and never give it another thought. . . . *Fugitive Lovers,* about passengers on a transcontinental bus, beat *It Happened One Night* to the theatres but, in spite of the attractiveness of Robert Montgomery and Madge Evans, it had missing ingredients—Frank Capra and the screenwriting of Robert Riskin. . . . Roland Young at his very best—Lillian Gish right, too—in *His Double Life.* . . . *I am Suzanne,* Rowland V. Lee's rather sweet little fantasy–comedy, had Lilian Harvey in her best American role, Gene Raymond, marionettes. . . . *Gay Bride,* another early Lombard comedy, for Carole, ZaSu Pitts, and Nat Pendleton. . . . Lombard again in *Lady by Choice* which was something of a ripoff on Capra's *Lady for a Day,* even to casting May Robson as the old reprobate—but she scored again. . . . *One More River* was James Whale's civilized version of a Galsworthy novel, hampered by dull leading actors. . . . *The President Vanishes* was effective topical melodrama, directed by William Wellman with good actors (Arthur Byron, Janet Beecher, Edward Ellis, Osgood Perkins, Paul Kelly, among others). . . . *The Pursuit of Happiness*

W. C. Fields captivates Princess Adrienne Ames in *You're Telling Me.*

and *Romance in Manhattan* were both vehicles for the considerable charm of Francis Lederer, the first a Revolutionary War comedy with Joan Bennett, Mary Boland, and Charlie Ruggles, the other a contemporary fairy tale with Ginger Rogers. . . . *The Richest Girl in the World* was lightweight but enjoyable fare for Miriam Hopkins with Joel McCrea, Fay Wray. . . . The old George Kelly hit, *The Show Off,* became a vehicle for Spencer Tracy. . . . ZaSu Pitts, Pert Kelton, Edward Everett Horton, Nat Pendleton, Ned Sparks had a high old time in *Sing and Like It.* . . . Another takeoff on Radioland, *Twenty Million Sweethearts,* had Dick Powell, Ginger Rogers, and good songs. . . . *Murder at the Vanities* had a popular cast, a rudimentary murder plot, songs like "Cocktails for Two" and a tribute to "Marijuana," and chorus girls like Toby Wing. . . . *We Live Again,* handsomely directed by Rouben Mamoulian, presented Anna Sten and Fredric March in the best of many screen versions of Tolstoy's *Resurrection.* . . . *Wednesday's Child,* particularly well-played by young Frankie Thomas . . .

Chapter Seven

The Movie Year of 1935

Much variety in movie styles in 1935. There are films comparatively daring for the time—*Private Worlds,* dealing with psychiatry; *The Story of Louis Pasteur,* a biography of a man of science; and *Black Fury,* poking a tentative finger into labor problems.

Pictures are big in scope—like *Mutiny on the Bounty,* for instance, and *Lives of a Bengal Lancer.* But one of the top ones is a low-budget sleeper, John Ford's *The Informer;* another is George Stevens's quiet little small town drama starring a luminous Katharine Hepburn in *Alice Adams.*

Technicolor returns with *Becky Sharp*—a soft, lifelike color far removed from the garish two-color postcard tints of the past. Back come the gangsters—but this time around the heroes are G-men. Hollywood delves into the classics—Shakespeare, Tolstoy, Dickens, Hugo, Dostoevsky, Thackeray among them—and sometimes the results are satisfying.

New stars make their appearance—Henry Fonda, Luise Rainer, Errol Flynn, Olivia de Havilland, Fred MacMurray, Rosalind Russell, Robert Taylor, Josephine Hutchinson, Walter Brennan. Nelson Eddy and Jeanette MacDonald begin their duets in *Naughty Marietta* while Fred Astaire whirls on with Ginger Rogers. Jean Arthur, a passé ingenue, returns as an able comedienne. Back, too, is Charles Boyer who had tried American movies unsuccessfully before. Merle Oberon, Peter Lorre are other imports.

But some faces are seen no more. Will Rogers is killed in a crash. Helen Hayes decides she prefers Broadway. Anna Sten, counted as a failure, is dropped after a tremendous build-up. Marlene Dietrich will survive her career difficulties but it's just about over for Al Jolson, Nancy Carroll, Marion Davies, Janet Gaynor, George Arliss, Constance Bennett, Ann Harding, and Ruby Keeler.

Besides those films already mentioned, there are many which survive—Eugene O'Neill's *Ah, Wilderness!* Garbo's *Anna Karenina;* Cukor's *David Copperfield;* the Marx brothers masterpiece, *A Night at the Opera;* Laughton's *Ruggles of Red Gap;* Noel Coward in the Hecht–MacArthur *The Scoundrel;* Hitchcock's *39 Steps,* with Robert Donat and Madeleine Carroll; the joyous Astaire-Rogers *Top Hat*—and *Roberta,* too. And there were others to note—just for starters, how about *The Bride of Frankenstein?* And Errol Flynn's *Captain Blood;* Gable/Harlow/Beery in *China Seas;* Dietrich's own favorite of her von Sternberg's *The Devil is a Woman;* *The Farmer Takes a Wife* with Janet Gaynor and a new boy who had played it on stage, Henry Fonda; the Fredric March-Charles Laughton *Les Miserables;* Irene Dunne's *Magnificent Obsession;* Max Reinhardt's *A Midsummer Night's Dream;* Leslie Howard's *Scarlet Pimpernel;* Ronald Colman's *Tale of Two Cities;* and a John Ford–Edward G. Robinson comic meller, *The Whole Town's Talking,* with Jean Arthur.

They're all well-remembered movies. There were others which are not but rate a thought or two.

Forgotten Films of 1935

It was unusual to see Sylvia Sidney, looking glamorous and without a problem in the world except whether to marry a young man or to continue loving an old one. One sometimes forgot that Sidney was an adroit comedienne who could flip out a bright line with the best of them. *Accent on Youth* reminded you. Herbert Marshall and Ernest Cossart helped, too. Wesley Ruggles directed the Claude Binyon adaptation of Samson Raphaelson's hit Broadway play.

The young ones (Philip Reed, Lon Chaney, Jr., and Nick Foran—later known as Dick Foran) can't understand Sylvia Sidney's infatuation with an older man, Herbert Marshall, in *Accent on Youth*.

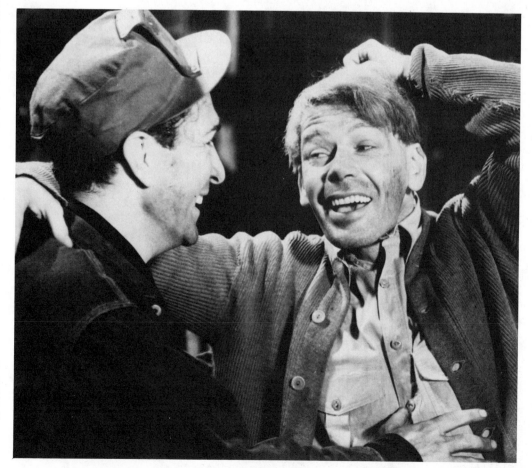

Paul Muni, as a Polish miner, whoops it up with J. Carrol Naish in *Black Fury*.

Black Fury was a gutsy and, for its time, courageous film with Warner Brothers, always into topical subjects, scoring with this sociological drama with a labor theme. Paul Muni gave one of his finest characterizations as a stupid Polish miner forced into a fight for rights he can scarcely comprehend. Michael Curtiz directed the Abem Finkel and Carl Erickson screenplay with Karen Morley, J. Carrol Naish, William Gargan, and John Qualen.

The Dark Angel was one of the better love stories when Samuel Goldwyn presented it in silent days with Ronald Colman and Vilma Banky. It worked just as well when Goldwyn remade it as a vehicle for Fredric March and Merle Oberon (the latter scrubbed of her exotic makeup for the occasion). Lillian Hellman and Mordaunt Shairp provided a literate adaptation of Guy Bolton's play, Sidney Franklin directed, and there was an extremely capable supporting cast (Herbert Marshall, Janet Beecher, Frieda Inescort, Henrietta Crosman, John Halliday, and George Breakston.)

Fredric March does not want Merle Oberon to know he is blind in The Dark Angel.

Elisabeth Bergner, who had originated the role on stage, ran through her remarkable repertoire of dramatic tricks —madcap waif to bereaved mother in *Escape Me Never*. The Margaret Kennedy play was soupy but it was something to see Bergner in action. Dr. Paul Czinner directed; Hugh Sinclair and Griffith Jones repeated their stage roles.

Before he went on to more serious things, William Wyler proved that he was something of a master at light romantic comedy, too. (He wasn't to return to the genre until *Roman Holiday* almost two decades later.) Neither of Wyler's 1935 films—*The Good Fairy* or, particularly, *The Gay Deception*—is remembered, nor were they treated with much attention even when they originally came out. But both are models of 1930s movie comedy.

Gay Deception had a prince masquerading as a bellboy in a luxury hotel, the prince being played by Francis Lederer in those happy days before his irrepressible charm began to fade. Frances Dee, one of our most neglected good actresses and a beauty, had her very best role as the girl in the case. And the supporting cast was dotted with people like Alan Mowbray, Ferdinand

Frances Dee is startled by an unorthodox bellhop, played by Francis Lederer, in *The Gay Deception*.

Gottschalk, Luis Alberni, and Akim Tamiroff. Screenplay by Stephen Avery and Don Hartman.

There were even better people in the supporting cast

Griffith Jones and Hugh Sinclair with Elisabeth Bergner, the gamine of *Escape Me Never*.

Alan Hale visits the orphanage, run by Beulah Bondi, in which Margaret Sullavan is the eldest orphan, in *The Good Fairy*.

George Raft's expression isn't exactly friendly to Ray Milland in *The Glass Key*. The woman was billed on screen as Rosalind Culli; in the ads she was called Rosalind Keith.

Fred MacMurray and Carole Lombard, both out for money but settling for love, in *Hands Across the Table*.

of *The Good Fairy,* most notably Frank Morgan, but also Herbert Marshall, Reginald Owen, Beulah Bondi, Alan Hale, and Cesar Romero. And Margaret Sullavan kept her character of the naive little orphan who learns about the wicked world from being insufferably cute. Preston Sturges adapted the Molnar play.

On the heels of the *Thin Man* hit came another Dashiell Hammett thriller, not nearly so merry but tough and exciting. This was *The Glass Key* which used George Raft's poker faced menace well and gave Edward Arnold a strong role as an honest politician beset by criminal forces. Guinn Williams stood out in the cast which also included the beauteous Claire Dodd. Frank Tuttle directed the screenplay by Kathryn Scola, Kubec Glasman, and Harry Ruskin.

By 1935 Carole Lombard had found her niche as probably the best glamour girl comedienne of her era. Each new Lombard picture after *Twentieth Century* furnished further proof and *Hands Across the Table* was the most satisfying to that date. Carole played a manicurist out for a rich man and Fred MacMurray, always at his best in roles like this, was the man with the same idea. Of course, she thinks he's rich—but you get the idea. Mitchell Leisen directed this (although Ernst Lubitsch is supposed to have had a hand in it, too) and the screenplay, from a Vina Delmar novel, was by Norman Krasna, Vincent Lawrence and Herbert Fields. Other cast members who helped included Ralph Bellamy, Marie Prevost, Astrid Allwyn, and Ruth Donnelly.

I'll Love You Always was a very unpretentious little picture about a pair of young marrieds trying to make it in Depression New York. Without approaching King Vidor's masterpiece, it had some of the feeling of *The Crowd.* However, Columbia, having apparently decided that Nancy Carroll was a has-been and George Murphy a never-would-be, just gave it "B" picture treatment and it quickly disappeared. Actually both stars were sincere and moving but their picture never had a chance. Leo Bulgakov directed. Screenplay by Vera Caspary and Sidney Buchman.

Although America really turned on to Alfred Hitchcock in *The 39 Steps,* the connoisseurs discovered him earlier in *The Man Who Knew Too Much.* Peter Lorre, in his first film since *M,* and Nova Pilbeam, for the few who saw *Little Friend,* may have brought audiences to the theater but it was the devilish build-up of Hitchcockian suspense that made it an event. Hitchcock made a glossy remake of this twenty years later (with James Stewart and Doris Day in the roles played here by Leslie Banks and Edna Best) but the original was more tight and tense. Written by Charles Bennett, D. B. Wyndham-Lewis.

Sylvia Sidney was in trouble with the law again in *Mary Burns, Fugitive,* branded a gun moll because her nice young man turned out to be a notorious desperado. Nobody played such roles as well as Sidney—and this was one of her best. Alan Baxter was icy as the bad man, Brian Donlevy had a new kind of menace as another relentless killer, and helpful also were Pert Kelton and Melvyn Douglas. The Gene Towne/Graham Baker story was directed in tense, staccato style by the underrated William K. Howard.

Bing Crosby crooned some Rodgers and Hart songs and made mild love to two beauties, Joan Bennett and Gail Patrick. But the real joy of *Mississippi* was W. C. Fields, as the boozy commodore of a river show boat in the antebellum South. The picture had some of the great Fields moments—especially a poker game in which he frantically attempts to lose the fifth ace he has dealt himself. Edward A. Sutherland directed. From a Booth Tarkington novel.

Newlyweds George Murphy and Nancy Carroll in *I'll Love You Always.*

You can tell that Frank Vosper and Peter Lorre are in the tradition of Hitchcock villains. Leslie Banks and Nova Pilbeam are their prisoners in *The Man Who Knew Too Much.*

Alan Baxter is ready for a shoot-out, despite Sylvia Sidney's pleas, in *Mary Burns, Fugitive*. Melvyn Douglas stands by.

Bing Crosby and Joan Bennett meet W. C. Fields and Queenie Smith in *Mississippi*.

Samuel Goldwyn gave up too quickly on his million-dollar star, Anna Sten. True, her American debut film, *Nana,* was close to disaster—and she didn't help. But she was very moving in *We Live Again* and, in her last Goldwyn movie, King Vidor's *The Wedding Night,* she was a true tragic heroine as a Polish farm girl whose love of a sophisticated novelist is doomed. Gary Cooper was less ill at ease than he normally would be in a role such as this and Helen Vinson was extremely sympathetic as his wife. Written by Edwin Knopf and Ruth Fitzgerald.

Other Forgotten 1935 Films Worthy of Note

Sylvia Sidney's beauty and poignant performance were enough to make *Behold My Wife* worth seeing but the story about the socialite and his Indian bride creaked with age. . . . Ann Harding was a bit too noble as the kiss-and-tell heroine of *Biography of a Bachelor Girl* and Robert Montgomery was hopelessly miscast but some of the S. N. Behrman wit came through. . . . Bette Davis stole *Bordertown* right away from Paul Muni as an unstable, and finally insane, wife with a letch for Mexican Muni. . . . Will Rogers did his same old thing in *Doubting Thomas* but people like Billie Burke, Alison Skipworth, Frank Albertson, Gail Patrick, and Sterling Holloway enlivened the movie version of George Kelly's *The Torch Bearers.* . . . *I Dream Too Much* was a tuneful trifle for Lily Pons, giving her songs from opera to Kern—and Henry Fonda as her leading man. . . . Joan Crawford looked every inch the star of *I Live My Life* and *No More Ladies* but what made them bright were other cast members—Brian Aherne, Aline MacMahon, Frank Morgan, Eric Blore, Arthur Treacher in the first, and Robert Montgomery, Franchot Tone, Edna May Oliver, Gail Patrick in *Ladies.* . . . W. C. Fields had some of his funnier moments in *The Man on the Flying Trapeze.* . . . Josephine Hutchinson, Pat O'-Brien, and Jean Muir played with sincerity in a big business drama, *Oil for the Lamps of China.* . . . Jean Muir radiated youth and beauty in *Orchids to You.* . . . *Public Hero Number One* was good G Man versus gangster melodrama, extremely well played by Jean Arthur, Joseph Calleia, Lionel Barrymore, Chester Morris. . . . Constance Cummings, Sally Eilers, Robert Young, and Edward Arnold headed the cast of *Remember Last Night* about murders among the smart set participants of a drunken orgy. . . . *Show Them No Mercy* was kidnap melodrama, well acted by Cesar Romero and Bruce Cabot playing two types of heavies—the suave and the sadistic.

Gary Cooper became leading man for Anna Sten in *The Wedding Night,* her best—but last—major movie.

Chapter Eight

The Movie Year of 1936

An extraordinary year . . . 1936 is loaded with big ones and good ones and sometimes the big ones are good, too. The theater and book worlds still supply a high percentage of product to be turned into celluloid but there are more and better originals.

Films like *Fury, The Black Legion,* and *Winterset* demonstrate a new awareness of social problems. So does *My Man Godfrey,* which is also an early entry in the screwball comedy cycle.

All kinds of promising young people are beginning to make their mark—James Stewart, Tyrone Power, Judy Garland, Simone Simon, Don Ameche, Ann Sheridan, Marsha Hunt, Frances Farmer, Burgess Meredith, Dorothy Lamour, and Gladys George among them. Madeleine Carroll returns to stay from England and back from Broadway comes Humphrey Bogart. Spencer Tracy, almost a has-been, finds new movie life—and what a life!

Sonja Henie starts her screen skating while Jeanette MacDonald and Nelson Eddy continue their duets in *Rose Marie.* Jeanette, without Eddy but with Clark Gable, sings through the *San Francisco* earthquake. Grace Moore keeps trilling, too, and so does Irene Dunne (in *Show Boat*) while also unexpectedly stepping out in comedy in *Theodora Goes Wild.* There is a lot of topflight comedy this year, ranging from the pixilated humor of Capra's *Mr. Deeds Goes to Town,* with Gary Cooper and Jean Arthur, to the madness of LaCava's *My Man Godfrey* with William Powell and Carole Lombard, not forgetting such others as the Loy–Powell–Harlow–Tracy *Libeled Lady,* the suavely romantic Lubitsch-type in the Dietrich–Cooper *Desire,* right down to such nonsense as *Sing Me a Love Song* with Hugh Herbert woo-wooing through a whole succession of

roles. Fred and Ginger have two lively outings—Irving Berlin's *Follow the Fleet* and their matchless Jerome Kern *Swing Time.*

Plays to films range all the way from *The Green Pastures* to *The Petrified Forest* and include a miscast Shearer and Howard in *Romeo and Juliet;* a glorious Garbo in *Camille;* an effective Rosalind Russell in *Craig's Wife;* and such fine film versions as the Burgess Meredith-Margo *Winterset* and two by William Wyler —the Walter Huston-Ruth Chatterton-Mary Astor *Dodsworth* and Lillian Hellman's *The Children's Hour* (retitled *These Three* and carefully eliminating any Lesbian tinge)—with performances to note by Miriam Hopkins, Bonita Granville, Marcia Mae Jones, Catherine Doucet, Alma Kruger, Merle Oberon, and Joel McCrea. The biggest book to film, *Anthony Adverse,* proves something of a bomb, but another all-time bestseller, *Trail of the Lonesome Pine,* scores as the first outdoor Technicolor movie with a cast that includes Sylvia Sidney, Henry Fonda, Beulah Bondi and Fred MacMurray.

Let's alphabetically list the pictures of the year as *Camille; Dodsworth;* Fritz Lang's *Fury* (with Spencer Tracy, Sylvia Sidney); *Mr. Deeds Goes to Town; My Man Godfrey; Swing Time;* and *These Three.* There are many more to note—the Errol Flynn *Charge of the Light Brigade;* the Howard Hawks–William Wyler *Come and Get It;* Gary Cooper and Madeleine Carroll in the Odets–Milestone *The General Died at Dawn;* Powell, Loy and Luise Rainer in *The Great Ziegfeld;* the Gary Cooper–Jean Arthur–DeMille *The Plainsman;* W. C. Fields's *Poppy;* Fredric March in Howard Hawks's *Road to Glory;* Hitchcock's *Secret Agent;* and a number of the others already listed. And those worthy ones that most people don't think about any more.

Forgotten Films of 1936 to Remember

Probably because Brian Aherne was not a box office name, *Beloved Enemy* was an overlooked film. It would be hard to imagine any other actor who could have better played the tragic hero of this drama of the Irish Rebellion of 1921. It had all the elements of Samuel Goldwyn's usual painstaking production—a literate script by John Balderston, Rose Franken, and William Brown Meloney, direction by H. C. Potter plus a fine cast (Merle Oberon, Jerome Cowan, Donald Crisp, David Niven, Ra Hould, Karen Morley *et al.*). And Gregg Toland continued to prove he was an artist with the camera.

The Black Legion was shattering—fictionalized, perhaps, but not too far from news reports of the actual Americanism cult that flourished in the midwest in the 1930s. Warners led Hollywood in turning out topical melodrama ripped from headlines. This was one of the best. Humphrey Bogart played an ordinary American working man who becomes a maddened convert to the cause. Erin O'Brien Moore, Robert Barrat, Helen Flint, Joseph Sawyer led a good cast. Archie L. Mayo directed. Screenplay by Abem Finkel and William Wister.

The kind of amiable musical entertainment that worked in the 1930s, *Born to Dance* had no special wit or style. What it did have was Eleanor Powell's rat-a-tat tapping, Jimmy Stewart's boyishness, Virginia Bruce's face, Frances Langford's voice, some comedy turns by Reginald Gardiner, Helen Troy, Barnett Parker, Una Merkel and others, and songs (like "Easy to Love" and "I've Got You Under My Skin") by Cole Porter. It was enough. Directed by Roy Del Ruth, screenplay by Jack McGowan, Sid Silvers, and B. G. DeSylva.

Leo Carillo played a Mexican bandit who has learned how to be a bad man from watching American gangster movies in *The Gay Desperado*, which Rouben Mamoulian directed with verve. Nino Martini, the operatic tenor, had plenty of opportunities to sing and joined the comedy as well. Ida Lupino, Mischa Auer, Harold Huber helped, too. Screenplay by Leo Birinski and Wallace Smith.

The Ghost Goes West (screenplay by Robert E. Sherwood, directed by Renê Clair) was a thoroughly delightful British comedy about a boorish American millionaire (Eugene Pallette in fine fettle) who transplants a landmark Scottish castle, complete with ghost, to his estate in Florida. Robert Donat was incomparable, both as the astral ancestor and as his more staid modern descendant.

Jerome Cowan, usually the hip comic, had a rare dramatic role, with Brian Aherne, in *Beloved Enemy*.

Humphrey Bogart begs for help from Dick Foran in *The Black Legion*.

Jessie Matthews was called "The Dancing Divinity" and the ad writers did not exaggerate. She was brightly pretty, had a cheerful sense of comedy, and sang pleasantly. But her dancing was a dream even though most of her numbers were shoddily choreographed and a promised union with Astaire never came off. Her two 1935 movies—*First a Girl* and *It's Love Again*—had the usual inconsequential story lines but gave Miss Jessie her best movie dancing opportunities. Both films were somehow spoiled by the memory that Sonnie Hale was also there. Victor Saville directed both.

Just to look at Madeleine Carroll in Georgian England period costumes is reason enough for including *Lloyds of London* in this book. Almost as pretty as Madeleine was an actor new to leading roles, Tyrone Power, but he played with dash and skill as well. The look of London in that era came impressively to the screen under Henry King's direction. Excellent actors—Virginia Field, George Sanders, Sir Guy Standing, C. Aubrey Smith, and most of Hollywood's featured British colony—contributed too. Screenplay by Ernest Pascal and Walter Ferris.

Harold Lloyd's usual comedies were slapstick and gags built around a Harold Lloyd type. *The Milky Way* put Lloyd into an already existing character albeit one that fitted him well—the timid milkman who believes he is a champ prizefighter. Director Leo McCarey surrounded him with other top clowns who were not just Lloyd slapstick stooges. Count Adolphe Menjou, Verree Teasedale, Marjorie Gateson, William Gargan, and Lionel Stander in their number along with two very likely leading ladies, Dorothy Wilson and Helen Mack. Grover Jones, Frank Butler, and Richard Cornell adapted the Broadway play by Lynn Root and Harry Clark.

Suppose that Richard Halliburton met and married Katharine Hepburn with neither aware of the identity of the other. That was the jumping-off point for *The Moon's Our Home* and let's credit Dorothy Parker (although other writers were also listed) for the bright adaptation of a routine Faith Baldwin novel. Credit also Henry Fonda and Margaret Sullavan as two of the most engaging young actors around. (The fact that they had once been briefly married in real life was good for the gossips but didn't relate to the happiness of their screen association.) And the supporting cast included people like Charles Butterworth, Beulah Bondi, Henrietta Crosmar Margaret Hamilton, Dorothy Stickney, and Walter Brennan. William A. Seiter directed.

(LEFT TOP)
Ida Lupino isn't frightened of Nino Martini, *The Gay Desperado*, but James Blakely respects that gun.

(LEFT)
Even Jimmy Stewart joined singers and dancers Frances Langford, Buddy Ebsen, Eleanor Powell, Una Merkel, and Sid Silvers in *Born to Dance*.

Robert Young came from America to join Jessie Matthews in *It's Love Again*.

When his ancestral castle is dismantled to be shipped to America, the castle's ghost, Robert Donat, goes too —*The Ghost Goes West*.

A very handsome couple, Madeleine Carroll and Tyrone Power, in *Lloyds of London*.

That's Harold Lloyd looking over the transom. Verree Teasdale, Adolphe Menjou, and Lionel Stander below in *The Milky Way*.

Henry Fonda is a writer, and Margaret Sullavan is a reader, in adjoining train compartments, in *The Moon's Our Home*. Beulah Bondi is her secretary; I think his is Brandon Hurst.

(Above) Jessie Matthews at door masquerades as a boy even though she's *First a Girl*. Griffith Jones and Sonnie Hale are seated. (Below) Henry Fonda and Margaret Sullavan in *The Moon's Our Home*.

Nova Pilbeam is ready for the executioner in *Nine Days a Queen*. Sybil Thorndike waits.

Britain didn't treat its two best juvenile actors of the 1930s very well. Nova Pilbeam, with *Little Friend* behind her, had undemanding roles in a couple of Hitchcock pictures and Desmond Tester had a great suspense scene in Hitchcock's *Sabotage* but nothing else of note. But in *Nine Days a Queen,* they both had their moments of glory as tragic pawns in plotting for the British throne. It stands among the best British historical films. Cedric Hardwicke, Sybil Thorndike, John Mills, Frank Cellier, Felix Aylmer, Martita Hunt, and Gwen Ffrangcon-Davies provided the kind of support that made every bit a gem. Robert Stevenson directed the Miles Malleson screenplay.

Robert Montgomery at his best, and before Cary Grant came into his own, was the foremost light comedian among movie leading men. And *Piccadilly Jim* did present Montgomery at his best. The P. G. Wodehouse story, directed by Robert Z. Leonard, gave bountiful opportunities to others as well, among them being Frank Morgan, Billie Burke, Robert Benchley, Eric Blore, Cora Witherspoon, and the always attractive Madge Evans. Charles Brackett and Elwin Knopf wrote the screenplay.

In Charles Laughton's gallery of extraordinary biographical characterizations, *Rembrandt* ranks high. There were notable portrayals also by Elsa Lanchester and Gertrude Lawrence. One of the most stunning art films ever made, directed by Alexander Korda, filmed by George Perinal, with screenplay by Carl Zuchmayer.

Unlike other studios which went in for more elaborate things, 20th Century-Fox produced unpretentious musicals, which were a melange of pleasant songs and singers, a story line that satirized—or more often burlesqued—topical themes and casts that leaned heavily on comics. One of its most enjoyable was *Sing, Baby, Sing* with Adolphe Menjou doing his take-off of John Barrymore, Alice Faye and Tony Martin singing a particularly tuneful score, and such worthies as the Ritz Brothers, Patsy Kelly, Gregory Ratoff, and Ted Healy gagging it up in support. Sidney Lanfield directed the screenplay by Milton Sperling, Jack Yellen, Harry Tugend.

Things to Come, H. G. Wells's conception of the world of the future made provocative cinema fare as brought to the screen by Alexander Korda and directed by William Cameron Menzies. Raymond Massey, Ralph Richardson and Sir Cedric Hardwicke headed the cast but the star was the imagination of Mr. Wells.

(LEFT)
Robert Montgomery and Madge Evens in *Piccadilly Jim.*

Charles Laughton is *Rembrandt;* Elsa Lanchester, his model and love (and real life wife).

Margaretta Scott taunts Raymond Massey in *Things to Come*.

Alice Faye and Adolphe Menjou in *Sing, Baby, Sing*.

Myrna Loy was the perfect wife in 1936, whether sharing the Dempsey-Tunney fight with Warner Baxter and friends Ian Hunter and Claire Trevor in *To Mary With Love* . . .

. . . or sharing breakfast with Clark Gable in *Wife vs. Secretary.*

Myrna Loy continued to be just about everybody's favorite screen wife, even when she was an unhappy one as in two 1936 movies, *To Mary With Love* and *Wife vs. Secretary. Mary* had a line that went "People always think movies should be more like life. I think life should be more like the movies." Life was very much like the movies in both films—the first having to do with ten years in a marriage from 1925, the other summed up in the title with Jean Harlow as the secretary and Clark Gable as their prize. John Cromwell and Clarence Brown respectively directed. Much more cool was Myrna in *After the Thin Man,* the second outing for Nick and Nora Charles, with William Powell, of course, back as Nick. W. S. Van Dyke again directed. The Hacketts wrote the screenplay based on Dashiell Hammet's characters with Richard Sherman and Faith Baldwin as original authors respectively of *Mary* and *Wife.*

Hollywood pretty well toned down that bawdy title lady of Barry Benefield's book, *Valiant Is the Word for Carrie,* but Gladys George, as always, played her so well that she remained interesting in spite of the Shirley Temple treatment. The happiest moments of the picture were those that detailed Carrie's involvement with a spunky little boy. This role was played by Jackie Moran, one of the very good child actors of his time. (His character grew much duller when he grew up to become John Howard.) With Harry Carey, Arline Judge, Dudley Digges, and Isabel Jewell. Wesley Ruggles directed Claude Beinyon's screenplay.

. . . And of course, she shared a murder mystery with William Powell in *After the Thin Man.*

Other Forgotten 1936 Films Worth Noting

Tod Browning, who used to do the same thing for Lon Chaney, dressed up Lionel Barrymore as a sinister old woman in *The Devil Doll* and had him shrinking people to a fraction of their normal size to further his nefarious plots. . . . *Garden of Allah* was heavy love in the desert à la Marlene and Boyer and the new Technicolor gave it all quite a shine. Joseph Schildkraut was jaunty in support . . . Booth Tarkington and Jane Withers turned out to be a good combination in *Gentle Julia,* with Marsha Hunt and Tom Brown a nice pair of young lovers . . . Beulah Bondi walked away with all the acting honors in *The Gorgeous Hussy* as the pathetic Rachel Jackson even though the rest of the cast included names like Joan Crawford, Robert Taylor, James Stewart, Franchot Tone, Lionel Barrymore, Melvyn Douglas all in cardboard roles. . . . Grace Moore, coyer than ever, turned to operetta in *The King Steps Out* which had a pretty Fritz Kreisler score beautifully sung, of course. . . . *Ladies in Love* gave us three soap operas in one movie but the protagonists—Janet Gaynor, Loretta Young, Constance Bennett, along with Simone Simon—were fetching and Alan Mowbray was funny. . . . Lots of suds in *Next Time We Love* but you can't neglect a Margaret Sullavan movie, particularly when she had a brand-new leading man named James Stewart. . . . *One Rainy Afternoon* had a Lubitschlike quality up to a point but petered out although Francis Lederer and Ida Lupino helped considerably. . . . *Pigskin Parade* was wacky football comedy which introduced a belting, singing kid named Judy Garland. . . . John Ford directed *Prisoner of Shark Island* about an innocent doctor (Warner Baxter) accused of complicity in Lincoln's assassination. John Carradine was arresting in his personification of malevolence. . . .

In *Valiant Is the Word for Carrie*, Gladys George adopted John Howard and Arline Judge.

Chapter Nine

The Movie Year of 1937

Every conceivable kind of movie entertainment is released in 1937, a rich year. You want big ones? We give you *Captains Courageous* and *The Good Earth, Lost Horizon,* and *Hurricane.* Or you can have a little gem like Leo McCarey's study of old age, *Make Way for Tomorrow,* with Beulah Bondi and Victor Moore breaking your heart. There is comedy at its hilarious high with McCarey's *The Awful Truth* and William Wellman's *Nothing Sacred.* There are stunning dramas like Fritz Lang's *You Only Live Once* with Sylvia Sidney and Henry Fonda, and the Goldwyn–Wyler–Sidney Kingsley *Dead End,* with Sidney again and Bogart. Watch Hepburn and Janet Gaynor hit stardom in *Stage Door* and *A Star is Born.* You can sob with Stanwyck as *Stella Dallas* and swashbuckle with Colman in *The Prisoner of Zenda.* Muni is another great man in *The Life of Emile Zola.* Still doing their thing are Fred and Ginger (*Shall We Dance?*), Jeanette and Nelson (*Maytime*), and the Marx Boys in *A Day at the Races.* Doing something very different are Robert Montgomery (*Night Must Fall*), Cary Grant moving into mirth with *Topper* and *Awful Truth,* and Claire Trevor in *Dead End.*

But the biggest news is, of all things, a cartoon. It's Christmas—any way you want to figure—when Walt Disney's *Snow White and the Seven Dwarfs* shows up. For years, we've known Donald Duck. The Three Little Pigs and their *Who's Afraid of the Big, Bad Wolf?* have had depression-weary people whistling. A magazine has run a cartoon showing a disgruntled customer leaving a theater whose marquee advertises "2 Big Features . . . Bank Night . . . Dishes . . . News" the caption—"What, no Mickey Mouse!"

But these were pastimes of a few minutes. Who would have thought that a feature Disney would have been more than mere novelty? But it is—much, much more.

Some names make news—Janet Gaynor is a star reborn and Luise Rainer wins her second successive Oscar for what turns out to be the last distinction of her film career. There are newcomers—a sweater girl named Lana Turner; a muscle boy named Jon Hall; a whole flock of "Dead End" kids; the singing sweetheart, Deanna Durbin; and a lovely Broadway character actress, Fay Bainter, transferring to movies. And don't

neglect Jane Bryan and Jane Wyatt, Andrea Leeds, Lucille Ball, Eve Arden, Joan Fontaine, the Lane Sisters, Alan Curtis, and Wayne Morris. In England, Laurence Olivier, once a Hollywoood failure, is looking good again and some new-to-movies faces like Vivien Leigh, Rex Harrison, Flora Robson, and Sara Allgood begin to be known.

But the names on everyone's lips are Dopey, Grumpy, Sleepy, Bashful, and the rest.

Most of the pictures of the year have already been mentioned. Let's list the best alphabetically—*The Awful Truth; Captains Courageous; Dead End; The Good Earth; The Life of Emile Zola; Make Way For Tomorrow; Night Must Fall; Nothing Sacred; Snow White and the Seven Dwarfs;* LaCava's *Stage Door;* Wellman's *A Star Is Born;* and *You Only Live Once.* And, of course, there were more—very worthwhile even though they may not come so readily to mind.

Forgotten Films to Remember of 1937

Call It a Day, Dodie Smith's little family comedy, made a very quiet but nice movie as directed by Archie Mayo and adapted by Casey Robinson. It was the cast that counted—the striking Frieda Inescort, usually given inferior things, as the wife and mother and the always-welcome Roland Young as her unlikely wooer. But the others—Ian Hunter, Olivia de Havilland, Alice Brady, Bonita Granville, Peggy Wood, Walter Woolf King, Una O'Connor, Beryl Mercer, and Anita Louise did well, too.

Perhaps because for the first time she was subordinated to her leading man, *Conquest* is a usually overlooked Garbo picture. Certainly the goddess had her divine moments but the interest of the story was centered around a brooding Napoleon, played by that master brooder, Charles Boyer. And there was a charming cameo by Maria Ouspenskaya. Clarence Brown directed with emphasis on the film's more spectacular moments. Samuel Hoffenstein, Salka Viertel, and S. N. Behrman wrote the screenplay.

Rebellious daughter Olivia de Havilland has a heart-to-heart talk with her mother, Frieda Inescort, in *Call It a Day*.

Charles Boyer is Napoleon, Greta Garbo his inamorata, in *Conquest*.

Another step in the upward rise of Jean Arthur as one of the best comediennes of the 1930s and 1940s was *Easy Living*, an amiably wacky farce in which Miss Arthur as a secretary riding the open deck of a double-decker bus is hit on the head with a Kolinsky coat thrown from a penthouse by an irascible tycoon. All manner of complications develop, of course. Edward Arnold was in his element in that role and there were plenty of opportunities for Luis Alberni and Franklin Pangborn to do their thing. Mitchell Leisen directed the screenplay by Preston Sturges.

Ray Milland and Jean Arthur in *Easy Living*. You can recognize Luis Alberni and Franklin Pangborne among the onlookers.

Flora Robson's marvelous Queen Elizabeth, with two attractive young people, Laurence Olivier and Vivien Leigh, in *Fire over England*.

Brian Aherne played the distinguished actor *The Great Garrick*. Olivia de Havilland portrays an admirer.

Flora Robson's stunning characterization of the ungainly, vain Queen Elizabeth dominated the Erich Pommer production, *Fire Over England,* even though Laurence Olivier and Vivien Leigh also appeared as a particularly handsome pair of young lovers. It was impressive historical drama with Raymond Massey and Leslie Banks among others in the cast. William K. Howard directed. Written by A. E. W. Mason, Clemence Dane, and Sergei Nolbandor.

Although he never won the screen reputation of someone like Fredric March, Brian Aherne was his equal in versatility in the few film chances he had to prove himself. *The Great Garrick,* hardly biographical but a lively farce built around a fanciful adventure involving eighteenth century England's most famous actor, called for vigorous romantics and adroit comedy playing and Aherne was more than up to it. Olivia de Havilland looked her prettiest and there were other honeys around, Lana Turner and Marie Wilson, as well as such comedy stalwarts as Edward Everett Horton, Luis Alberni, and Etienne Girardot. Mervyn Le Roy produced and James Whale directed the Ernest Vajda script.

With a bright, if inconsequential, screenplay by Claude Binyon and expert direction by Welsey Ruggles, *I Met Him in Paris* needed only very accomplished comedy actors. You could find few better than Claudette Colbert, Melvyn Douglas, and Robert Young. It all happily worked. Fritz Feld in one of his earliest bits—he's still doing them—grabbed some special attention.

Bette Davis had four films in 1937—one, *Marked Women,* certainly not forgotten; another, *That Certain Woman* with Henry Fonda, deservedly so. The other two, while hardly in her gallery of unforgettable characterizations, were too good to disappear as they practically have. She wasn't the title or principal character in Michael Curtiz's fast moving prizefight yarn, *Kid Galahad.* That was Wayne Morris—and good, too. But Davis, along with Edward G. Robinson, Humphrey Bogart, Jane Bryan, and Harry Carey, gave it quality. *It's Love I'm After* was much more valuable for her—one of her few opportunities to play all-out farce in a role that anticipated her Margo Channing of *All About Eve.* She, with Leslie Howard, played a Lunt/Fontanne sort of team of theater idols with a wide-eyed Olivia de Havilland as his adoring fan. Archie L. Mayo directed with people like Eric Blore, Bonita Granville, Spring Byington, George Barbier, and Patric Knowles all helpful in the cast. Seton I. Miller adapted Frances Wallace's *Galahad* novel; Casey Robinson wrote *It's Love I'm After.*

After Arthur Miller's *Crucible,* Frank Lloyd's *Maid of Salem* looks silly indeed with its tiresome love story and its last-minute movie rescue. But the Salem witchcraft hysteria was a new subject for movies then and the cast was extraordinary. Bonita Granville played another of her monstrous children and the adults included Claudette Colbert, Beulah Bondi, Louise Dresser, Gale Sondergaard, Edward Ellis, Donald Meek, and Mme. Sultewan.

Robert Young, Claudette Colbert, and Melvyn Douglas frolic in the snow in *I Met Him in Paris.*

Two for Bette: as one of a pair of battling Shakespearean actors with Leslie Howard in *It's Love I'm After* . . .

. . . and as the nightclub-singer paramour of Edward G. Robinson, with Wayne Morris as *Kid Galahad*.

On the Avenue had so many attractions in its cast and in its Irving Berlin songs that one could forget the mildly idiotic story that went with it. Who cares about story when you could look at Madeleine Carroll, listen to Dick Powell and Alice Faye sing songs like "I've Got My Love to Keep Me Warm," "You're Laughing at Me" and "This Year's Kisses" and enjoy the antics of the Ritz brothers leading a pack of capable comics. Roy Del Ruth directed.

William Wister Haines's story about the danger-filled lives of electrical linemen made a very good minor movie, *Slim,* directed by Ray Enright. Nobody could match the young Henry Fonda in a role like this and he played the idealistic youngster, hardening into a veteran, with his expected grace. Pat O'Brien and Margaret Lindsay were well cast, too.

An early example of the kind of flavorsome British comedies that would predominate in the 1950s was *Storm in a Teacup* which had to do with the excitement stirred up in a small Scottish town by the impounding of an unlicensed dog. One of the charms of this kind of British comedy was the use of just such a tiny incident to start it all off. Sara Allgood was a joy as the dog's owner, so were the others including the young romantic team played by actors whose names, Vivien Leigh and Rex Harrison, would soon mean much more to the world. Victor Saville and Ian Dalrymple directed James Bridie's script.

Ward Greene's novel, *Death in the Deep South*, given an engrossing screenplay by Aben Kandel and Robert Rossen, tautly produced and directed by Mervyn Le-Roy, became the film, *They Won't Forget*. Based on the true-life Robert Franks case, the film was a violent and uncompromising indictment of perverted small town justice. Claude Rains was eloquent as the opportunistic prosecutor but so was all the cast—notably Allyn Joslyn, Gloria Dickson, Edward Norris, Elisha Cook, Jr., Clinton Rosemond, and the girl who was making her debut as the sweater-wearing victim—Lana Turner.

England's first Technicolor film, *Wings of the Morning*, was the most natural up to that time. It had other virtues, most notable of which was the French actress, Annabella, in her first English-language role and bewitching in a dual role as the gypsy bride of a prologue

One of the best songs in *On the Avenue* was "You're Laughing at Me," as sung by Dick Powell to a gorgeous Madeleine Carroll.

Edward Ellis lays down the law, Puritan style, to the *Maid of Salem*, Claudette Colbert. Among others involved, not counting the uncredited actors at the rear left, are Mme. Sul-Te-Wan, Zeffie Tilbury, Mary Treen, Beulah Bondi, Bonita Granville, and Virginia Weidler.

Lana Turner sips a soda in her movie debut in *They Won't Forget*. Linda Perry is her companion.

Otto Kruger and Claude Rains square off in court in *They Won't Forget*. Leonard Mudie is the judge, and Clifford Soubier the witness. The court stenographer is uncredited.

and her great granddaughter impersonating a boy. She was lucky enough to have Henry Fonda as leading man, his American accent explained by making him Canadian. Harold Schuster directed, Donn Byrne and Tom Geraghty were the writers.

Unlike his usual pictures which had a very light touch for all of their suspense, Alfred Hitchcock's *Sabotage* (retitled *The Woman Alone* for its American release) was very somber drama all the way. But it was one of his most compelling in its story of the owner of a small London cinema who is also a terrorist employed by foreign powers. Oscar Homolka here gave his strongest screen portrayal, with Sylvia Sidney anguished as his unknowing wife. There were all manner of tantalizing Hitchcock touches. The sequence nobody who saw it can forget, although the film itself has become obscure, is that in which Desmond Tester, as Sidney's young brother, is sent to deliver what he thinks is a can of film

Gus McNaughton is making trouble for Sara Allgood because she has an unlicensed dog, and Rex Harrison and Vivian Leigh get into it too, in *Storm in a Teacup*.

Henry Fonda as the idealistic young linesman, *Slim*.

Instead it is a bomb set at a specific time to blow up Piccadilly. Hitchcock follows him on the trip as the boy dawdles, is delayed, and then . . . But catch it yourself some time—brave revival theatres still sometimes show it. Charles Bennett adapted Joseph Conrad's book.

Other Forgotten 1937 Films Worthy of Note

Broadway Melody of 1938 had, starting with Eleanor Powell's tapping, all the familiar elements but it also had Judy Garland singing to a photograph of Clark Gable and making movie musical history. . . . Fred Astaire didn't quite make history with *Damsel in Distress*, one of his lesser efforts, but Joan Fontaine attractively replaced Ginger, Burns and Allen helped with the comedy, and there was a Gershwin score, including "A Foggy Day." Kay Francis was somewhat out of her element in bitchy comedy but Verree Teasedale thrived on it so *First Lady* was amusing. . . . Because of dimpled Irene Hervey and some Gilbert and Sullivan numbers featuring real Savoyards, *The Girl Said No* overcame its trite story. . . . Although it lacked the spectacle of a later American remake, *King Solomon's Mines* was good ad-

venture stuff with Paul Robeson, Sir Cedric Hardwicke, and Roland Young heading the cast. . . . Although somewhat shaded by the greater impact of the similar *Night Must Fall*, *Love From a Stranger* was a good chiller with Ann Harding menaced by homicidal Basil Rathbone. . . . Although the plot was a weak variation on Capra (*It Happened One Night* and *Platinum Blonde*), *Love Is News* made it because of the personalities of such pretty people as Loretta Young and Tyrone Power. . . . The Jacques Deval/Robert E. Sherwood play, *Tovarich*, about titled White Russians turning Parisian domestics, made good screen fare for Claudette Colbert and Charles Boyer. . . . Carole Lombard, this time hamming it up a little, and John Barrymore, hamming it up a lot, were reunited for *True Confession* and, while no *Twentieth Century*, it was diverting. . . . *Victoria the Great* was a solemn, episodic biography with Anna Neagle and Anton Walbrook impressive as the queen and her consort. . . . *Wake up and Live* was one of the better of those unpretentious Fox musicals with a good Gordon and Revel score, an amusing story about a mike-shy radio singing sensation (Jack Haley, with the voice of Buddy Clark—excellent) and one of those Fox musical comedy casts (Alice Faye, Patsy Kelly, Ned Sparks, Walter Winchell, Ben Bernie, *et al.*). . . .

Henry Fonda, in his bath in *Wings of the Morning*, doesn't realize that the "boy" is really Annabella.

Desmond Tester dawdles on his way to deliver a reel of film (which is really a time-bomb) in one of Hitchcock's most famous sequences from *Sabotage*.

Sylvia Sidney faints when she hears bad news in Alfred Hitchcock's *Sabotage*

Chapter Ten

The Movie Year of 1938

Dishes, Bank Night and other gimmicks designed to lure them into the movie houses in 1938 are not working any more. So Hollywood announces that 1938 is "Motion Pictures' Greatest Year" and gives away thousands in a contest. The contest, designed to prove that "Motion Pictures Are Your Best Entertainment," is a failure. The five extraordinary films of the year—*Pygmalion, Grand Illusion, The Lady Vanishes, The Citadel,* and *Un Carnet de Bal* are all from Europe. It's a routine year for Hollywood.

Even so, there is some popular fare—Errol Flynn's lively *Adventures of Robin Hood*; an Irving Berlin cavalcade, *Alexander's Ragtime Band*; Jimmy Cagney as the criminal idol of the Dead End Kids in *Angels With Dirty Faces*; the Spencer Tracy–Mickey Rooney *Boys' Town*; Fredric March in DeMille's *The Buccaneer*; Flynn in *The Dawn Patrol*; a silly but melodious Strauss festival; *The Great Waltz*; *In Old Chicago*; the Gable–Loy–Tracy *Test Pilot*, and Frank Capra's felicitous transfer of *You Can't Take It With You* to the screen. You mustn't neglect Bette Davis's forerunner of Scarlett O'Hara in William Wyler's *Jezebel*, or Margaret Sullavan's gallant dying girl in *Three Comrades*, or the way Katharine Hepburn and Cary Grant make the old Philip Barry play, *Holiday*, seem written especially for them under the direction of George Cukor.

There are new people to appreciate—like Wendy Hiller from *Pygmalion*, Michael Redgrave and Margaret Lockwood of *The Lady Vanishes*, Robert Morley in *Marie Antoinette*. Hedy Lamarr comes in on the wave of her *Ecstasy* publicity and becomes a likely reason for Charles Boyer to desert the Casbah of *Algiers*. John Garfield begins with a bang and others who make a start are Bob Hope, Eddie Albert, David Niven, Phyllis Brooks, Red Skelton, John Payne, Nancy Kelly, Richard Greene, and Jane Wyman while there's a new lease on movie life for such as Mickey Rooney, Lew Ayres, and Ann Sothern.

There are movies of 1938, forgotten now but worthy of another thought.

Forgotten Films of 1938

Trust David O. Selznick to come up with the right movie version of a literary classic. His *Adventures of Tom Sawyer* was glossily Technicolored in those mostly black-and-white days but it had the true Mark Twain feeling. Maybe that's because the more unfamiliar Tommy Kelly, Jackie Moran, and Ann Gillis seemed so much more believable as Tom, Huckleberry Finn and Becky Thatcher than did, say, Jackie Coogan, Mickey Rooney, and Mitzi Green. And characters like Muff Potter, Aunt Polly, and the rest were well cast with Walter Brennan, May Robson, Victor Jory, Victor Killian, and others. Norman Taurog (he had done the first talkie *Huckleberry Finn* as well as *Skippy, Mrs. Wiggs* and others) directed with screenplay by John V. A. Weaver.

Tommy Kelly in the title role, Jackie Moran as Huckleberry Finn, and Victor Jory as Injun Joe in *The Adventures of Tom Sawyer*.

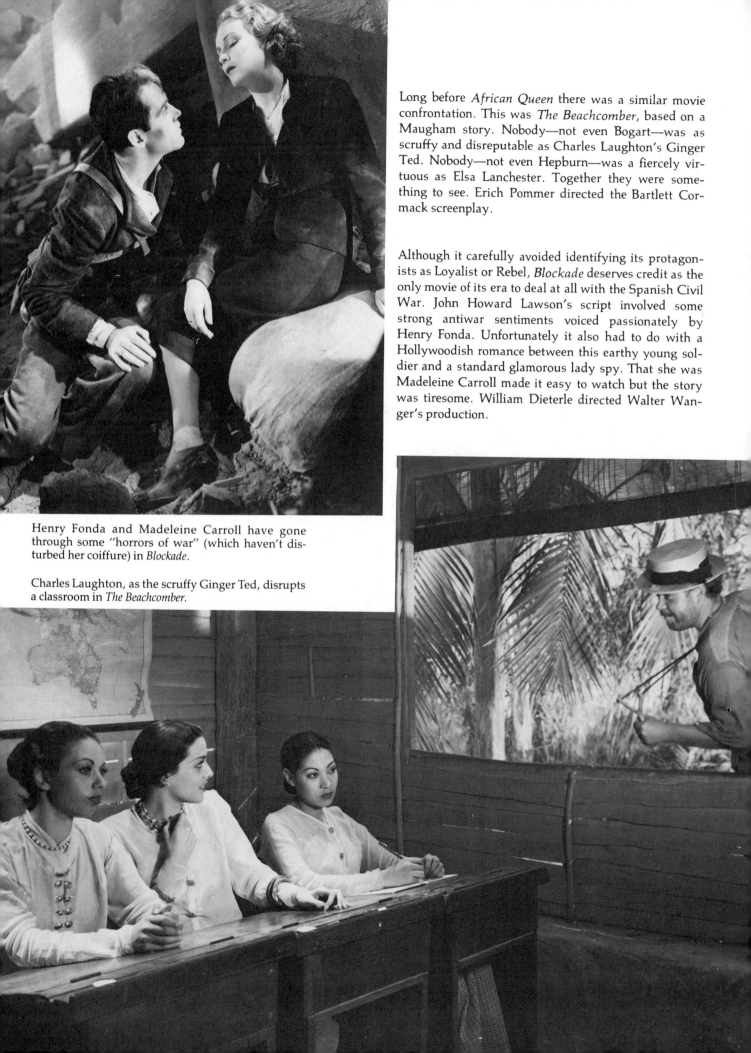

Long before *African Queen* there was a similar movie confrontation. This was *The Beachcomber*, based on a Maugham story. Nobody—not even Bogart—was as scruffy and disreputable as Charles Laughton's Ginger Ted. Nobody—not even Hepburn—was a fiercely virtuous as Elsa Lanchester. Together they were something to see. Erich Pommer directed the Bartlett Cormack screenplay.

Although it carefully avoided identifying its protagonists as Loyalist or Rebel, *Blockade* deserves credit as the only movie of its era to deal at all with the Spanish Civil War. John Howard Lawson's script involved some strong antiwar sentiments voiced passionately by Henry Fonda. Unfortunately it also had to do with a Hollywoodish romance between this earthy young soldier and a standard glamorous lady spy. That she was Madeleine Carroll made it easy to watch but the story was tiresome. William Dieterle directed Walter Wanger's production.

Henry Fonda and Madeleine Carroll have gone through some "horrors of war" (which haven't disturbed her coiffure) in *Blockade*.

Charles Laughton, as the scruffy Ginger Ted, disrupts a classroom in *The Beachcomber*.

Irving Berlin wrote some of his brightest songs (like "Change Partners" and "I Used to Be Color Blind") for Ginger Rogers and Fred Astaire in *Carefree*.

Maybe the reason you don't think *"Carefree"* when Astaire and Rogers movies come up is because it just wasn't as good as most of the others. The silly little story line didn't matter—all their movies had that. But there was nobody like Blore, Rhodes or Victor Moore, Helen Broderick or Alice Brady in support. The Irving Berlin songs (except for *Change Partners*) were bottom drawer. And even the dancing, except for an Astaire golf routine, seemed like numbers they had done before. Mark Sandrich directed.

The British gave us what Hollywood never could—not in *Men in White*, not even in *Arrowsmith*. *The Citadel*, from the novel by A. J. Cronin, then, was a well-nigh definitive study of a man of medicine—his dedication, his temptations, and his eventual triumph. There were some worthy Hollywood names involved—Director King Vidor and leading actress Rosalind Russell—but basically the British deserved the cheers. Robert Donat played the central figure brilliantly but all the others made themselves felt—Ralph Richardson, Rex Harrison, and Emlyn Williams to name three. Williams, with Ian Dalrymple, Frank Wead, Elizabeth Hill scripted.

Robert Donat and Ralph Richardson, in the days before Donat becomes a fashionable Mayfair doctor, in *The Citadel*.

Andrea Leeds looked for a while as if she would make it. She didn't though—her career petered out but her best part in that period was in John M. Stahl's *Letter of Introduction*. Here she played a girl arriving with the title letter to a Broadway matinee idol, who happened to be her father. (He had also forgotten her existence.) Adolphe Menjou did his Barrymore thing in this part and was helped by ladies like Eve Arden, Ann Sheridan, and Rita Johnson. Edgar Bergen with Charlie McCarthy and Mortimer Snerd were present, too. Screenplay by Sheridan Gibney and Leonard Spiegelgass.

Adolphe Menjou collapses, to the embarrassment of Frank Jenks, Jonathan Hale, Doris Lloyd, Andrea Leeds, Kathleen Howard, and others less immediately recognizable, in *A Letter of Introduction*.

As all the understanding fathers, sympathetic mothers, and mixed-up kids of today's TV family situation series come along, you forget the granddaddy of them all. (Gosh, Mickey *is* a granddad today, isn't he!) This was the Hardy family, headed by the fine old Judge (Lewis Stone) himself and particularly including the irrepressible Andy. That was Mickey Rooney and, although he was to do much more important things, it's because of his Andy that any memory of the series still endures. *Love Finds Andy Hardy* may be our favorite of the series because in addition to the constant Ann Rutherford, it also introduced a couple of new feminine distractions for Andy—Judy Garland and Lana Turner. George B. Seitz directed. Screenplay by William Ludwig.

Deanna Durbin, by withdrawing from the mainstream, has successfully made her name a shadowy one from the past but, in the 1930s, she was one of the top box-office stars. A couple of her pictures still show up occasionally but not *Mad About Music* which was her brightest. Although it borrowed its story of an adolescent who must hide the fact that her parent is a glamour star (see *Desirable*, and *Letter of Introduction*) and "invents" a father of her own (as in Barrie's *Old Lady Shows her Medals*), it was all done with verve. Deanna was sunny but you liked everyone—Jackie Moran, Gail Patrick, Herbert Marshall, Marcia Mae Jones, and the rest. Norman Taurog directed. Screenplay by Bruce Manning and Felix Jackson.

A Man To Remember was a very simple little movie. Like *The Citadel*, it dealt with a medical man. Unlike *The Citadel*, this had to do with a very ordinary small town doctor, unfolding his life and the effect of it upon an unaware community. Edward Ellis was notable in the role; so were the screenplay by Dalton Trumbo and the direction of Garson Kanin.

Merrily We Live was an absolute ripoff of one of the previous year's top hits, *My Man Godfrey*. Figuring you had seen it all before, it wasn't too hard to see it again because director Norman Z. McLeod managed to round up such a cast of bright people—Constance Bennett, Brian Aherne, Bonita Granville, Tom Brown, Billie Burke, Patsy Kelly, Alan Mowbray, Marjorie Rambeau, Ann Dvorak, and Clarence Kolb.

Almost nobody knows about *Of Human Hearts*—it didn't really receive its due even in its day—but it is one of the most moving dramas of parental devotion ever filmed. A story of a backwoods family in the period before and during the Civil War, it gave Walter Huston an impressive characterization as the Godfearing, stern

Love Finds Andy Hardy: Mickey Rooney is surrounded by his steady, Ann Rutherford, his buddy Judy Garland, and the tempting Lana Turner.

Herbert Marshall is somewhat taken aback by the reception he receives from Deanna Durbin and her classmates (Helen Parrish and Marcia Mae Jones among them) and headmistresses Nana Bryant and Elizabeth Risdon in *Mad About Music*.

Another screwball family—Billie Burke, Tom Brown, Constance Bennett, and Bonita Granville—had their day in a *My Man Godfrey* ripoff called *Merrily We Live*. Brian Aherne had the "William Powell role."

Walter Huston, Beulah Bondi, and James Stewart played a frontier family in the days before the Civil War in *Of Human Hearts*.

Edward Ellis, with William Henry and Anne Shirley, in the title role of a small-town doctor, in *A Man to Remember*.

father. Both Gene Reynolds and James Stewart gave something special to the rebellious son—as a boy and grown up. You could single out others—Charles Coburn, Leona Roberts, Guy Kibbee, John Carradine, and Gene Lockhart. But it was Beulah Bondi's completely unsentimental but deeply felt portrait of a sacrificing mother which ranks among the great achievements of this beautiful actress. Clarence Brown directed with screenplay by Bradbury Foote from a novel by Honore Morrow.

Room Service, a funny Broadway play in its own right, was not an ideal vehicle for the Marx brothers, seeming to confine them a bit. Nor did their very special brand of madness always fit in with a different comedy style. More in the spirit of the original were Frank Albertson, as the innocent from Oswego, and Donald MacBride, who had played his part in the play. Ann Miller and Lucille Ball were there, too, but with Groucho, Harpo, and Chico around, nobody else really had much of a chance. William A. Seiter directed. Morrie Ryskind reworked the screenplay for the Marxes.

The Shopworn Angel had become a little shopworn itself in the decade since Nancy Carroll and Gary Cooper had originally touched you with its bittersweet love story. How many naive boys had loved hard-boiled girls in the movies since? But who could resist Margaret Sullavan, even though her role was considerably softened from the original? And Jimmy Stewart was just the boy to take over from Gary. H. C. Potter directed. Dana Burnett's original was adapted by Waldo Salt.

Writer Claude Binyon and director Wesley Ruggles presented the Bing Crosby everybody liked best in *Sing You Sinners*—a nonchalant, engaging rascal with all kinds of charm. The easy-going movie had that, too, and so did the rest of the cast—Fred MacMurray, Elizabeth Patterson, Ellen Drew and, particularly, a new "small fry," Donald O'Connor.

The Sisters were Bette Davis, Jane Bryan, and Anita Louise and their parents were Beulah Bondi and Henry Travers. It was good to see them all but you know which one would be singled out. The others got fairly short shrift but Bette had all sorts of experiences—from love and marriage to ne'er do well Errol Flynn to being caught in the San Francisco earthquake. She carried on bravely and you always want to see Bette. Anatole Litvak directed Milton Krim's screenplay of the Myron Brinig novel.

Edward G. Robinson had a part absolutely tailored to his measure in *A Slight Case of Murder* in which his

Between Errol Flynn and the San Francisco earthquake, there were not many quiet moments for Bette Davis, the eldest of *The Sisters*. Siblings Anita Louise and Jane Bryan had an easier time of it.

Lucille Ball and Ann Miller are the ladies between Groucho, Chico, and Harpo in *Room Service*.

Jimmy Stewart, World War I, meets Margaret Sullavan, a chorus girl, in the remake of the Nancy Carroll–Gary Cooper *Shopworn Angel*.

tough guy persona was enjoyably caricatured. Eddie G. hadn't had so much fun since Little Caesar was a sprout. The Damon Runyon/Howard Lindsay play furnished the basis for a movie that was broadly funny as directed by Lloyd Bacon and with people like Ruth Donnelly, Edward Brophy, Allen Jenkins, Harold Huber, and Bobby Jordan (as a juvenile delinquent named Douglas Fairbanks Rosebloom) helping out the boss. But the main thing was Robinson sending up all the old gang characters he had ever played. Damon Runyon and Howard Lindsay wrote the play adapted by Earl Baldwin and Joseph Schrank.

Director Tay Garnett took Fredric March and Joan Bennett to lots of exotic locales in *Trade Winds*. It was a combination of mystery and romantic comedy, neither being all that original but the result being diverting anyway. This was mainly due to the stars with blonde Miss Bennett showing up for the first time as a Hedy Lamarr-ish brunette. Ann Sothern showed new comedy possibilities, too—after this she had a whole new career. Dorothy Parker, Alan Campbell, and Frank R. Adams wrote the screenplay.

Edward G. Robinson, in high society, is still buddies with his former associates—Edward Brophy, Allen Jenkins, and Harold Huber—in *A Slight Case of Murder*.

The song is "Small Fry" and Small Fry is Donald O'Connor, in *Sing You Sinners*. The bearded gent is Bing Crosby and Old Ma is Fred MacMurray.

Vivacious Lady was just about as frothy as a movie can get with its tale of a Broadway-wise night club girl marrying the squarest young professor in the world. But because they were Ginger Rogers and Jimmy Stewart and because George Stevens had such a knack in his direction of movies like this, it seemed far better than it might have been with any other stars and director. And, of course, Charles Coburn and Beulah Bondi helped no small bit as the parents of the groom. It was just a comedy drama and a nice relief from all the screwball slapstick they shoved at you those days. I. A. R. Wylie wrote the original with P. J. Wolfson and Ernest Pagano scripting.

The Young in Heart was just about as happy a movie as you could hope to find—in every detail from the impeccable Selznick production through the screenplay of Paul Osborn and Charles Bennett (based on an I. A. R. Wylie novel) and the direction of Richard Wallace. And, first and foremost, the cast—Roland Young, Billie Burke, Janet Gaynor, and Douglas Fairbanks, Jr., all at their very best as the most disarming family of amiable con artists out to fleece a sweet little old lady. Minnie Dupree was just about the sweetest little old lady you'd want to meet. And you couldn't forget Richard Carlson, new boy to movies here, and Paulette Goddard, turning out to have a nice brittle comedy sense to match her famous glamour.

The most engaging family of rascals the screen has brought us—there may be runners-up I don't immediately remember—are Billie Burke, Douglas Fairbanks, Jr., Roland Young, and Janet Gaynor in *The Young in Heart*.

Blonde Joan Bennett got a new look and a new persona in *Trade Winds*. She appears here with Ralph Bellamy and Fredric March.

Ginger Rogers and Jimmy Stewart (he's busy in forgotten films this year) are embarrassed by a motorcycle cop in *Vivacious Lady*.

Other Forgotten 1938 Pictures to Be Noted

Since the central figure in *The Amazing Dr. Clitterhouse* was a mild doctor whom you wouldn't suspect of being a criminal, the casting of Edward G. Robinson was a mistake but the story line had interest and Claire Trevor made her final step away from "B" pictures. . . . Gary Cooper was badly cast, too, in *Bluebeard's Eighth Wife*—even Lubitsch couldn't make you believe Gary as a roué—but Claudette Colbert and David Niven were more at home. . . . Nor were Jimmy Cagney and Pat O'Brien ideal casting for the manic leads in *Boy Meets Girl* although Marie Wilson certainly was. . . . *Four Men and a Prayer* was pretty mild for John Ford but any Ford should be noted. . . . *Garden of the Moon* had tuneful songs and the always attractive Margaret Lindsay. . . . *The Girl Was Young* was second-drawer Hitchcock but, in the general run of movies, that's more than good enough. . . . Let's call *Spawn of the North* a North Western—and a good one—with Henry Fonda and George Raft as brawling buddies, along with others like John Barrymore, Akim Tamiroff, Dorothy Lamour and a trained seal. . . . *There's Always a Woman* was in the *Thin Man* mold with Melvyn Douglas duplicating the William Powell style but Joan Blondell doing her own special thing. . . . *Three Blind Mice* was pleasant romantic comedy, chiefly because of such very pleasant people as Loretta Young, Binnie Barnes, Joel McCrea, Majorie Weaver, and David Niven. . . . Will Fyffe's extraordinary characterization highlighted the British dog film *To the Victor*. . . . With names like Sylvia Sidney, Fritz Lang, Kurt Weill involved, how could a picture go wrong? But *You and Me*, with its mixture of juvenile story line and heavy impressionism, went very wrong indeed. . . . The locale and the British supporting cast may have made the difference between *A Yank at Oxford* and your run-of-the-mill college movie but the difference was there and so were a couple of particular girls, Maureen O'Sullivan and Vivien Leigh, to play opposite Robert Taylor. . . . *Yellow Jack* was effective scientific semidocumentary with a notable performance by Robert Montgomery speaking in one of those brogues he loves so well. . . .

Chapter Eleven

The Movie Year of 1939

The movies ride high in 1939! There's action galore—all the way from the frantic excitement of *Gunga Din* to Westerns of the caliber of *Stagecoach, Jesse James,* and *Destry Rides Again.* Such characters as the Hardys and Dr. Kildare roll along, and another, Maisie, gets going. There are more and more Technicolor pictures, fewer straight musicals.

Gone With the Wind finally comes to the screen—and sets a standard for sheer magnitude. The well-publicized search for a Scarlett O'Hara has passed Norma Shearer, Jean Arthur, Loretta Young, Paulette Goddard, and others and turned up such contenders as Susan Hayward and Evelyn Keyes. But Vivien Leigh, little known except to British audiences, gets the role. After *GWTW,* she's never little-known again.

Among those with a fresh start in 1939 are John Wayne, who had played bits in big pictures and leads in quickie Westerns, Marlene Dietrich, so recently named box-office poison, Lana Turner, Marsha Hunt, and Jackie Cooper. And we meet such welcome strangers as Ingrid Bergman, William Holden, Robert Preston, Geraldine Fitzgerald, Betty Field, Greer Garson, Ruth Hussey, Lee J. Cobb, Patricia Morison, Gloria Jean, Alan Marshal, Edmond O'Brien, Linda Darnell, and Maureen O'Hara.

And what a year for movies! Let's list our favorites in alphabetical order—Garson Kanin's *Bachelor Mother* with Ginger Rogers and David Niven; Bette Davis dying beautifully in *Dark Victory;* Robert Donat's *Goodbye, Mr. Chips; GWTW,* of course; George Stevens's *Gunga Din;* Garbo laughing in the Lubitsch *Ninotchka;* Lewis Milestone's filmization of John Steinbeck's *Of Mice and Men;* John Ford's *Stagecoach;* the joy of *The Wizard of Oz;* the bitchery of *The Women;* the dark romance of Wyler's *Wuthering Heights,* with its superb adaptation of Hecht and MacArthur; and Henry Fonda ideal as Ford's *Young Mr. Lincoln.*

But so many others to note—the Gary Cooper *Beau Geste; Confessions of a Nazi Spy;* Dietrich and Stewart in *Destry Rides Again;* Fonda and Colbert in Ford's *Drums Along the Mohawk;* Laughton's *Hunchback of Notre Dame;* Ingrid Bergman's American debut in *Intermezzo;* the Power-Fonda *Jesse James;* the Muni–Davis–Aherne *Juarez;* Bette Davis and Miriam Hopkins in *The Old Maid;* Beulah Bondi, Lionel Barrymore and Sir Cedric Hardwicke in *On Borrowed Time;* Cagney's *Roaring Twenties;* and W. C. Fields's *You Can't Cheat An Honest Man.* Still more with virtues outweighing such faults as the casting of Norma Shearer and Errol Flynn in unsuitable roles—*Idiot's Delight,* and *The Private Lives of Elizabeth and Essex.* And Bob Hope's *Cat and the Canary,* as well as *Four Feathers, Hound of the Baskervilles, The Story of Vernon and Irene Castle,* and *Union Pacific.*

And then there were others, not so well remembered but worth thinking about again.

Forgotten Movies of 1939

John Barrymore, who had been making something of a spectacle of himself on and offscreen in the preceding few years, could still bring his magic to a role when he cared about it. He seemed to care about the erudite alcoholic he played in Garson Kanin's *The Great Man Votes*. It was a witty, stylish performance, rather than the hammed-up caricatures he had been giving us, and it could be touching, too. Virginia Weidler and Peter Holden held up their end neatly as his children with Donald MacBride taking care of the ham as a political ward heeler. Screenplay by John Twist.

Hollywood Cavalcade was a sketchy attempt to put the whole history of the movies into one picture. Here we had three protagonists—the girl star (Alice Faye) and the romantic hero (Alan Curtis), both combinations of silent screen and early talkie real-life greats, as well as the director (Don Ameche) who, according to Ernest Pascal's screenplay, is responsible for every innovation that any of the pioneers brought to the medium. Where it was most fun was in its recreation of the Mack Sennett/Keystone Kops era, possibly because, although Irving Cumming directed, Sennett was listed as technical adviser. And the cast here included not only Buster Keaton but Ben Turpin, Chester Conklin, and a whole slew of slapstick kings.

John Barrymore, in an unexpectedly amusing and moving role, shared scenes with Peter Holden and Virginia Weidler in *The Great Man Votes*.

Alice Faye re-created a whole world of Hollywood heroines in *Hollywood Cavalcade*, going back to the Mack Sennet days for a pie from Buster Keaton.

Because its remake by the same director, Leo McCarey, (*An Affair to Remember* with Deborah Kerr and Cary Grant) was so successful, the original tends to be overlooked. This was *Love Affair,* with McCarey's skilled directorial hand skirting the shoals of soap opera but combining sentiment, comedy, and romance effectively. And Irene Dunne and Charles Boyer moved gracefully from pink champagne sophistication on to closing scenes that may have strained credibility but seemed terribly touching while you watched. Also note the bright dialogue by Delmer Daves and Donald Ogden Stewart and a sweet bit by Maria Ouspenskaya.

Altering the old Jean Harlow/Clark Gable *Red Dust* to fit a ''B'' picture cast and budget didn't do a thing for it except in one instance. This was Ann Sothern, getting a role she could do something with—you had a hint of what she could do in *Trade Winds*—and turning out to be a fresh and individual comedienne. The picture was *Maisie* and Miss Sothern played the title character so successfully that there would be several more screen adventures of Maisie to come. Edward L. Marin directed May McCall's screenplay.

Midnight, directed like a Lubitsch by Mitchell Leisen, had a merry script by Charles Bracket and Billy Wilder, and some extremely competent actors to play it. These included Claudette Colbert, always at her most zestful in high style comedy like this; John Barrymore, waiting

Irene Dunne and Charles Boyer as the lovers of *Love Affair* in an idyllic moment with Maria Ouspenskaya.

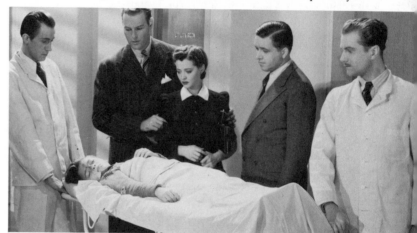

The youngster on the stretcher is now-distinguished director Sidney Lumet. The hospital personnel are not credited, but the three concerned civilians are Leif Erikson, Sylvia Sidney, and Hiram Sherman. The movie—*One Third of a Nation.*

A lively group in *Midnight*—Francis Lederer, John Barrymore, Don Ameche, Claudette Colbert, Mary Astor, and, looking in from the back, Rex O'Malley, Hedda Hopper, Elaine Barrie

Ann Sothern played *Maisie* in the first of a popular series of movies, this time with Robert Young and Cliff Edwards.

for the scene-stealing bits and then coming through like a Barrymore; Don Ameche, much more relaxed than usual; along with Francis Lederer and Mary Astor, making the most of second leads. A very saucy Cinderella story.

. . . One Third of a Nation had been a controversial play (by Arthur Arent) and in Dudley Murphy's screen adaptation (he also directed) it remained strong although necessarily losing much of its theatrical effect. Sylvia Sidney again played the bitter slum girl, the last of the Depression heroines at which she excelled. An interesting New York cast (Myron McCormick, Leif Erikson, Hiram Sherman, a youngster named Sidney Lumet— yes, the same one—among others) gave it realism. Yet dominating them all was the tenement itself, becoming virtually a real character.

These Glamour Girls was a sort of junior version of *The Women*, in its tale of the debutantes who make things tough for a taxi dancer on a college prom weekend. Some of Hollywood's most promising young talent— like Jane Bryan, Richard Carlson, Ann Rutherford, Anita Louise, and Peter Lind Hayes—were well cast as were Tom Brown and Lew Ayres, still college boys even though they had been around for a decade. But the girls to watch were that sexy Lana Turner, making a big step from the sweater girl bits she had been playing, and Marsha Hunt, an unexpected character actress, who broke your heart as the desperate college widow. S. Sylvan Simon directed. Screenplay by Jane Hall, Marion Parsonnet.

In the 1970s, *We Are Not Alone* was an advertising catch phrase for the movie, *Close Encounters of the Third Kind*. Back at the end of the 1930s, it was a movie title—the title of one of the most arresting films of its time. James Hilton and Milton Krims adapted it from Hilton's novel and Edmund Goulding directed with his usual care. The story deals with tragedy that explodes in a quiet town among ordinary people. Paul Muni had played many "Mr. Paul Muni" roles; he never was more simply moving, less pretentious, than here. Flora Robson made his termagant wife pitiable, not merely shrewish. Una O'Connor, James Stephenson, and Henry Daniell headed a strong supporting cast. And a glowing Jane Bryant was poignant as the innocent, doomed young German girl. (Having thus achieved such a peak, she shortly quit the screen forever for marriage—our great loss.)

They're all *These Glamour Girls*, but Lana Turner is the outsider among debutantes Ann Rutherford, Jane Bryan, Mary Beth Hughes, Anita Louise, and Marsha Hunt.

You may remember being amused, and eventually bored, by that perennial high school boy, Henry Aldrich, in his various incarnations in "B" movies, radio and early TV. You might not remember the play and movie that started it all. This was Clifford Goldsmith's *What a Life* and, with the help of a Brackett and Wilder script, the movie version was as engaging as George Abbott's Broadway play. Hollywood wisely brought in two of the stage cast to repeat their roles—a fresh and pretty Betty Field and Vaughan Glaser as the very model of a high school principal. Home-grown Jackie Cooper was Henry Aldrich—and quite all right, too.

Other Forgotten 1939 Films to Note

Madeleine Carroll was always so lovely to look at that *Cafe Society* rates higher memory marks than its tired spoiled heiress/newspaper reporter plot should justify. . . . The legendary Nathaniel West received one of his screenwriting credits (along with Dalton Trumbo, Jerry Cady) for John Farrow's tense little thriller, *Five Came Back*, in which a good cast (Chester Morris, Lucille Ball, Wendy Barrie, Kent Taylor, Joseph Calleia, and C. Aubrey Smith) appeared. . . . Although *the* Wyatt Earp/Doc Holliday movie was yet to be made (John Ford did it in *My Darling Clementine* a few years later), Alan Dwan's *Frontier Marshal* was a better-than-average try with Cesar Romero's Doc better than that. Good work by Randolph Scott, Binnie Barnes, Nancy Kelly, too. . . . The Hayes Office, safeguarding public morals, insisted the last word of the title *Good Girls Go to Paris, Too* be eliminated. Joan Blondell was at her perkiest as a sort of sassy Lorelei Lee, with Melvyn Douglas, Alan Curtis, and Walter Connolly all in good form. . . . Fred MacMurray was unexpectedly effective as a prizefighter married to a socialite (Irene Dunne, good, too, not unexpectedly), in Wesley Ruggles's *Invitation to Happiness* but the story let them down. . . . Because of its cast (Myrna Loy, Tyrone Power, Maria Ouspenskaya, Brenda Joyce, and others) and its storm and flood sequence, *The Rains Came* deserves mention here, in spite of its Readers Digest treatment of Louis Bromfield's popular novel. . . .

Paul Muni is a doctor called to attend a German dancer (Jane Bryan) in *We Are Not Alone.*

Jackie Cooper is Henry Aldrich, Betty Field his high school heroine, in *What a Life.*

Chapter Twelve

The Movie Year of 1940

The start of a new decade in 1940 is the year of the Okies and *Grapes of Wrath* but also of Main Line society in *The Philadelphia Story* . . . of Walt Disney's *Fantasia* and of John Ford's version of Eugene O'Neill's *The Long Voyage Home* . . . of movies at such opposite poles as *Pride and Prejudice* and *The Great McGinty.*

It's common enough now, in 1940, for the screen to come right out and say "Nazi." Thus, one might say that Chaplin's *Great Dictator* isn't quite as revolutionary as it would have been even a year earlier.

There are new stars on the screen—Joan Fontaine, previously just another ingenue, is one. Rita Hayworth and Betty Grable, who have been around in a minor capacity, are doing better now—although they don't know yet that they will be top pin-up girls of World War II.

Others who are making their debuts or attracting special attention for the first time on the screen are Arthur Kennedy, Martha Scott, Judith Anderson, Ruth Gordon, James Stephenson, Victor Mature, Carole Landis, Dennis Morgan, Dan Dailey, Gene Tierney, Paul Henried, Robert Sterling, Dean Jagger, Carmen Miranda, Elia Kazan, Mildred Natwick, Anne Baxter, Mary Martin, Glenn Ford, Jack Carson, Brenda Marshall, Desi Arnaz, and Joan Brodel (later known as Joan Leslie).

John Ford's filmization of John Steinbeck's *The Grapes of Wrath,* starring Henry Fonda, is the Great American Motion Picture. (The years have passed but we have seen no reason to change that statement, even today.) But there are many more of special distinction, the foremost, listed in alphabetical order, including Raymond Massey's *Abe Lincoln in Illinois;* W. C. Fields's masterpiece, *The Bank Dick;* Disney's fantastic *Fantasia;* Hitchcock's first American movie, *Foreign Correspondent;* Chaplin's *Great Dictator;* Sturges's *Great McGinty;* Howard Hawks's reworking of *The Front Page* for Rosalind Russell; Cary Grant in *His Girl Friday;* Bette Davis in Wyler's *The Letter; The Long Voyage Home* (Cameraman Gregg Toland was a hero of this as well as many others—*Grapes of Wrath, Citizen Kane,* among others of the era); Thornton Wilder's *Our Town,* the Hepburn–Grant–Stewart–Hussey–George Cukor filmization of Philip Barry's *Philadelphia Story;* Disney's *Pinocchio;* a beautifully cast *Pride and Prejudice;* Hitchcock's *Rebecca,* with Olivier, Fontaine, Judith Anderson *et al.;* and that utter delight, Lubitsch's *Shop Around the Corner,* with Margaret Sullavan and James Stewart heading a perfect cast. There was something to be said for many others—the Davis–Boyer *All This and Heaven, Too;* the Gable–Tracy–Colbert–Lamarr *Boom Town; Broadway Melody of 1940,* in which Fred Astaire found an ideal dancing partner in Eleanor Powell; Cagney's *Fighting 69th;* Ginger Rogers's *Kitty Foyle;* Pat O'Brien's *Knute Rockne, All American;* DeMille's *Northwest Mounted Police;* Spencer Tracy's *Northwest Passage;* the first outing for Bing, Bob and Dotty, *Road to Singapore;* Errol Flynn's *Sea Hawk;* Raoul Walsh's *They Drive by Night;* Korda's *Thief of Bagdad;* the Alice Faye–Betty Grable *Tin Pan Alley,* Vivien Leigh and Robert Taylor in *Waterloo Bridge;* and Gary Cooper's *The Westerner*—all worthy of their strong popularity.

And there were others, many others, of note even though they may have faded from memory.

Forgotten Films of 1940

We always knew she was, but *And One Was Beautiful* was just about the first concentrated effort to make Jean Muir appear that way. Up to then, they usually treated her like a road company Lillian Gish, very short on glamorizing. And they cast hardly homely Laraine Day as the "one" who wasn't. The picture was magazine novelette and the only reason for including it here is that it was the last real movie opportunity for the courageous Miss Muir.

Ben Hecht, as writer, director, producer of *Angels Over Broadway,* had everything his way and the picture was striking work. His fable of three Broadway hangers-on who thwart the suicide of a frightened little man and make his life worth living again took place in a single night and may have been quite preposterous but intriguing. There were uncommonly good performances by Douglas Fairbanks, Jr., and John Qualen, while Rita Hayworth, for the first time, made herself felt as more than an especially pretty girl. Thomas Mitchell, as an alcoholic playwright, reveled in his role as the mouth-piece for some of Hecht's most flamboyant lines. The camera of Lee Garmes had artistry.

Nobody was better suited than Henry Fonda to the roles of the shy, gentle young heroes of Walter D. Edmonds's historical novels of upper New York State. Fonda, who had already played two of them (*The Farmer Takes a Wife, Drums Along the Mohawk*), now became *Chad Hanna,* the farm boy who joins a traveling circus. The story line was meandering but director Henry King caught the atmosphere of a small circus in an earlier period and Fonda's relaxed performance made you care about his character.

Preston Sturges very quickly became virtually a household name, at least in movie-aware households—and, seemingly as quickly, fell out of favor. His best films as writer/director are frequently revived except for one, the rather Capraesque *Christmas in July.* This was a happy movie about what happens when a $20-a-week clerk thinks he has won a fortune in a contest. Dick Powell and Ellen Drew had the leads and there were a lot of those people who became Sturges's stock company— William Demarest, Franklin Pangborn, Raymond Walburn, Georgia Caine, and the like.

(TOP)
They both lived up to the title of the movie *And One Was Beautiful,* but Jean Muir was given the title role, and Laraine Day was the "plain" sister. They are shown here with Robert Cummings and Billie Burke.

(RIGHT)
Linda Darnell and Henry Fonda as members of a small circus traveling New York State's canals in *Chad Hanna.*

John Qualen, Douglas Fairbanks, Jr., and Rita Hayworth as three people of the night in *Angels over Broadway.*

Nazimova, Robert Taylor, and Norma Shearer in *Escape*.

Robert Montgomery, as a hoodlum who becomes *The Earl of Chicago*, shown here with Edward Arnold, and Ian Wulf.

Robert Montgomery cultivated the screen image of the cocktail shaking playboy but every so often (*Night Must Fall, Here Comes Mr. Jordan*), he came up with a decidedly different characterization. One of these was *The Earl of Chicago* in which he was a hoodlum who discovered he was a member of the peerage and found himself responding to the best British traditions. It was Montgomery at his offbeat best. Richard Thorpe directed with screenplay by, among others, Gene Fowler.

Melodramas about concentration camp victims and escapes from the Nazi threat would become routine and taken for granted in just a few months but *Escape*, based on the Ethel Vance novel, was one of the earliest and one of the best. Mervyn LeRoy directed vividly and there were the Norma Shearer and Robert Taylor names for the box office. But the cast excitement was in its character actors—Nazimova, Conrad Veidt, Albert Basserman, Philip Dorn, Felix Bressart, Bonita Granville, and Blanche Yurka—all contributing arresting cameos. Screenplay by Arch Oboler and Marguerite Roberts.

Why did Pare Lorentz, one of our most exciting film makers, stop working in the medium? Why is his a name virtually forgotten by even most knowledgable movie mavens? We wish we knew the answer. He has

Ellen Drew and Dick Powell help celebrate *Christmas in July.*

It's a happy group before the Nazi threat takes over in *The Mortal Storm*. Clockwise around table from left, the diners are Frank Morgan, Robert Young, Margaret Sullavan, James Stewart, Robert Stack, William T. Orr, Gene Reynolds, and Irene Rich.

left us with only three motion pictures—all magnificent, all unknown today except perhaps in college class-rooms. These were the documentaries—*The River* and *The Plough That Broke the Plains*—as well as one that was as real in its treatment and technique although it used professional actors of the caliber of Myron McCormick, Dudley Digges, and Will Geer. This was *The Fight for Life,* a stunning study of the patients and doctors in a maternity clinic. The throbbing musical score of Louis Gruenberg still remains a high point in the history of motion picture music.

In 1940 Brian Aherne played a couple of widely varying father roles—as a particularly versatile actor, his roles were inclined to be varied. But *My Son, My Son,* for the most part, was a plodding sobber. Much more pleasant was Charles Vidor's *The Lady in Question,* a good American remake of a French film, *Heart of Paris.* Aherne was the Paris tradesman who brings a girl acquitted of murder into the bosom of his family. Irene Rich played his wife and you took note of three young actors, none of them yet established—Rita Hayworth, Glenn Ford, and Evelyn Keyes. Screenplay by Lewis Meltzer.

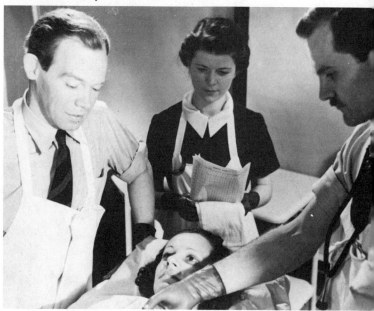

Myron McCormick (left) played the interne in Pare Lorentz's *The Fight for Life.* The other players, probably nonprofessional, are unidentified.

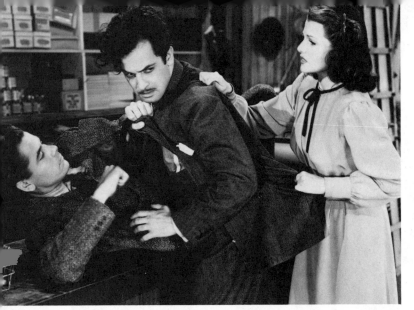

Glenn Ford and Edward Norris are at odds over *The Lady in Question*, Rita Hayworth.

Irene Dunne returns to civilization after having been a castaway for years, in *My Favorite Wife*. Cary Grant is her husband, who has remarried, and Randolph Scott is her fellow castaway.

Margaret Lockwood, Rex Harrison, and Paul von Hernreid (he changed it to Henreid when he came to America) in *Night Train*.

An early anti-Nazi drama—and one of the most searing —was *The Mortal Storm*, adapted from Phyllis Bottome's novel and directed by Frank Borzage. So many similar films have followed it that it might look pretty old hat today. Perhaps that is why it is seldom revived. But it was strong and moving then. Not the least of its virtues was the acting of a cast, one of the best ever assembled, including Margaret Sullavan, James Stewart, Frank Morgan, Irene Rich, Robert Young, Bonita Granville, Maria Ouspenskaya, Robert Stack, Dan Dailey, William T. Orr, Gene Reynolds, Ward Bond, and Esther Dale. Screenplay by Claudine West, Anderson Ellis, and George Froeschel.

Irene Dunne, Cary Grant and Leo McCarey, the trio who made *The Awful Truth* one of the merriest movies of the 1930s, were at it again in *My Favorite Wife*. It was more of the same and just about as much of a joy (although unaccountably its reputation has not endured like that of its predecessor). This time Cary marries beauty Gail Patrick only to discover that Irene, his wife presumed dead for seven years, has returned from the island where she has been shipwrecked with Randolph Scott. Everyone was in fine fettle—a word should be said for Granville Bates as the judge in a hilarious courtroom scene. Garson Kanin was listed as director in McCarey's production; Samuel and Bella Spewack wrote the screenplay (again with McCarey).

Since *The Lady Vanishes* was such a hit, why not another using as many of the same elements as possible? *Night Train* didn't have Hitchcock—but a comparatively new director, Carol Reed, proved quite up to the master. It didn't have Michael Redgrave—but you couldn't do better as a substitute than Rex Harrison. Paul von Hernreid (soon to become Paul Henreid in America) was as suave as Paul Lukas. Otherwise, Margaret Lockwood was still the lady in distress and the Basil Redford/Naunton Wayne team still provided chuckles as very British tourists. And the screenplay was by Sydney Gilliat and Frank Launder who had done the same job for Hitchcock. This one was almost as exciting.

Gregory La Cava made a mildly bawdy, frequently funny, and occasionally touching movie out of *The Primrose Path*, the story of a girl growing up in a family in which her mother and grandmother are both former members of the world's oldest profession. Ginger Rogers was a little too much—well, Ginger Rogers—to be completely convincing as the girl but she gave it a good try. Much better cast were Queenie Vassar, Joan Carroll, Miles Mander and, especially, Marjorie Rambeau as the blowsy, good-hearted mother. La Cava and Allan Scott based their screenplay on a Broadway play by Robert L. Budner and Walter Hart.

An assistant district attorney takes a girl he is prosecuting back to his family in Indiana for the Christmas holidays. She is regenerated. Sounds sentimental, doesn't it? It was—but *Remember the Night* was never cloying. Not with a sharp script by Preston Sturges, perceptive direction by Mitchell Leisen, some of their best acting by Barbara Stanwyck, Fred MacMurray, and Beulah Bondi. They made a nice movie—the kind you don't see much any more.

Henry Fonda had walked away with the picture as the laconic outlaw in *Jesse James*. He was back in the same role in *The Return of Frank James*, perhaps a little less scruffy, a little more conventionally heroic, but Fonda's quiet menace always worked in such a role. Fritz Lang directed and Jackie Cooper, growing up fast, played Fonda's youthful accomplice.

John Garfield and Anne Shirley were so ingratiating as the young couple in a third movie version of Maxwell Anderson's *Saturday's Children* that you didn't mind if it seemed slightly warmed over this time around. There was a great deal of help from Claude Rains, too, and from Lee Patrick, Dennie Moore, and the others. Vincent Sherman directed with screenplay by Julius and Philip Epstein.

There certainly wasn't anything new about the story Jerry Wald and Richard Macaulay concocted for *Torrid Zone*. But the story was just a framework for some fast and furious dialogue, delivered pungently by Jimmy Cagney and, surprisingly, by Ann Sheridan, who had one of her rare chances to show that she was more than just an "Oomph Girl." Pat O'Brien, Helen Vinson, George Tobias, Andy Devine, and Jerome Cowan were also prominent. William Keighley directed.

Other Forgotten 1940 Films to Note

Arise My Love was fairly typical Claudette Colbert/Ray Milland romantic comedy drama with wartime background. . . . Wesley Ruggles fell down on making the epic Western he thought *Arizona* would be but Jean Arthur, William Holden and Edgar Buchanan made it worth viewing. . . . *The Biscuit Eater* was a very good little boy and dog yarn. . . . Jeanette MacDonald was ever so arch in *Bitter Sweet* while Nelson Eddy was merely stolid but there was that Noel Coward score and a very handsome finale staged in shades of brown. . . . Dean Jagger was impressive in the title role of *Brigham Young* but the film grew ponderous. . . . Beulah Bondi played one of her wonderful old ladies in *The Captain Is*

Marjorie Rambeau and Ginger Rogers as mother and daughter of *The Primrose Path*.

Once again Henry Fonda played the title role in *The Return of Frank James*. Jackie Cooper is his youthful sidekick.

Beulah Bondi, Fred MacMurray, and Elizabeth Patterson welcome Barbara Stanwyck to a down-home Christmas in *Remember the Night*.

a Lady and there were other worthies like Charles Coburn, Billie Burke, Helen Broderick, Helen Westley, and Majorie Main with Virginia Grey and Dan Dailey, too. . . . *Castle on the Hudson* was standard prison melodrama but John Garfield had vigor and Burgess Meredith had an effective bit. . . . *A Child Is Born* was a remake of the old maternity ward movie but it was worth seeing for performances by Geraldine Fitzgerald, Gale Page, Gladys George, Eve Arden, and Fay Helm. . . . *City for Conquest* was good big city melodrama before it dissolved in bathos; Jimmy Cagney, Elia Kazan, Arthur Kennedy were arresting. . . . Edward G. Robinson created strong characters in two biographical dramas, *A Dispatch From Reuter's* and *Dr. Ehrlich's Magic Bullet*—the first sincere but stodgy; the second much more dramatic (with kudos for Ruth Gordon and Albert Basserman, too). . . . *Dr. Cyclops* was entertaining foolishness about a mad doctor who shrinks humans to thumb size. . . . Spencer Tracy, as *Edison the Man,* may have been better cast than Mickey Rooney as *Young Tom Edison* but Mickey was a good enough actor to overcome it and the two pictures made solid screen biography. . . . Bob Hope and Paulette Goddard, who had done it before in *The Cat and the Canary,* had another and quite as funny bout with the horrors in *The Ghost Breakers.* . . . Cary Grant seemed to walk through *The Howards of Virginia* but Martha Scott was a lovely leading lady in the slow paced but interesting drama of the Revolutionary War period. . . . *I Love You Again* was that old standby, amnesia, played for laughs this time and who better for those than William Powell and Myrna Loy? . . . *Joe and Ethel Turp Call on the President* was Damon Runyon stuff with Ann Sothern and William Gargan properly Brooklynese and Marsha Hunt taking another stride in her burgeoning career as a young character actress. . . . *My Love Came Back* was romatic comedy presenting Olivia de Havilland at her most beguiling, aided no end by Charles Winninger and Eddie Albert. . . . Jeanette and Nelson went back to *Naughty Marietta* territory for *New Moon* but with not nearly as successful results—although the lovely score was vintage Romberg. . . . Easygoing Bing Crosby and vivacious Mary Martin made an easygoing, vivacious movie out of *Rhythm on the River.* . . . In *Santa Fe Trail*, the brave Errol Flynn got all mixed up with John Brown, played as a rolling-eyed fanatic by Raymond Massey. . . . Marlene Dietrich was back in *Destry* form in *Seven Sinners,* leading on John Wayne this time. . . . Booth Tarkington's *Seventeen* seemed pretty outdated in those days of Andy Hardy but Jackie Cooper, Norma Nelson and, particularly, baby vamp Betty Field were properly Tarkingtonian. . . . Charles Laughton, Vivien Leigh, and Rex Harrison were a likely threesome in *The Sidewalks of London* but the promising story line petered out. . . . Laughton was inclined to ham up his Italian fruit grower role in *They Knew What They Wanted* and Carole Lombard was just too glamorous to be a weary waitress but the old Sidney Howard play still had some dramatic punch. . . . Let's say Myrna Loy was the main reason for including *Third Finger, Left Hand* here—but isn't she always?

Torrid Zone featured moustached Jimmy Cagney, flanked by Ann Sheridan and Helen Vinson.

Saturday's Children—Anne Shirley and John Garfield.

Chapter Thirteen

The Movie Year of 1941

There are comedies and dramas, musicals and costume pictures, Westerns and mysteries—all the movie staples in 1941. And, starting to show up, are the service pictures, things like Bob Hope's *Caught in the Draft*, Fred Astaire's *You'll Never Get Rich*, and *Buck Privates* with Abbott and Costello.

But it is *Citizen Kane* which will make movie history.

From Lou Costello to Orson Welles—that's the gamut of new 1941 film personalities. Welles brings in a considerable group—Joseph Cotton, Dorothy Comingore, Agnes Moorehead, Ruth Warrick, Everett Sloane, and others. Roddy McDowall, Sara Allgood, and Anna Lee arrive from England. Deborah Kerr, new to British films, won't come to Hollywood for a few more years. Other faces, new at least to major screen roles, are Teresa Wright, Patricia Collinge, Dan Duryea, Kathryn Grayson, Richard Whorf, Rosemary DeCamp, Sterling Hayden, Laird Cregar, Maria Montez, Patricia Dane, Dana Andrews, Susan Hayward, and, hair over her eye, Veronica Lake. Garbo fails for the first time—and will never give it another try.

Besides *Citizen Kane* there are some major movies. Right at the very top are Preston Sturges's delicious *Lady Eve*, with Henry Fonda and Barbara Stanwyck, John Huston's classic Bogart version of *The Maltese Falcon*, and John Ford's *How Green Was My Valley*.

But others of particular note include (alphabetically) Walt Disney's *Dumbo*; Robert Montgomery's *Here Comes Mr. Jordan*; Bette Davis in Wyler's version of Lillian Hellman's *The Little Foxes*; Shaw's *Major Barbara* with a strong British cast; Gary Cooper in Howard Hawks's *Sergeant York*; Preston Sturges's *Sullivan's Travels*; and Hitchcock's *Suspicion* (Cary Grant, Joan Fontaine).

And the following had their merits, popularity, or both—the Margaret Sullavan *Back Street*; Tyrone Power–Rita Hayworth's *Blood and Sand*; the Bette Davis–Mary Astor *Great Lie*; Bogart in Raoul Walsh's *High Sierra*; the Boyer–DeHavilland *Hold Back the Dawn*; Robert Taylor–Lana Turner's *Johnny Eager*; a field day for some great actors in *King's Row*; Fritz Lang's *Man Hunt*; Monty Woolley in *The Man Who Came to Dinner*; W. C. Fields's *Never Give a Sucker an Even Break*; Edward G. Robinson in *The Sea Wolf*; Josef von Sternberg's *The Shanghai Gesture*; the James Cagney–Olivia de Havilland–Rita Hayworth *Strawberry Blonde*; Vivien Leigh and Laurence Olivier in *That Hamilton Woman*; *The Wolf Man*; Joan Crawford's *A Woman's Face*, and *Ziegfeld Girl* with Judy, Hedy, Lana, and lots of others.

Then there are the good ones you're not as apt to remember.

Forgotten Films of 1941

In spite of some atrocious miscasting (primarily James Craig as a Yankee farmer who sells his soul to the devil), *All That Money Can Buy* worked as a screen version of Stephen Vincent Benet's *The Devil and Daniel Webster.* The best thing about it was Walter Huston's persuasive devil known as Mr. Scratch; Edward Arnold's Webster being good enough, too. William Dieterle directed.

The combination of a script by Charles Brackett and Billy Wilder, direction by Howard Hawks, production by Samuel Goldwyn, performances by the likes of Gary Cooper, Barbara Stanwyck, S. Z. Sakall, Richard Haydn, Oscar Homolka, Henry Travers, Dana Andrews, Dan Duryea, and others—if they were all up to par—would make a particular treat of the picture for which they combined talents. They were—and so was *Ball of Fire.*

Martha Scott aged beautifully in *Cheers for Miss Bishop*, going from a fresh young girl in her first assignment to an elderly retired teacher being given the cheers of all those students whose lives she touched. If anything could have saved the movie from turning maudlin, it would have been that performance. Unfortunately it wasn't quite enough. Tay Garnett directed and the cast included good actors like William Gargan, Marsha Hunt, Edmund Gwenn, John Arledge, with a fine bit by Rosemary DeCamp.

You couldn't find a more perfectly matched romantic team than Jean Arthur and Charles Coburn in *The Devil and Miss Jones.* Of course, the movie paired them off respectively with Robert Cummings and Spring Byington but it was the Arthur/Coburn combination you cared about. And you really did care in this very engaging Norman Krasna script as directed by Sam Wood. They were both at their absolute peak up to that time. (They'd get together again in *The More the Merrier*—and that would turn out to be even better.)

(TOP)
James Craig is tempted by Walter Huston as Mr. Scratch, a rural Mephistopheles, in *All that Money Can Buy.*

(CENTER)
A battered Gary Cooper winds up with Barbara Stanwyck—Richard Haydn is present too—in *Ball of Fire.*

The teacher grows old—Martha Scott in *Cheers for Miss Bishop.*

Spring Byington, Charles Coburn, Jean Arthur, and
Robert Cummings in a confrontation with the police,
(Edward McNamara), in *The Devil and Miss Jones.*

MGM presented three young candidates for stardom,
Donna Reed, Robert Sterling, and Dan Dailey, in *The
Getaway.*

Sterling also teamed with better-established Marsha
Hunt in *I'll Wait for You.*

Robert Sterling, a personable young actor who had
shown up well in *Manhattan Heartbreak,* a 1940 "B"
picture remake of *Bad Girl,* moved to MGM for more of
the same in 1941. These were *I'll Wait For You* and *The
Get Away,* remakes respectively of *Hideout* and *Public
Hero Number One,* with two of the more welcome leading ladies, Marsha Hunt and Donna Reed, to bolster
the romance. Sterling moved into "A" pictures playing
second leads to stars like Gable and Taylor and was on
his way to stardom when military service cut in. In spite
of some good work after the war, he never regained his
career momentum.

I Wake Up Screaming was a strange, moody little detective story in which Betty Grable, Carole Landis, and
Victor Mature were the leads. But the picture was carried by its character people—Elisha Cook, Jr., Alan
Mowbray, Allyn Joslyn and, particularly, Laird Cregar, a dark, heavy figure of psychological menace as the
investigating detective. H. Bruce Humberstone directed. Dwight Taylor's script was based on a novel by
Steve Fisher.

On the stage, Flora Robson gave a performance of shattering intensity as the housekeeper in *Ladies in Retirement.* Ida Lupino, in Charles Vidor's fine film version,
was obviously hampered by her youth and movie star
looks. Still Lupino has proved her intensity, too, and
she used everything in her repertoire to carefully build
her characterization. None of the supporting people
could be faulted—Isobel Elsom, Elsa Lanchester, Edith
Barrett, Louis Hayward, and Evelyn Keyes. It was a
suspenseful thriller with Reginald Denham, who had
written the play (with Edward Percy) collaborating
with Garrett Fort on the screenplay.

Mr. and Mrs. Smith is the Alfred Hitchcock movie that
is never included in his retrospectives. Actually it seems
like somebody else's movie. Nary a corpse litters the
scene. Not a moment of shrieking suspense. Norman
Krasna's screenplay was straight comedy, amusing but
derivative. Still when you have two of the most attractive comedy talents around—Carole Lombard and Robert Montgomery—guided through their paces by Hitch,
the movie has to be above average. Not above the average of any of these three but still pleasant enough.

Hartzell Spence's biography of his preacher father, *One
Foot in Heaven,* came to the screen as a heartwarming
film, full of honest sentiment and unhackneyed Ameri-
cana. Credit Casey Robinson's script, Irving Rapper's
direction, and particularly the actors—Fredric March
and Martha Scott—surrounded by people like Beulah
Bondi, Laura Hope Crews, Gene Lockhart, and Frankie
Thomas.

Victor Mature has two women on his hands, Betty Grable and Carole Landis, in *I Wake Up Screaming*.

Ida Lupino introduces her dotty sisters, Elsa Lanchester and Edith Barrett, to her employer, Isobel Elsom, in *Ladies in Retirement*.

Carol Reed's uncompromising study of the tragedy of a Welsh mining town and its people, *The Stars Look Down*, made an absorbing motion picture. Not for this one, the sunny sentimentality that suffused John Ford's *How Green Was My Valley*—and none of the well-earned popularity of the Ford film either. Extraordinary characterizations by Michael Redgrave, Nancy Price, Margaret Lockwood, Emlyn Williams, and Edward Rigby. The A. J. Cronin novel had a screenplay by J. B. Williams.

It's mild mayhem for Carole Lombard and Robert Montgomery in *Mr. and Mrs. Smith.*

Cesar Romero, who had played his share of snarling gangland menaces, kidded the breed in *Tall, Dark and Handsome* as a big shot with a reputation as a cold killer. Actually he has a heart of marshmallow and wouldn't kill a fly. Romero had a field day and so did Milton Berle, Sheldon Leonard, and Stanley Clements. H. Bruce Humberstone directed. Screenplay by Karl Tunberg and Darrell Ware.

Ginger Rogers had a run of delightful comedies after she took off her dancing shoes and went on her own. One of the most joyous was *Tom, Dick and Harry* in which Ginger as a telephone operator has romantic flings, complete with dizzy daydreams, with a titular threesome, and then tries to make her choice. The gentlemen in the case, all just right for the occasion, were Burgess Meredith, Alan Marshal, and George Murphy. Garson Kanin's deft direction of Paul Jarrico's script kept it all merrily rolling along. The contributions of them all can be measured by hindsight when one remembers how dreary the same material was when brought to the screen in a late 1950s remake.

Fredric March and Martha Scott as a minister and his wife in *One Foot in Heaven.*

It might not have been a *Lady Eve*—after all, how many films are?—but *You Belong to Me* reunited Henry Fonda and Barbara Stanwyck quite attractively. She was a doctor; he, her husband, was jealous of her male patients. The Claude Binyon–Dalton Trumbo script was pretty trivial but served well as a showcase for the ingratiating stars. Wesley Ruggles directed.

Other Forgotten 1941 Films to Note

Bing Crosby and Mary Martin teamed again most pleasantly in *Birth of the Blues* from which a special memory is of Ruby Elzy's electrifying singing of "St. Louis Blues." . . . Vivid performances by Elia Kazan and Betty Field and that Harold Arlen title song helped make *Blues in the Night* more than routine melodrama. . . . Jack Benny got into the skirts of *Charley's Aunt* to prove there was life in the old girl yet. . . . John Steinbeck's script, narrated by Burgess Meredith, was an

Welsh mother Nancy Price and her son Michael Redgrave lead the villagers to a mine disaster in *The Stars Look Down.*

especially noteworthy element in Herbert Kline's *The Forgotten Village*, a documentary of Mexican peasants. . . . Carol Reed gave us an intriguing suspense film in *Girl in the News*. . . . Another small, virtually unknown, British film of merit was *Laburnum Grove* with Edmund Gwenn, Sir Cedric Hardwicke. . . . *Love Crazy* was wild farce—the kind of thing William Powell and Myrna Loy did with such sparkle between their sophisticated *Thin Man* outings. . . . Flora Robson, Robert Newton, Catherine Lacey, and Ann Todd made *Poison Pen* an interesting little British melodrama. . . . Claudette Colbert made the most of the life of a school teacher in *Remember the Day* although *Mr. Chips* and *Miss Bishop* had pretty well taken the bloom from this particular rose. . . . An eager young Glenn Ford stood out in the marvelous cast (Margaret Sullavan, Fredric March, Anna Sten, Frances Dee, Erich Von Stroheim) of *So Ends Our Night* although the film itself was strangely undramatic. . . . Ford again and William Holden were immensely likable young cowboys in *Texas*. . . . *That Uncertain Feeling* was bottom-drawer Lubitsch but it had its moments, most contributed by an ebullient Burgess Meredith. . . . Irene Dunne and Robert Montgomery are an irresistible combination and Gregory La Cava was just the director to bring out the best in them but the script of *Unfinished Business* wasn't up to their efforts. . . . Fritz Lang gave plenty of sweep to *Western Union*, which had Randolph Scott in one of his best Westerns. . . . John Barrymore, in a role reminiscent of his *Twentieth Century* Oscar Jaffe, played the harum-scarum thing called *World Premiere* with all stops out, while Fritz Feld and Luis Alberni were his equals in the comedy department. . . .

Cesar Romero as the soft hearted gangster introduces Virginia Gilmore to the kid, Stanley Clements, who will be her charge in *Tall, Dark and Handsome*. The maid is Charlotte Greenwood.

Ginger Rogers can't choose among *Tom, Dick and Harry* but fantasizes about life with irresponsible Harry (Burgess Meredith).

Henry Fonda and Barbara Stanwyck, back in their *Lady Eve* comedy mood, in *You Belong to Me*.

113

Chapter Fourteen

The Movie Year of 1942

In 1942 more and more of the movies these days have war in their theme. Actors are disappearing as the services call up Gable, Fonda, Power, James Stewart, Robert Preston, Robert Sterling, Arthur Kennedy, William Holden, and dozens of others. Madeleine Carroll finishes as Bob Hope's *Favorite Blonde* and quits movies for war work. Other screen personalities are already very active in camp show appearances and bond selling tours. Carole Lombard, returning from a bond rally, is killed in a plane crash.

But, as familiar faces disappear, new ones pop up—faces like those of Gene Kelly and Danny Kaye, Margaret O'Brien, Alan Ladd, MacDonald Carey, Van Johnson, Janet Blair, Glynis Johns, Diana Barrymore, and Lynn Bari. Some, like Ladd and Bari, have been around but are only now beginning to move up. Jean Gabin comes over from France but doesn't quite hit here. Dorothy Comingore, despite her *Citizen Kane* triumph, proves difficult to handle and begins her tragic descent.

Everyone enjoys Bogart and Bergman in *Casablanca* but no one can predict its immortality. There are many more critical kudos that year for Wyler's *Mrs. Miniver*, which doesn't keep its reputation. The other "bests" would include (alphabetically) Disney's *Bambi*; Noel Coward's *In Which We Serve*; Welles's butchered but brilliant *Magnificent Ambersons*; the first teaming for Hepburn and Tracy in George Stevens's *Woman of the Year*; and Jimmy Cagney's rousing *Yankee Doodle Dandy*. You might add Gary Cooper's *Pride of the Yankees* and the Lubitsch–Jack Benny–Carole Lombard *To Be or Not to Be* to that list. And Bette Davis's *Now Voyager*. But there are others of merit or popularity to note—Val Lewton's *Cat People*; Judy Garland and Gene Kelly in *For Me and My Gal*; the Crosby–Astaire *Holiday Inn*; Ginger Rogers in Bracket and Wilder's *The Major and the Minor*; Henry Fonda in *The Male Animal*; Rosalind Russell in *My Sister Eileen*; Ronald Colman's *Random Harvest*; Duvivier's all-star *Tales of Manhattan*; George Stevens's *Talk of the Town* with Cary Grant, Jean Arthur, Ronald Colman; Alan Ladd's *This Gun for Hire*; Spencer Tracy and John Garfield in Steinbeck's *Tortilla Flat*; John Farrow's *Wake Island* with Robert Preston, Brian Donlevy, Astaire; and Hayworth in *You Were Never Lovelier*. And, just for camp, *White Cargo* with Hedy ("I am Tondeleyo") Lamarr, luring men to ruin in the tropics.

Then there were those others that don't come as quickly to mind.

Forgotten Films of 1942

Damon Runyon's Broadway fables always presented his Big Apple touts and hangers-on as the quaintest folk in the world and usually had a finish so tearily sentimental that it almost slopped over into the maudlin. *The Big Street* was one of the prime examples in its tale of the bus boy, Little Pinks, who worships the hardhearted night club singer, becomes her slave when she is crippled. And the finish where she dies in his arms after the high spot of their dance is probably the most shamelessly sobby of all. That it all worked—even jerked a few tears—is a tribute to the stars. Only Henry Fonda could make you believe in his incredibly naive Pinks. And Lucille Ball was brassy but pathetic. Good people like Eugene Pallette, Agnes Moorehead, Sam Levene, and Ray Collins helped out as standard Runyon types. Irving Reis directed.

Raoul Walsh, one of the best for this kind of thing, made a good, brawling period movie in *Gentleman Jim.* Errol Flynn was ideally cast as the prizefighting dandy and Ward Bond was just what you'd expect the great John L. Sullivan to be. Alexis Smith was a decorative lead and the supporting cast included people like Alan Hale, Jack Carson, William Frawley, Arthur Shields, and Rhys Williams. Vincent Lawrence and Horace McCoy scripted.

Thorne Smith, of *Topper* fame, dreamed up the plot of *I Married a Witch* and Rene Clair transferred it to screen. It wasn't the best work of either but, with an especially good cast, it managed to be quite amusing most of the time. Fredric March played the title *I*, a stuffy New Englander whose Puritan ancestors burned a witch. Just as in Clair's *Ghost Goes West*, the long-burned witch turns up. She was Veronica Lake at her most fetching. Robert Benchley, Cecil Kellaway, and Susan Hayward were around, too. Script by Robert Pirosh and Marc Connelly.

One of the early anti-Nazi war films—the screens would be full of them for the next couple of years—was the British *The Invaders* (also called *The 49th Parallel*). Michael Powell directed Emeric Pressburger's tale of six survivors of a sunken Nazi submarine making their way across Canada with Eric Portman scoring as their leader. Some pretty distinguished actors—Laurence Olivier, Anton Walbrook, Leslie Howard, Glynis Johns, and Raymond Massey—played brief, but telling roles as people encountered by the Nazis on their journey.

Journey for Margaret introduced Margaret O'Brien and

Nightclub singer Lucille Ball has taken a bad fall, but as always, "Little Pinks" (busboy Henry Fonda) is there to help, in *The Big Street.*

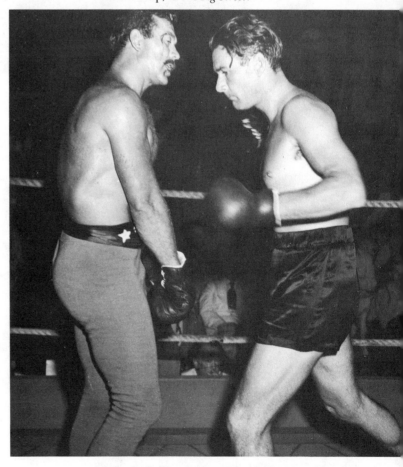

John L. Sullivan versus Jim Corbett—or Ward Bond versus Errol Flynn—in *Gentleman Jim.*

(TOP) Fredric March as "I" and Veronica Lake, the other half of the title, in *I Married a Witch* with Cecil Kellaway and Robert Benchley.

Eric Portman is an escaping Nazi and Leslie Howard is his prisoner in *The Invaders* (also known as *49th Parallel*).

she was so real in her depiction of a child haunted by wartime experiences that it was possible to believe that her performance must have been a fluke—not acting at all. Of course, we grew to realize in other films that Margaret O'Brien was one of the most amazing child actors we have seen. Robert Young, Laraine Day, Fay Bainter, William Severn were also in the cast and W. S. Van Dyke 2d directed. Screenplay by David Hertz and William Ludwig.

Kid Glove Killer may have been just a program picture but it was a particularly taut little thriller. With good actors like Van Heflin and Marsha Hunt, it was the first feature for a director who had been working in MGM's shorts department. After another 1942 "B" picture worth noting (*Eyes in the Night* with Edward Arnold as a blind detective), Fred Zinnemann was promoted to bigger things. He never went back to shorts or program pictures again.

Carol Reed took time out from stronger things (like *Night Train, The Stars Look Down*) to bring us *Kipps*, a pleasant little period piece based on a novel by H. G. Wells. Reed's favorite actor of the period, Michael Redgrave, was of course perfectly right for the title role.

After his stage and screen hits in *The Man Who Came to Dinner*, Monty Woolley briefly became a screen star on his own in two 1942 films and one (*Holy Matrimony*) in 1943. None of them was any great shakes at the box office and they haven't been revived for years, even on TV. Woolley returned to supporting roles. Even so, they were interesting pictures—particularly the two from 1942. In *The Pied Piper*, he was an irascible English gentleman leading a group of youngsters (Roddy McDowall, Anne Baxter, and Peggy Ann Garner among them) out of the clutches of Nazi Otto Preminger and his minions. In *Life Begins at 8:30*, he was an alcoholic has-been actor, adding some welcome humor to the role Paul Muni had played straight in the stage play by Emlyn Williams. Ida Lupino, Sara Allgood, and Cornel Wilde helped. Nunnally Johnson wrote both screen plays and both were directed by Irving Pichel.

Although most of the films coming to us from England in the early 1940s were wartime melodramas, they still could give us a human, unpretentious little film about something no more momentous than the problems faced by an ordinary boy and girl in preparing to be married. This was *Quiet Wedding* directed by Anthony Asquith, written by Terrence Rattigan and Anatole de Grunwald. It presented people like Margaret Lockwood and Derek Farr as the couple, and others involved were Athene Seyler, A. E. Matthews, and Peggy Ashcroft.

Anatole Litvak made a good wartime romance out of a more complicated novel by Eric Knight in *This Above All*. Since Tyrone Power and Joan Fontaine were the particularly attractive leads, the film concentrated on them. Thomas Mitchell headed the supporting cast which was composed of most of the best British talents then working in Hollywood. They included Gladys Cooper, Sara Allgood, Nigel Bruce, Henry Stephenson, Philip Merivale, Alexander Knox, Melville Cooper, Jill Esmond, Rhys Williams, and Arthur Shields.

Other Forgotten 1942 Films to Note

Jules Dassin directed *The Affairs of Martha*, hardly

Robert Young comforts a little girl (Margaret O'Brien) who has seen the horrors of war in *Journey for Margaret*.

Fred Zinnemann's first feature, *Kid Glove Killer*, with Van Heflin, Lee Bowman, Marsha Hunt.

Michael Redgrave is the outsider in *Kipps* with Helen Haye, Michael Wilding, Diana Wynyard, and the back of Max Adrian.

Two for Monty Woolley: (TOP) as a has-been actor with Ida Lupino and Cornel Wilde in *Life Begins at 8:30*.

. . . and (ABOVE) as an Englishman rescuing youngsters Roddy McDowall and Anne Baxter from the clutches of Nazi Otto Preminger in *The Pied Piper*.

notable in his career but pleasant with one of those excellent MGM casts, headed by pert Marsha Hunt and including Richard Carlson, Marjorie Main, Spring Byington, Virginia Weidler, Allyn Joslyn, Barry Nelson, Margaret Hamilton among others. . . . *The Fleet's In* was a tame movie version of the rowdy play *Sailor Beware* but it had Dorothy Lamour and William Holden surrounded by entertaining people like Cass Daley, Gil Lamb, Betty Hutton and the Jimmy Dorsey Band, playing songs that are still whistled. . . . Cesar Romero was amusing enough in *Tall, Dark and Handsome* that Fox gave him more of the same in *A Gentleman at Heart*. . . .

Dashiell Hammett's *The Glass Key* which had served in the 1930s as a vehicle for George Raft and Edward Arnold was dusted off for Alan Ladd and Brian Donlevy effectively enough. . . .

Michele Morgan came to the American screen in still another wartime resistance melodrama, *Joan of Paris*, well made and with a good cast (Paul Henreid, Thomas Mitchell, Laird Cregar, James Monks, Alan Ladd, and May Robson). . . . Two more of the better wartime melodramas, both from England, were *Mister V* produced, directed by and starring Leslie Howard, and *One of Our Aircraft is Missing*, with a cast of competent British character actors. . . . People like Cesar Romero, Lynn Bari, George Montgomery, Ann Rutherford, and Carole Landis were in *Orchestra Wives* but the only reason for including it here was Glenn Miller and his orchestra playing numbers like "Serenade in Blue" and "Kalamazoo." . . . Preston Sturges wasn't at his wittiest with *Palm Beach Story* but any Sturges has its moments and Claudette Colbert, Rudy Vallee, Mary Astor, and Sturges regulars like William Demarest and Franklin Pangborn made them amusing . . .

Dalton Trumbo's screenplay for *The Remarkable Andrew* surrounded William Holden with ghosts of the country's founding fathers—most notably, Andrew Jackson (Brian Donlevy) in fantasy that frequently sputtered. . . . Henry Fonda practically repeated his *Lady Eve* characterization in a ripoff of that picture only mildly helped by Rouben Mamoulian's directorial skill and that of such actors as Fonda, Laird Cregar, Spring Byington, as well as the face of Gene Tierney. . . . Alfred Hitchcock's *Saboteur* was most notable for a wild Hitchcock chase through and over Manhattan landmarks. . . . Gable and Lana Turner again in *Somewhere I'll Find You*, with Robert Sterling as third point on the triangle. . . . Tyrone Power swashbuckled through the most convoluted costume melodrama since *Anthony Adverse* in *Son of Fury*, with a cast worth a second look (Frances Farmer, Roddy McDowall, George Sanders, Gene Tierney, Elsa Lanchester, John Carradine, Dudley Digges, and Kay Johnson). . . . John Wayne and Randolph Scott were the brawlers in still another version of *The Spoilers* but it was Marlene Dietrich who made it fun to watch. . . . *Street of Chance* was a moody little Cornell Woolrich melodrama with Claire Trevor and Burgess Meredith as an amnesiac trying to prove he is innocent of murder. . . .

Margaret Lockwood and A. E. Matthews in *Quiet Wedding*.

Joan Fontaine and Tyrone Power in *This Above All*.

Chapter Fifteen

The Movie Year of 1943

Another war year in 1943—and most of our movies are of the *Guadalcanal Diary–Bataan* genre. More and more actors have gone into service and even the ladies are off entertaining the boys. Marlene Dietrich, for instance, virtually shelves her career, traveling wherever there are servicemen to whom she can sing. Leslie Howard leaves on a wartime flight. The plane and its passengers are never seen again. (The same will happen a year or so later to orchestra leader Glenn Miller. Onetime leading man Phillips Holmes has been the first to perish in a service-related crash.)

Back on the home front, new people keep coming through—like Robert Walker and Jennifer Jones, June Allyson, Farley Granger, Dorothy McGuire, Lena Horne, Nancy Walker, Ella Raines, Gloria DeHaven, William Eythe, Robert Ryan, to name just a few. Lassie begins a career. So does a little girl named Elizabeth Taylor. And a big girl named Jane Russell. The latter runs into some difficulty when *The Outlaw* is leaped upon by censors. Producer Howard Hughes withdraws and holds it for several years but Jane is established as a star on the strength of the publicity.

War is exploding all over the movie screens. Some of the more notable examples—Brackett and Wilder's *Five Graves to Cairo;* Fritz Lang's *Hangmen Also Die;* Disney's *Victory Through Air Power;* Goldwyn's *North Star;* Jean Renoir's *This Land is Mine;* Bogart in *Sahara* and *Action in the North Atlantic;* Fonda in *Immortal Sergeant;* Cary Grant and John Garfield in Destination Tokyo; Garfield in *Air Force, Hitler's Children, Next of Kin,* and, on the lighter side, the screen version of Irving Berlin's *This Is the Army* and the fantasy–comedy–drama of *A Guy Named Joe* with Spencer Tracy, Irene Dunne, Van Johnson. But these are just a sampling. There are many, many more including a couple of bad ones about women in war—*So Proudly We Hail* and *Cry Havoc.*

Nor does Hollywood neglect the home front—with such varying examples as George Stevens's very merry *The More the Merrier,* Saroyan's sentimental *Human Comedy,* Lillian Hellman's forceful *Watch on the Rhine,* and Cary Grant's *Mr. Lucky.*

But there's no war at all in what, to us, are the pictures of the year—Henry Fonda in William Wellman's *The Ox Bow Incident* and Alfred Hitchcock's *Shadow of a Doubt* with Teresa Wright and Joseph Cotten.

Others among the better pictures of 1943 would include Minnelli's *Cabin in the Sky,* Dorothy McGuire's radiant *Claudia* debut, Gary Cooper and Ingrid Bergman in Hemingway's *For Whom the Bell Tolls,* Lubitsch's enchanting *Heaven Can Wait,* and Bette Davis trading bitcheries with Miriam Hopkins in *Old Acquaintance.* Jennifer Jones's *Song of Bernadette* and Greer Garson's *Madame Curie* are greatly admired. And others to note would range from the well-meaning *Mission to Moscow* to *I Walked With a Zombie.*

Then there are those others that don't come so readily to mind.

Charles Boyer falls in love with one of those unconventional families (Joyce Reynolds, Montagu Love, Joan Fontaine, and Jean Muir) in *The Constant Nymph*.

It's Ann Sheridan and Errol Flynn in *Edge of Darkness*. You may be able to make out some notables who show up, very fuzzily, in the background—Walter Huston, John Beal, Roman Bohnen, Ruth Gordon, Nancy Coleman, Judith Anderson, Helene Thimig, and Richard Fraser.

Forgotten Films of 1943

Margaret Kennedy's *The Constant Nymph* was already showing signs of age by its second movie remake. But this is the kind of lush romantic drama at which director Edmund Goulding excelled. He was helped no end by his cast, particularly the leads, Joan Fontaine and Charles Boyer. But there were other beauties—Alexis Smith, Jean Muir, Brenda Marshall, and Joyce Reynolds—and solid character actors like Charles Coburn, Peter Lorre, and Dame May Whitty. Screenplay by Kathryn Scola.

Robert Rossen wrote and Lewis Milestone directed *Edge of Darkness*, still another melodrama about citizens of yet another Nazi-occupied country—Norway this time —rebelling against their captors. But the picture's strength was in its actors—not so much in the conventional movie star leads, Errol Flynn and Ann Sheridan, as the rest of the cast. It included Walter Huston, Judith Anderson, John Beal, Ruth Gordon, Nancy Coleman, Roman Bohnen, Charles Dingle, Helmut Dantine, Morris Carnovsky, and Art Smith.

Other than the occasional *Dead of Night*, anthology films with their various episodes are largely unsatisfy-

ing dramatically. Some have an interesting vignette here and there but usually they are too briefly anecdotal for any cumulative or lasting effect. After his triumph with one of the very best of the genre, *Un Carnet de Bal*, Julien Duvivier tried several times again without similar successful results. One was *Flesh and Fantasy*, three stories in which the fantasy overwhelmed all. The cast was notable though—Charles Boyer, Betty Field, Barbara Stanwyck, Edward G. Robinson, Robert Benchley, Thomas Mitchell, Dame May Whitty among the actors. Screenplay by Ernest Pascal, Samuel Hoffenstein, and Ellis St. Joseph.

Another episodic film, conceived as a tribute to wartime England, was *Forever and a Day*, written and directed by a great number of famous names. The story was of the people who live in an English house from the time it is built (1804) until it is destroyed by a bomb in a World War II air raid. The cast was what made it of particular interest, although few of the actors—Ida Lupino, Claude Rains, Charles Laughton, Brian Aherne, Jessie Matthews, Wendy Barrie, Merle Oberon, Anna Neagle, and Ray Milland were just a sampling—had very special opportunities. The exceptions were Gladys Cooper and Roland Young, who had a heartbreaking moment as bereaved parents in World War I.

Betty Field as the spinster sister, with Marjorie Lord, in *Flesh and Fantasy*.

Some of the dozens of stars of *Forever and a Day*— Robert Cummings, Merle Oberon, Elsa Lanchester, and Roland Young.

Ida Lupino's unyielding characterization of an avaricious and scheming woman on a climb to the top at anyone else's expense was the chief merit of *The Hard Way.* A few more roles like this in better pictures might have put Lupino in the Crawford–Davis league but what's a girl to do when she's at the same studio and apparently only gets their castoffs? Joan Leslie was a lovely ingenue, Jack Carson had a rare dramatic role, and Gladys George had a strong bit. Vincent Sherman directed with screenplay by Daniel Fuchs and Peter Viertel.

Certainly a bonnie little comedy–drama, *Jeannie* was sweetly unpretentious but most delightful. Barbara Mullen was so winning as the title character, a rather homely Scottish Cinderella, that it was a shame she never had another worthy screen role, only a few character bits. Michael Redgrave was stalwart as always as her unlikely Prince Charming. Harold French directed the screenplay by Anatol de Grunwald and Roland Pertwee.

John Steinbeck's novel and play, *The Moon Is Down,* are barely remembered today in any mention of his more important works. Small wonder then that the

Helene Thimig, Margaret Wycherly, Henry Travers, Lee J. Cobb, and various Nazis in *The Moon Is Down.*

Ida Lupino dominates her younger sister, Joan Leslie, in *The Hard Way.*

Michael Redgrave and Barbara Mullen in *Jeannie.*

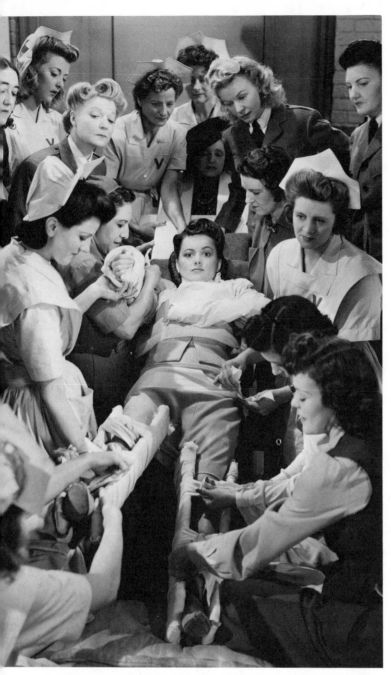

The women are practicing on Olivia de Havilland in
Princess O'Rourke.

The one about the masquerading royal lady and the
commoner who falls in love with her would be best
served by Audrey Hepburn, Gregory Peck, and William
Wyler in the 1950s. But it made a very pleasant romantic comedy in 1943 as *Princess O'Rourke,* thanks particularly to Norman Krasna's script and direction. Olivia
de Havilland was the fetching girl in the cast, brightly
supported by Charles Coburn, Robert Cummings, Jane
Wyman, and Jack Carson.

Other Forgotten 1943 Films to Note

That cute little Broadway musical of George Abbott's
Best Foot Forward made a cute little movie musical with
Lucille Ball making the most of her role of fading movie
star at the military school prom. And from the stage
cast came kids like Tommy Dix, Kenny Bowers, Jack
Jordan, June Allyson and that funniest of all blind
dates, Nancy Walker. . . . John Garfield was arresting
in an otherwise rather routine anti-Nazi melodrama,
The Fallen Sparrow. . . . And still another anti-Nazi
melodrama, *Hangmen Also Die,* was given some distinction by Fritz Lang's direction. . . . *Holy Matrimony*
pleasantly paired Monty Woolley and Gracie Fields in
the old Arnold Bennett *Buried Alive* story, previously
filmed with Roland Young and Lillian Gish. . . . Eric
Ambler's *Journey Into Fear* made bizarre movie fare but
even second-rate Orson Welles fare was fascinating.
. . . Dolores Del Rio joined Joseph Cotten, Ruth Warrick, Agnes Moorehead, and other Welles regulars.
. . . Gypsy Rose Lee's *G-String Murders* was the basis
for *Lady of Burlesque* which had Barbara Stanwyck
enjoying herself in the title role aided by such hard-
boiled honeys as Iris Adrian and Marion Martin. . . .
Jean Arthur found adventure and romance with John
Wayne in *A Lady Takes a Chance* and she was, as
always, a joy in spite of a tired story line. . . . One of the
least known of Val Lewton's horror movies was *The
Seventh Victim* but Lewton cultists relish it. . . . Although Sinatra popularized it years later, Harold Arlen
and Johnny Mercer wrote "One for My Baby (And One
More for the Road)" for Fred Astaire in *The Sky's the
Limit*—a bright memory but not quite enough to put the
movie in any list of memorable Astaire pictures. . . .
Thank Your Lucky Stars had an awful story line and
some (except for Dinah Shore and one or two others)
amateur night specialty numbers by all the big Warners
stars. But it also had Bette Davis doing the Frank Loes-
ser–Arthur Schwartz "They're Either Too Young or Too
Old," which, come to think of it, is the only thing about
the movie that can't be forgotten. . . . Michael Redgrave
was customarily effective in *Thunder Rock* but the mysticism of the story became muddled. . . .

movie version, made without box-office names and
without a fashionable director, is virtually forgotten.
Yet it was a fine film for its time—sober and eloquent in
its treatment of a Norwegian town under control of the
Nazis. It avoided the melodramatics common to such
pictures and thus, perhaps, may have seemed dramatically uninvolving. Nunnally Johnson wrote the screenplay, Irving Pichel directed, and Sir Cedric Hardwicke,
Henry Travers, Lee J. Cobb, Peter Van Eyck, and Dor-
ris Bowden headed the cast.

Chapter Sixteen

The Movie Year of 1944

There are fewer straight battle movies of the *Wake Island–Bataan* type in 1944 but servicemen are principal characters in every other movie. The war is seldom forgotten on the screen unless the picture turns to another era. Even then (in *Wilson,* for example), the past events can be made very contemporary in their implications.

Tallulah Bankhead is a returnee, Danny Kaye a refugee from Broadway—both arriving in some triumph. A sultry siren, Lauren Bacall, teaches Bogart how to whistle. Esther Williams splashes in. Gregory Peck is new and exciting. Dick Powell, almost through, gets a new lease on movie life as a tough guy. Other new names in the cast lists belong to Angela Lansbury, Phyllis Thaxter, Eleanor Parker, Diana Lynn, Gail Russell, Peggy Ann Garner—and they're only a few.

Our choices for movies of the year would be Vincente Minnelli's enchanting *Meet Me in St. Louis* with Judy Garland and Margaret O'Brien heading a happy cast; the tough Billy Wilder–Raymond Chandler adaptation of James Cain's *Double Indemnity* with Stanwyck, MacMurray, Robinson; Preston Sturges's twosome, *Hail the Conquering Hero* and *Miracle of Morgan's Creek,* and Otto Preminger's stylish *Laura* with Clifton Webb, Gene Tierney, Dana Andrews. But there are many more, worthy or popular or sometimes both—Capra's *Arsenic and Old Lace,* the Rita Hayworth–Gene Kelly *Cover Girl;* Ingrid Bergman and Charles Boyer in Cukor's *Gaslight;* Bing Crosby and Barry Fitzgerald in Leo McCarey's *Going My Way;* Bankhead in the Hitchcock-Steinbeck *Lifeboat;* Bette Davis doing her thing with Claude Rains in *Mr. Skeffington;* *National Velvet* starring a very young and very beautiful Elizabeth Taylor; Van Johnson in Mervyn LeRoy's *Thirty Seconds Over Tokyo;* Bogart and Bacall in Howard Hawks's *To Have and Have Not;* and Darryl Zanuck's *Wilson.* And, with certain reservations, we'd add *Jane Eyre; Keys of the Kingdom; Kismet* (for Marlene); *Since You Went Away; Up in Arms;* and *White Cliffs of Dover.*

And then there were those notable ones you probably don't quite remember.

Forgotten Films of 1944

In spite of its title, *The Curse of the Cat People* was not like one of those "adult" horror films that came out of the Val Lewton factory, more an exploration into the fantasy world of an impressionable child. Perhaps that is why it really never became one of the Lewton "cult" films. DeWitt Bodeen, author of the original *Cat People,* wrote this script; Gunther V. Fritsch and Robert Wise directed; Ann Carter played the child; and Simone Simon repeated her role from the first picture, this time as an apparition.

You'll seldom see *The Great Moment* in any Preston Sturges retrospective and, even in 1944, it was a failure. But although it dealt with a serious subject—it was based on the biography, *Triumph Over Pain,* of Dr. William Morton who discovered the use of ether as an anesthetic—it was filled with those Sturges comic bits and people, some of which fit and some which did not. Joel McCrea, Betty Field, and Harry Carey carried the leads and a lot of the usual Sturges stock company (William Demarest, Franklin Pangborn, Louis Jean Heydt, and Porter Hall among others) were present. A curious movie but interesting.

Alfred Hitchcock once made a silent screen version of Mrs. Belloc-Lowndes's novel, *The Lodger,* about a Jack the Ripper who stalked London in the gaslight era. Presumably the "master" injected more suspense into it than John Brahm was able to do in the 1944 version. Laird Cregar played the title role in a style that was hammy and heavy (as he also did in a 1945 melodrama, *Hangover Square*). Yet there were some good creepy moments and the period atmosphere was well sustained. There were also some dependable performers, notably Sara Allgood, Sir Cedric Hardwicke, George Sanders, and Merle Oberon. Screenplay by Barre Lyndon.

William Demarest, as the patient, and Joel McCrea and Betty Field as Dr. Morton and his wife, in Sturges's *The Great Moment*.

(ABOVE LEFT) The emphasis is on fantasy rather than horror in *The Curse of the Cat People* with Simone Simon and Ann Carter.

Merle Oberon is menaced by *The Lodger* (Laird Cregar). George Sanders can't help much.

It became fashionable to deride Margaret O'Brien and perhaps she did become a little bit sticky in some of her later movies. But she was a remarkable tiny actress in *Journey for Margaret, Meet Me in St. Louis,* and we'd add her *Lost Angel* to make a trilogy. This was a kind of quasi-Damon Runyon story in which some Broadway characters see the light when exposed to a little girl, raised scientifically and having her first adventure in the world outside. It gave Miss Margaret a chance to be quaint and irresistible. Marsha Hunt, James Craig, and Keenan Wynn were among those affected. Roy Rowland directed Isabel Lennart's screenplay.

Margaret O'Brien is the *Lost Angel*, and James Craig is her protector. The hat-check girl is a bit player named Ava Gardner.

An intense but murky film, *None but the Lonely Heart* drove customers away from the box office in spite of Cary Grant's popularity. Yet Grant's characterization of a restless Cockney trying to come to terms with his life is one of his finest. And Ethel Barrymore brought her theatrical majesty intact to the screen as his mother. June Duprez and Barry Fitzgerald had other roles. Clifford Odets, who also adapted the Richard Llewellyn novel, made his debut as a film director.

Cornelia Otis Skinner and Emily Kimbrough wrote blithely about their youthful adventures on a trip abroad in the early 1920s. *Our Hearts Were Young and Gay* made very pleasant movie fare, too, as adapted by Sheridan Gibney. Gail Russell and Diana Lynn had above-average ingenue charm as Cornelia and Emily. Both dead now (Russell tragically), neither lived up to her early promise. James Brown, Charles Ruggles, Dorothy Gish, and Beulah Bondi were in support; Lewis Allen directed.

Cockney Cary Grant and his strong mum (Ethel Barrymore) in *None but the Lonely Heart.*

Robert Siodmak's direction of *Phantom Lady* was sometimes consciously arty but the filmization of a good William Irish mystery was still an arresting film. Ella Raines, one of the most striking young actresses of the period, appeared to her best advantage and there were vivid bits by Franchot Tone, Fay Helm and, particularly, Elisha Cook, Jr., as a near-psychopathic jazz drummer. Screenplay by Bernard C. Shoenfeld.

Marion Hargrove wrote entertainingly about his own experiences as a young recruit in *See Here, Private Hargrove* and the book was a best seller. It transferred as happily to the screen particularly since it had one of the brightest young actors, Robert Walker, in the title role. Donna Reed was nice to have around, too, and so was Keenan Wynn. Wesley Ruggles directed the Harry Kurnitz screenplay.

James Brown meets Cornelia Otis Skinner and Emily Kimbrough (Gail Russell and Diana Lynn) in *Our Hearts Were Young and Gay.*

Ella Raines pretends to be a floozy to get some information out of Elisha Cook, Jr., in *Phantom Lady*.

Robert Walker as a typical G.I. in *See Here, Private Hargrove*.

Very much different from the run of wartime anti-Nazi movies was the filmization of Anna Seghers's *The Seventh Cross*. Even though the period was prewar, it was unusual for movies to show "good Germans" helping an anti-Nazi in his desperate flight from a concentration camp. This was a strong role for Spencer Tracy at his best and Hume Cronyn and Jessica Tandy were priceless as people who help. But the whole cast—Signe Hasso, Herbert Rudley, Felix Bressart, Agnes Moorehead, Katherine Locke, and Paul Guilfoyle most prominently—was impressive. So was the direction of Fred Zinnemann whose first major movie this was. Screenplay by Helen Deutsch.

Two Girls and a Sailor was the kind of wartime musical that would look very old hat today. As stories go, it was pretty old hat then. But it had everything going for it in the way of entertainment—Jimmy Durante for one of his most welcome appearances, sprightly music by people ranging from Lena Horne to Virginia O'Brien, Harry James to Xavier Cugat—and even Jose Iturbi. And, far from least in that year, some really winning young people—Van Johnson, June Allyson, Gloria De-Haven, and Tom Drake. Joe Pasternak produced, Richard Thorpe directed, Richard Connell and Gladys Lehman wrote the screenplay.

George Cukor put Moss Hart's Army Air Force stage show, *Winged Victory*, rousingly on screen with all male roles played by AAF enlisted men, most of them from the original Broadway production. Hence we had Private Lon McCallister, Sergeant Edmond O'Brien, Corporal Lee J. Cobb, and many others (such as Peter Lind Hayes, Red Buttons, Barry Nelson, Gary Merrill, Martin Ritt, Karl Malden, Sascha Brastoff, Mark Daniels, Don Taylor and more, all identified by rank). We also had some civilian girls playing civilian girls—Jeanne Crain, Jo-Carroll Dennison and a newcomer, Judy Holliday. It was standard stuff even then, with all the clichés—but it made the kind of service picture audiences wanted in those days.

Jessica Tandy and Hume Cronyn aid Spencer Tracy in *The Seventh Cross*.

Gloria De Haven, June Allyson, and Van Johnson as *Two Girls and a Sailor*.

Mark Daniels, Barry Nelson and Edmond O'Brien were all actually in the Air Force when they appeared in *Winged Victory*. Various mothers, wives, and sweethearts were played by civilians including Geraldine Wall, Jo-Carroll Dennison, Jeanne Crain, and a newcomer, Judy Holliday.

Other Forgotten 1944 Pictures to Note

Between Two Worlds transplanted the old Sutton Vane play *Outward Bound* to war-torn London with its cargo of souls having been killed in an air raid. Some of the casting (Sara Allgood, Edmund Gwenn, Sydney Greenstreet) worked well; most of the picture seemed contrived. . . . Nor could you really believe in most of the cast of *Dragon Seed* as Chinese peasants, particularly Katharine Hepburn and most of her associates although Walter Huston and Aline MacMahon were impressive. . . . Paul Lukas and Olive Blakeney gave interesting performances in *Experiment Perilous* but the picture was inclined to linger on Hedy Lamarr, much more photogenic but much less animated. . . . By the time Maxwell Anderson's *The Eve of St. Mark* transferred to the screen, it became just another, although much more pretentious, movie about men in service. . . . *It Happened Tomorrow* had an intriguing idea—a man who could foretell tomorrow's headlines—and Rene Clair's wit made as much as possible of it but the story didn't hold up and Dick Powell wasn't the man for the role. . . . *The Mask of Dimitrios* took a fascinating Eric Ambler story, cast it well (particularly with Zachary Scott, Sydney Greenstreet, and Peter Lorre) but the picture had only flashes of the Ambler suspense. . . .

The Purple Heart dealt with Japanese atrocity against captured American airmen with Richard Loo (who else?) providing the major menace against Dana An-

drews, Farley Granger, Kevin O'Shea, Richard Conte, and others in the Lewis Milestone-directed movie. . . . *The Sullivans* was a sentimental, entertaining reconstruction of the wartime real-life story of five brothers lost together in the sinking of a ship, with a pleasant cast (notably John Campbell, James Cardwell, Edward Ryan, Thomas Mitchell, Ward Bond, and Anne Baxter). . . . Cardwell and Campbell showed up again along with Linda Darnell and Lynn Bari in a little swing movie, *Sweet and Low Down*, but the honors here went to the Benny Goodman band. . . . Skippy Homeier gave a chilling performance (repeating his Broadway role as the child Nazi) in *Tomorrow the World* but the picture grew over-melodramatic and the usually able adult actors (Fredric March, Betty Field, Agnes Moorehead) were dull. . . . Quite an effective adult ghost movie was *The Uninvited* with Ray Milland, Cornelia Otis Skinner, Ruth Hussey, and a hauntingly lovely Gail Russell, complete with a hauntingly lovely music theme, "Stella by Starlight.". . . *Woman of the Town* was a minor Western about the legendary Bat Masterson and there have been more exciting movie Mastersons than that played by Albert Dekker. But Claire Trevor, always effective, had a good role and there were supporting people of merit like Henry Hull, Percy Kilbride, and Porter Hall.

Chapter Seventeen

The Movie Year of 1945

The war ends in 1945 but war movies don't stop. Some of the best (*A Walk in the Sun, The Story of G. I. Joe, The True Glory*) win acclaim but not much box-office loot. Audiences go for other problems now—alcoholism (*The Lost Weekend*), travails of adolescence in the slums (*A Tree Grows in Brooklyn*), suffering motherhood (*Mildred Pierce*)—or for movies like *The Bells of St. Mary's* and *Anchors Aweigh* which dispense with problems altogether.

One advertising catchphrase, "Gable's Back—and Garson's Got Him," tells the story as servicemen stars begin to troop back to the screen. For many, it's not difficult to pick up where they were before. Some actors, however, who were just on the verge of hitting it big when they left—Robert Sterling is a good example—find that their former spots have been preempted by the Van Johnsons who came along later.

Not only are the servicemen returning. Joan Crawford, James Dunn, Joan Blondell, Ray Milland, Sylvia Sidney, and Ann Harding all make new starts with their flagging film careers. All are welcomed back, but not all make it in the long run. Attracting attention for the first time are Robert Mitchum, Ann Blyth, Rhonda Fleming, Jeanne Crain, John Dall, Joan Lorring, Nina Foch, Hurd Hatfield, Robert Alda, Virginia Mayo, Anne Jeffreys, Lizabeth Scott, Lawrence Tierney, and Yvonne DeCarlo, among others.

Our own special favorites among the movies of the year would be Brackett and Wilder's *Lost Weekend*, Elia Kazan's *A Tree Grows in Brooklyn,* and Lewis Milestone's *A Walk in the Sun*. But there are so many others deserving of special mention—Gene Kelly and Frank Sinatra in *Anchors Aweigh*; Ingrid Bergman and Bing Crosby in *The Bells of St. Mary's*; Judy Garland and Robert Walker in Minnelli's *The Clock*; the Michael Powell–Emeric Pressburger *Colonel Blimp*; Bette Davis in *The Corn Is Green*; Joan Crawford's *Mildred Pierce*; Bergman and Gary Cooper in *Saratoga Trunk*; Bergman and Peck in Hitchcock's *Spellbound*; and Mitchum and Burgess Meredith in Wellman's *Story of G. I. Joe*. To add a few more, Val Lewton's *Body Snatcher* and *Isle of the Dead*; Dorothy McGuire and Robert Young in *The Enchanted Cottage*; Albert Lewin's *Picture of Dorian Gray*; and John Ford's *They Were Expendable* with Robert Montgomery, John Wayne. There were also some musicals ranging from the Chopin biopic—more "pic" than "bio"—*A Song to Remember* through the Rodgers and Hammerstein reworking of *State Fair* to Danny Kaye's *Wonder Man*, and including *Rhapsody in Blue*, which at least presented its Gershwin music effectively.

Then there were those others which have retreated into the mists of memory.

Joseph Cotten and Ginger Rogers in *I'll Be Seeing You*.

Intensive searches of archives in London, New York, and Los Angeles failed to turn up a single usable still from *Love on the Dole*. Here's the next best—an early (but not that early) portrait of its leading lady, Deborah Kerr, considerably more glamourized than she appeared in the film. But unglamourous portraits of Kerr just don't exist.

Forgotten Films of 1945

Noël Coward's *Blithe Spirit* was wittily directed by David Lean and acted by a cast which knew just what to do with Coward dialogue. Who could be more right for such a Coward hero than Rex Harrison? Constance Cummings and Kay Hammond were also quite correct. But the joy of the picture was Margaret Rutherford's brusque and hearty medium, Mme. Arcati. Other Coward–Lean films are frequently available but *Blithe Spirit* has all but disappeared, even from television showings.

I'll Be Seeing You had a lot going for it—a handsome Selznick–Dore Schary production, a sentimental storyline that was right for its time, a competent cast and, of course, that evocative title tune. Joseph Cotten and Ginger Rogers played two who meet on furlough—he's a shell-shocked veteran, she a prisoner on parole. Spring Byington, Tom Tully, Shirley Temple were small-town American types with whom they are involved. William Dieterle directed a Marion Parsonnet screenplay.

It was an odd period—in 1945—to release a grim study of British life in the 1930s Depression. As a result, *Love on the Dole* had no audience and vanished quickly from theatres. Walter Greenwood wrote the screenplay from his own 1936 play and John Baxter directed. Deborah Kerr, Clifford Evans, Marie Ault, and Marjorie Rhodes were in the cast. It was a worthy film out of its time.

J. Carrol Naish, after years of yeoman service usually as secondary heavies, came into his own with a moving characterization in *A Medal for Benny*. Irving Pichel directed a film based on a story by John Steinbeck (with Jack Wagner and Frank Butler). Steinbeck's *paisano* characters were blood brothers of those of his *Tortilla Flat*. They were well played by Mikhail Rasumny, Dorothy Lamour, Arturo de Cordova, and particularly Naish as the father who receives a posthumous Medal of Honor for his son, who had been driven out of town as a bad boy.

A very minor little mystery but a surprisingly effective one was *My Name Is Julia Ross.* This gave Nina Foch one of the very rare chances she ever had in films to demonstrate her dramatic talents as the frightened heroine while Dame May Whitty and George Macready were particularly sinister. Joseph H. Lewis directed the screenplay by Muriel Roy Bolton.

Margaret Rutherford, the medium, helps bring back the ghost (Kay Hammon) of Rex Harrison's first wife in *Blithe Spirit*.

J. Carrol Naish (second from left) scored in *A Medal for Benny* with Charles Dingle, Dorothy Lamour, and Frank McHugh.

133

Nina Foch in *My Name Is Julia Ross*.

Clive Brook, Roland Culver, and Beatrice Lillie in *On Approval*.

Beatrice Lillie had dazzled Broadway and was a radio staple, but Hollywood never knew what to do with her. It was England that gave her her best film outing in *On Approval*. She kept it richly amusing and sometimes hilarious in spite of pedestrian direction by Clive Brook (who also co-starred, produced and adapted the Frederick Lonsdale play). Googie Withers and Roland Culver helped, too.

Although it was later overshadowed by such postwar films as *The Best Years of Our Lives* and *Bright Victory* (which may explain why it has so seldom been seen since), *Pride of the Marines* was a strong and compassionate drama of a blinded war hero learning to readjust. Delmer Daves directed the Albert Maltz script with John Garfield giving one of his most striking performances. There were notable contributions by others (John Ridgely, Rosemary DeCamp and, particularly, Eleanor Parker and Dane Clark).

Although the script sometimes let her down, Tallulah Bankhead had a field day as Catherine the Great in *A Royal Scandal*. It was much more Tallulah than her dismal dramas of the 1930s. Otto Preminger directed and you could sense the touch of producer Ernst Lubitsch, too. Charles Coburn, Vincent Price, William Eythe, and Anne Baxter were also present. Screenplay by Edwin Justus Mayer.

Although Jean Renoir used his camera and treated his protagonists in an almost documentary style, *The Southerner* was rich in human drama and blessed by uncommonly fine performances. These included Zachary Scott as a poor white sharecropper, Betty Field as his wife, Beulah Bondi as the senile grandmother and others in the cast, such as J. Carrol Naish, Charles Kemper, Blanche Yurka, and Norman Lloyd. From George Session Perry's novel, *Hold Autumn in Your Hand*.

Robert Siodmak directed two murder dramas released in 1945, both moodily effective, both with some impressive performances but both ultimately failures. Charles Laughton played with restraint in *The Suspect,* while Rosalind Ivan and Henry Daniell were fascinatingly evil. The picture though lacked sustained suspense. *The Strange Affair of Uncle Harry* had more serious flaws, including the miscasting of suave George Sanders as the henpecked title character. And there was the despicable ending which made it all a dream. But Geraldine Fitzgerald, miscast, too, but rising above it, Sara Allgood and Moyna Magill were effective, and so was the picture up to that ending. The most attractive Ella Raines was the rather strange choice as leading lady in both films. It was hard to conceive of her being attracted to either Laughton or to Uncle Harry.

Eleanor Parker and John Garfield in *Pride of the Marines*.

William Eythe, Tallulah Bankhead (she's Mother Russia) in *A Royal Scandal*.

Robert Siodmak directed two effective 1945 murder dramas—*The Strange Affair of Uncle Harry*, with Geraldine Fitzgerald, Sara Allgood, George Sanders, and Moyna McGill . . .

. . . and *The Suspect*, with Ella Raines and Charles Laughton.

Zachary Scott played Renoir's *The Southerner* with Betty Field as his wife, Beulah Bondi as Granny, and Jay Gilpin and Bunny Sunshine (or Jean Vanderwilt, depending on the source) as the children.

The lovely performances of Robert Donat and Deborah Kerr (aided by Glynis Johns, Ann Todd, Roland Culver) made *Vacation From Marriage* a very endearing little wartime comedy drama. They played a very stuffy British married couple who blossom out when each joins the service. Alexander Korda directed with screenplay by Clemence Dane and Anthony Pelessier.

The Way Ahead, another excellent British wartime film, was a tribute to the infantryman. It covered familiar ground but, under the direction of Carol Reed and as written by Eric Ambler and Peter Ustinov, it did it extremely well. David Niven, James Donald, Billy Hartnell, Raymond Huntley, and Stanley Holloway headed the cast. Another Carol Reed wartime film of 1945, *The True Glory,* was even more distinguished. This, a documentary detailing all stages of the Allied Forces over the Germans, was co-directed by Garson Kanin, then a captain in the U.S. Army.

Apparently the director and stars couldn't decide which of two similarly-themed melodrams they would film—so they made them both. Both *The Woman in the Win-*

Deborah Kerr and Robert Donat, who have been a mousey married couple, discover how life in the service has changed them in *Vacation from Marriage.*

137

Two Carol Reed wartime films: one a documentary, *The True Glory* (that's General Eisenhower with the soldiers) . . .

. . . the other a dramatic tribute, *The Way Ahead*, with (from left) Peter Ustinov, David Niven, Billy Hartnell, and John Laurie.

dow (script by Nunnally Johnson) and *Scarlet Street* (script by Dudley Nichols) dealt with the fearsome consequences of the infatuation of a mild, middle-aged, respectable man for a casual pickup. Edward G. Robinson and Joan Bennett played these roles impressively while Dan Duryea completed the triangle effectively in both pictures. Rosalind Ivan (only in *Scarlet Street*) was a loathsome shrew. Fritz Lang directed both in his moodiest style. *Window* was the more satisfying film all the way to the big letdown of an awful "it was all a dream" ending.

Fred Astaire acted and danced adroitly in *Yolanda and the Thief* and Vincente Minnelli may never have staged a film more dazzling to behold. But the leaden humors and flat fantasy of the script defeated them. And the totally blank personality of Lucille Bremer (although she was beautiful and danced well) was a final numbing blow. Still it was something special just to look at.

Joan Bennett led Edward G. Robinson into trouble
twice during 1945: first in *Woman in the Window* . . .

Other Forgotten 1945 Films to Note

Some of the best character actors around—like Walter Huston, Roland Young, Barry Fitzgerald, Judith Anderson, and the like—were knocked off one after the other in Rene Clair's version of Agatha Christie's murder classic, *And Then There Were None* (also known as *Ten Little Indians*). . . . John Hersey's novel and play, *A Bell for Adano,* was a good movie for its time although John Hodiak lacked charisma for the central role. . . . Jimmy Cagney transferred his gangster-baiting tactics to Japan in *Blood on the Sun*, with a particularly sultry Sylvia Sidney as a mysterious Eurasian. . . . Humphrey Bogart was too well established in his final persona to be acceptable as a weak wife-murderer in *Conflict* although Rose Hobart was unpleasant enough to drive even Sam Spade to the step. . . . *The House on 92nd Street* benefited from the semidocumentary treatment given it by *March of Time* producer Louis de Rochemont and director Henry Hathaway. . . . *Johnny in the Clouds* (also called *The Way to the Stars*) was

another of those very good British wartime films, impeccably acted, of course, by a cast headed by Michael Redgrave, John Mills, and Rosamund John. . . . *Our Vines Have Tender Grapes* was a nice little family pastoral with Edward G. Robinson, Agnes Moorehead, Margaret O'Brien, and Jackie Jenkins. . . . *Out of This World* was a slight but pleasant lampoon of the Sinatra phenomenon with Eddie Bracken (complete with Bing Crosby's voice) as the swooned-over one. . . . Marcia Davenport's sprawling novel, *The Valley of Decision,* was virtually skeletonized for the screen but what a cast it had—Greer Garson, Gregory Peck, Gladys Cooper, Marsha Hunt, Jessica Tandy, Donald Crisp, and Lionel Barrymore for starters. . . . In spite of songs by Kurt Weill and Ira Gershwin and an amusing Morrie Ryskind idea, *Where Do We Go From Here* was labored fantasy particularly in the performance of Fred MacMurray who is just not cut out for such things. A word though for the girls—Joan Leslie and June Haver . . .

... then in *Scarlet Street*. Fritz Lang directed both.

Lucille Bremer, Fred Astaire, and Mildred Natwick in
Yolanda and the Thief.

Chapter Eighteen

The Movie Year of 1946

The tempo of the times in 1946 is reflected in the theme of the most successful film of the year. *The Best Years of Our Lives* deals with returning servicemen and their readjustments. Goldwyn has done it over the protests of those who say the public is fed up with war problems.

Some of the best movies of the year—a good many of them—come from Britain. We begin to see French films in American movie theaters again and Italy startles us with Roberto Rossellini's *Open City,* the beginning of a whole new era for Italian cinema. But the emphasis in homegrown products is entertainment without too many problems.

As British films come back, we begin to meet some of the most interesting new actors. Some have been seen before—Celia Johnson, for instance, in a couple of lesser roles. But now she's bigger news and so are Trevor Howard, Jean Simmons, Stewart Granger, James Mason, Ann Todd, Patricia Roc, naming just a few. Among American faces becoming familiar are those of Burt Lancaster, Ava Gardner, Steve Cochran, Larry Parks, Van Heflin, Kirk Douglas, John Lund, Mark Stevens, Cathy O'Donnell, Celeste Holm, Guy Madison, and, in one unforgettable screen appearance only,

Harold Russell, of *Best Years of Our Lives.*

Besides *Best Years* there are others in a very special niche—the Noel Coward–David Lean *Brief Encounter,* Olivier's *Henry V,* and John Ford's *My Darling Clementine* with Henry Fonda. But there are so many others of note—the Bogart/Hawks *Big Sleep;* Robert Siodmak's *The Killers;* Alfred Hitchcock's *Notorious* (Bergman–Grant–Rains); and Garfield, Turner and Hume Cronyn in *The Postman Always Rings Twice.* And a lot of others of varying merit crowd for recognition—*Anna and the King of Siam; Caesar and Cleopatra; Duel in the Sun; Gilda; Humoresque; The Razor's Edge; The Seventh Veil; Sister Kenny; The Spiral Staircase; Stolen Life; To Each His Own;* and *The Yearling.* So many popular musicals, too—*The Jolson Story,* of course, and Astaire–Crosby in *Blue Skies;* Judy Garland's *Harvey Girls;* Danny Kaye's *Kid From Brooklyn;* Disney's *Make Mine Music;* Minnelli's all-star *Ziegfeld Follies;* with mention of *Night and Day* and *Till the Clouds Roll By,* only because some of the Cole Porter and Jerome Kern songs were effectively presented.

Those are the ones you remember. But there were some more.

Forgotten Films of 1946

You wouldn't normally expect Jennifer Jones to be particularly adept at light comedy but, under the guidance of the master Ernst Lubitsch, she was an engaging *Cluny Brown*. And Charles Boyer had even more than his usual charm. But best of all were bits by people like Una O'Connor, Sara Allgood, Reginald Owen, and a rabbity Richard Haydn. An amusing filmization of Margery Sharp's novel, with screenplay by Samuel Hoffenstein and Elizabeth Reinhardt.

Closer in style and spirit to Jean Renoir's French masterpieces than any of his other American films was *The Diary of a Chambermaid* which also gave Paulette Goddard probably her best role. She was the servant girl of the title, using her wiles to advance herself. Francis Lederer, Burgess Meredith (who also scripted and co-produced), Judith Anderson, Hurd Hatfield, and Reginald Owen were well-cast, too.

A. J. Cronin's novel, *The Green Years*, of an Irish orphan boy growing to young manhood in an alien land, made a fine, sentimental motion picture as directed by

Charles Boyer and Jennifer Jones meet her local swain, Richard Haydn, in *Cluny Brown*.

Judith Anderson, the mistress of the house; Francis Lederer, the darkly glowering butler; and Paulette Goddard as she who writes *The Diary of a Chambermaid*.

Tom Drake, Gladys Cooper, and Hume Cronyn in *The Green Years*.

(BELOW) A different Hume Cronyn with Marsha Hunt in *A Letter for Evie*.

Victor Saville. Tom Drake and Dean Stockwell were both excellent as the boy in different ages.

But the high spots of the film were characterizations by seasoned actors, particularly Charles Coburn as a roistering old rogue and Hume Cronyn as a dour Scot. The fine cast also included Jessica Tandy, Gladys Cooper, Selena Royle, and Richard Haydn. Screenplay by Robert Ardrey and Sonya Levien.

In *A Letter for Evie*, once again a girl falls for a correspondent she has never met. But, being nervous about his own attractiveness, he has enclosed a picture of his handsome wolfish buddy. This old chestnut (shades of *They Knew What They Wanted, Shop Around the Corner, et al.*) managed to provide fresh and amusing entertainment. This was due to the directorial touch of Jules Dassin, the loveliness of Marsha Hunt but especially to the little gem provided by Hume Cronyn in a rare screen comedy role.

A Notorious Gentleman presented Rex Harrison, absolutely fascinating as one of the most unprincipled cads ever to make his "rake's progress" across a screen. There was also a striking performance by Lilli Palmer as one of his victims. Sidney Gilliat directed, produced and (with Frank Launder) wrote the screenplay.

While *The Searching Wind* may be a lesser Lillian Hellman play, there is much of Hellman's scathing anger in its depiction of appeasers in government. The film version, scripted by Miss Hellman and directed by William Dieterle, was a faithful treatment of the play but suffered from some bad casting in Robert Young's rather weak characterization and Ann Richards's uninteresting leading woman. But Sylvia Sidney gave a performance of intensity and there was effective support by Dudley Digges, Albert Basserman, and Douglas Dick.

Stairway to Heaven was a witty and inventive British fantasy of the *Here Comes Mr. Jordan* type in which a British pilot pleads his case (that he be allowed to remain alive and to love an American servicewoman) before a celestial court. David Niven had one of his very best roles here but all the actors (Roger Livesey, Marius Goring, Kim Hunter, Raymond Massey, and the rest) were commendable. So was the work of Michael Powell and Emeric Pressburger who wrote, produced, and directed.

Rex Harrison as *A Notorious Gentleman* with Lilli Palmer, Margaret Johnston, and Godfrey Tearle.

David Niven is at the foot of the *Stairway to Heaven*. Kim Hunter is at the head of the group. Among others you can probably pick out are Marius Goring, Roger Livesey, Abraham Sofaer, Raymond Massey, Robert Coote, and Kathleen Byron.

Robert Young and Sylvia Sidney in an air raid in *The Searching Wind.*

Robert Rossen wrote and Lewis Milestone directed *The Strange Love of Martha Ivers* which gave Barbara Stanwyck a chance to play a coldly evil woman, unequaled in viciousness by any in the Stanwyck roster except, perhaps, by the murdering wife in *Double Indemnity.* Kirk Douglas, Roman Bohnen, and Judith Anderson were thoroughly unpleasant, too, with Van Heflin standing out as a more normal leading man. It was intriguing melodrama.

Three Strangers were played by three superb actors—Geraldine Fitzgerald, Sydney Greenstreet, and Peter Lorre—in a vivid and suspenseful film. Rosalind Ivan

and Joan Lorring gave gripping performances, too. John Huston wrote the original story and, with Howard Koch, the screenplay. Jean Negulesco directed.

Other Forgotten 1946 Films to Note

Bedlam provided a striking recreation of the Hogarthian madhouse in the Val Lewton–Mark Robson film with Boris Karloff. . . . Alan Ladd tried to find out who had murdered his estranged wife and pinned it on him in *The Blue Dahlia.* . . . *The Chase* was murky melodrama but with some interesting bits and a sharp performance by Steve Cochran. . . . Dorothy McGuire was as bewitching as originally in *Claudia and David* a not-unworthy sequel to the *Claudia* that had introduced her. . . .

Mark Stevens showed promise, never developed, in an interesting melodrama, *The Dark Corner*, with Clifton Webb and Lucille Ball. . . . Famed theatre director/critic Harold Clurman had his only screen directing in Clifford Odets's *Deadline at Dawn*, minor but exciting melodrama with Susan Hayward, Bill Williams. . . . Claude Rains was notable in *Deception* with Bette Davis subdued but hardly effaced. . . . Robert Montgomery followed Dick Powell and Humphrey Bogart as super-detective Philip Marlow in *Lady in the Lake.* The film was notable for Montgomery's use of the camera (he also directed) as the picture was seen completely through the protagonist's eyes. . . . *Margie* had a beguiling Jeanne Crain in a nice little movie about flaming youth in the 1920s. . . . Sylvia Sidney was striking as a ruthless political candidate in *Mr. Ace* although George Raft's performance left something to be desired as the political boss of the title. . . . Eddie Albert was at his most likable in an amusing little wartime comedy, *Rendezvous With Annie.* . . . Orson Welles movies are not all *Citizen Kane. The Stranger* was lesser Welles with a wildly overboard performance by the master but it had its moments.

Sydney Greenstreet, Peter Lorre, and Geraldine Fitzgerald as *Three Strangers.*

Barbara Stanwyck restrains Van Heflin in *The Strange Love of Martha Ivers*. Kirk Douglas has conked out at the foot of the stairs.

Chapter Nineteen

The Movie Year of 1947

More and more major pictures are arriving in 1947 from Great Britain while French and Italian films are once more regulars on the art house circuit.

In America it is a year to bring pictures like *Gentlemen's Agreement*, *Crossfire*, and others which explore issues previously untouched by Hollywood.

Among new or little-known personalities making an impact are the scrubbed and sunny Janet Leigh, the giggling Richard Widmark, along with others like Pedro Armendariz, Wanda Hendrix, Alastair Sim, Barbara Bel Geddes, Mona Freeman, Jane Greer, Doris Day, Rory Calhoun, Alec Guinness, Natalie Wood, Thelma Ritter, and Claude Jarman.

Let's list our particular favorite pictures of the year alphabetically—John Garfield in Robert Rossen's *Body and Soul*; Elia Kazan's *Boomerang*; Robert Ryan in Dmytryk's *Crossfire*; David Lean's *Great Expectations*; Chaplin's *Monsieur Verdoux*; and James Mason in Carol Reed's *Odd Man Out*. But also worth special note would be such as Dassin's *Brute Force*; Kazan's *Gentlemen's Agreement*; Hathaway's *Kiss of Death*; and a flock of others. Not all are particularly distinguished but are worth noting for one reason or another—*The Bachelor and the Bobbysoxer*; *Dear Ruth*; *The Egg and I*; *The Farmer's Daughter*; *The Ghost and Mrs. Muir*; *Good News*; *Life With Father*; *Miracle on 34th Street*; *Mother Wore Tights*; *The Perils of Pauline*; *Possessed*; and *The Secret Life of Walter Mitty*. It was also a year of some major disasters—*Forever Amber* and *Mourning Becomes Electra* (except for Michael Redgrave's performance) among the heaviest clinkers.

There were others—forgotten but notable films.

Deborah Kerr and Trevor Howard in *The Adventuress*.

Forgotten Films of 1947

The most irresistible Irish patriot you've seen on screen was Deborah Kerr in *The Adventuress*. Miss Deborah was a saucy colleen (it was before America decided she could play only elegant ladies) who, in her anti-British zeal, got herself thoroughly mixed up with the Nazis.

Trevor Howard, British to the core, helped her out of her problems. Frank Launder directed and, with Sidney Gilliat, wrote and produced.

The heavenly figure who comes down to earth to help right things was a very overworked figure of 1940s movie whimsy—although *Mr. Jordan* and Henry Travers's role as an angel in *Wonderful Life* rose triumphantly above the general run. Not in their league but charming nonetheless was Cary Grant's suave spirit in *The Bishop's Wife.* Add people like David Niven, Loretta Young, Elsa Lanchester, Gladys Cooper, Monty Woolley, and others under the direction of Henry Koster and you had an enjoyable movie. Screenplay by Robert E. Sherwood and Leonardo Bercovici.

Speaking of *Mr. Jordan*, he returned to us (this time as played by Roland Culver rather than Claude Rains) in a fantasy musical, *Down to Earth*, in which Rita Hayworth, looking every inch a goddess, took on human form as a musical comedy queen. Jimmy Gleason and Edward Everett Horton had brief chances to repeat their

Loretta Young is *The Bishop's Wife*, David Niven is her husband, and Cary Grant, believe it or not, is an angel come to help them.

Rita Hayworth is another divinity who has come *Down to Earth*.

Dolores Del Rio is the woman, Henry Fonda the priest, in *The Fugitive*.

Wendy Hiller, Nancy Price, and Roger Livesey in *I Know Where I'm Going*.

Sylvia Sidney begins to realize that her husband (John Hodiak) isn't what she believed him to be in *Love from a Stranger*.

original *Jordan* characterizations but this picture wasn't a patch on its predecessor. Still the dance numbers (with Marc Platt starring) were lavishly staged and you could always just look at Rita. Alexander Hall directed.

Even though Dudley Nichols's script watered down Graham Green's story of a whisky priest, *The Fugitive,* as directed by John Ford, was a taut and thoughtful motion picture with an impassioned performance by Henry Fonda. Also rating bravos were Pedro Armendariz, Dolores Del Rio, Ward Bond, and Cinematographer Gabriel Figueroa.

The films of Michael Powell and Emeric Pressburger (*Colonel Blimp,* for instance, or *Stairway to Heaven, Black Narcissus, The Red Shoes*) were generally presented on a wide canvas, full of vivid incident. But their *I Know Where I'm Going* was much more simple, though none the less impressive for that. The story had to do with a sophisticated London girl marooned on a Scottish island, with its plain inhabitants and their primitive customs. The marvelous Wendy Hiller was surrounded by fine actors—Roger Livesey, Pamela Brown, Finlay Currie, Nancy Price, and Petula Clark being just a few of them.

The Long Night was moody, sometimes arresting, melodrama with Henry Fonda remarkably sympathetic and sensitive as a murderer, barricaded in his tenement room. But compromises in the screenplay of John Wexley and the direction of Anatole Litvak weakened this remake of Jean Gabin's French film, *Daybreak.* Ann Dvorak did well but Barbara Bel Geddes's screen debut was lackluster and Vincent Price was totally miscast.

John Hodiak didn't have the frightening malevolence that Basil Rathbone could summon up but there were still some thrills in the Richard Whorf remake of *Love From a Stranger.* Of course, nobody can be more convincingly terrorized than Sylvia Sidney and she made the final moments gripping in spite of the inadequacy of Hodiak.

Ernest Hemingway's *The Short, Happy Life of Francis Macomber* was one of his classic stories and, as directed by Zoltan Korda, it came to the screen almost as impressively with the title *The Macomber Affair.* The "almost" was due to a screenplay that softened and confused a vital issue. But Joan Bennett, Gregory Peck and, particularly, Robert Preston as the cowardly blowhard never compromised their performances for a moment.

Henry Fonda is an ordinary guy with eyes for the charms of Ann Dvorak in *The Long Night* . . .

Joan Bennett has contempt for Robert Preston's cowardice in *The Macomber Affair*.

Tyrone Power with some of his carnival cronies, including Joan Blondell, James Flavin, and Coleen Gray, in *Nightmare Alley*.

Although it never went as far in its depiction of the sordid side of carnival life as William Lindsay Gresham's book, *Nightmare Alley* was still far off the beaten track for movie melodrama. Tyrone Power never played such a completely unsavory character—but he played it well while Joan Blondell was notable in a showy, untypical role. Edmund Goulding directed Jules Furthman's screenplay.

RKO virtually threw *Out of the Past* away as a "B" picture when it originally came out. Now it is regarded by the few who still know it as one of the prime examples of *film noir*. Robert Mitchum's extraordinary screen presence was there to see if anyone had seen it

and Jane Greer should have zoomed to major stardom as his glittering nemesis—but somehow the public and most critics passed this picture by. Jacques Tourneur directed and Geoffrey Homes wrote the screenplay from his own novel. Kirk Douglas and Rhonda Fleming also appeared.

Robert Montgomery directed as well as starred in *Ride a Pink Horse.* As an actor, he gave one of his best tough-guy performances. As director, he kept the action in a vivid melodrama (written by Ben Hecht and Charles Lederer from a Dorothy Hughes original) moving without letup. Producer Joan Harrison, once closely associated with Hitchcock, probably deserved some of the credit. Certainly the supporting cast with sharp performances by Thomas Gomez, Fred Clark, Art Smith, and Andrea King helped. And so did the delicately lovely Wanda Hendrix. Why didn't she become a star?

Martha Scott never received the attention she merited for her playing of a selfish, vicious wife in *So Well Remembered* nor did John Mills in a more typical role as a gentle humanitarian. But then neither did their picture in spite of a fine screenplay by John Paxton from James Hilton's novel, good direction by Edward Dmytryk, and supporting performances by an excellent cast (Trevor Howard, Patricia Roc, Richard Carlson). But then RKO never treated what it considered a less-than-blockbuster movie with much attention.

Noël Coward's *Cavalcade* technique—the passing years of English life as seen through the eyes of one family—were used again in his *This Happy Breed.* This time it wasn't the elegant *Cavalcade* set but a lower middle class family with which he dealt. David Lean scored directorially again and Celia Johnson, Coward's favorite actress (ours, too), headed the cast. No collection of actors could have been more genuine than she, Robert Newton, John Mills, Kay Walsh, Amy Veness, Alison Leggatt, and Stanley Holloway.

Robert Mitchum and Jane Greer in *Out of the Past*.

Other Forgotten 1947 Films to Note

It was a big year for the British. In addition to *Great Expectations* and *Odd Man Out,* both far from forgotten, and those covered more extensively in this section (*The Adventuress, I Know Where I'm Going, So Well Remembered,* and *This Happy Breed*) there were others which deserve a special note—*Beware of Pity,* but only for the performances of Lilli Palmer, Gladys Cooper, Sir Cedric Hardwicke . . . *Black Narcissus,* a slow, but often striking and beautifully filmed, study of British nuns in the Himalayas, with Deborah Kerr, Flora Robson, Kathleen Byron, Jean Simmons, David Farrar . . . *Captain Boycott,* a lively piece about an Irish rebellion with Stewart Granger, Cecil Parker, and a cameo by Robert Donat . . . *The Captive Heart,* drama of British prisoners of war with Michael Redgrave's expected fine performance . . . *Green for Danger* with a delightful Alastair Sim solving a reasonably baffling murder mystery . . . *Nicholas Nickelby,* a fairly faithful but sketchy and pretty uninspired version of the Dickens's novel . . . *Tawny Pipit,* an unpretentious but fresh and funny village comedy . . . *The Years Between,* an interesting problem drama with fine performances by Michael Redgrave, Valerie Hobson, and Flora Robson. . . .

And non-British films deserving a mention—*Blaze of Noon* with William Holden and Sterling Hayden as

Wanda Hendrix and Robert Montgomery in *Ride the Pink Horse*.

Richard Carlson has been disfigured in the war. Martha Scott is his mother, using the injuries to hold on to him, in *So Well Remembered*.

Robert Newton, Amy Veness, and Celia Johnson arrive at the house in which they will spend two decades of British history in *This Happy Breed*.

early barnstorming flyers . . . *Carnegie Hall*, pretty awful soap opera but with marvelous music and a touching performance by Marsha Hunt . . . *Cynthia*, just to watch Elizabeth Taylor emerging into young womanhood . . . *Daisy Kenyon* was a glossy woman's picture but a pretty good one, thanks primarily to its cast, with Joan Crawford in the title role, Henry Fonda and Dana Andrews as points on the triangle. . . . *Dark Passage* and *Dead Reckoning* were typical Humphrey Bogart melodramas, the first more interesting than the second primarily because Lauren Bacall had the feminine lead while Bogart had to make do with Lizabeth Scott in *Reckoning*. . . . Max Ophuls brought style to *The Exile* and Douglas Fairbanks, Jr., was always in his element in such dashing roles but the script was tired. . . .

Glenn Ford starred in a tight little melodrama, *Framed*, with Janis Carter, sexy and intelligent in one of the few movies to take advantage of her potential. . . . Marlene Dietrich playing a filthy gypsy was almost enough—but it's the only reason for mentioning *Golden Earrings*. . . . A poignantly youthful Janet Leigh made her scenes count in *If Winter Comes* but a good cast (Walter Pidgeon, Deborah Kerr, Angela Lansbury, Dame May Whitty, and Binnie Barnes) couldn't make the old-hat story less than tiresome. . . . Joan Fontaine was the personification of well-bred evil as *Ivy* and there was one of the best groups of character actors (Sara Allgood, Rosalind Ivan, Herbert Marshall, Sir Cedric Hardwicke, Lucile Watson, Una O'Connor, and Isobel Elsom, among others) that could be gathered—but you couldn't believe a moment of it. . . . Robert Rossen's script and direction gave *Johnny O'Clock* some distinction and Evelyn Keyes was attractive but, for Dick Powell, it was just more of the same in his new style of tough-guy heroes. . . . J. P. Marquand's proper Bostonian, *The Late George Apley*, just wasn't for the still-glamorous likes of Ronald Colman and, except for some apt casting in lesser roles (Percy Waram, Mildred Natwick, and Edna Best), the movie Hollywoodized Marquand . . . Let's give *The Romance of Rosy Ridge* a mention just because it introduced Janet Leigh—and that was something for which to give thanks. . . . *Song of the Thin Man* gave us our last visit with William Powell and Myrna Loy as Nick and Nora Charles (we never really accepted Peter Lawford and Phyllis Kirk, or even David Niven and Maggie Smith). . . . Robert Young was well cast in *They Won't Believe Me*, an intriguing psychological drama with three likely leading ladies (Susan Hayward, Jane Greer, and Rita Johnson). . . . Jean Renoir's directorial artistry made as much as possible of a routine story line in *Woman on the Beach*. While Joan Bennett and Robert Ryan were interesting, the hamminess of Charles Bickford, in a pivotal role, pulled it down. . . .

Chapter Twenty

The Movie Year of 1948

There's no special movie trend in 1948. But there are a great many special movies and they come, not only from the United States, but from France, England, Italy, and even Mexico.

There are the beginnings of the practice, to be followed more and more in succeeding years, to desert Hollywood sound stages for actual locales when filming a movie.

Montgomery Clift is representative of the new names on cast lists and there are others who come to the fore—actors known previously only to the stage, such as Jose Ferrer and Paul Douglas, and foreign imports, such as Louis Jourdan and Valli. Others who qualify as 1948 new faces include Richard Basehart, Wendell Corey, Shelley Winters, Stephen McNally, Jan Sterling, John Agar, Moira Shearer, Kieron Moore, Betsy Drake, Betty Lynn, Dan O'Herlihy, Richard Attenborough, Viveca Lindfors, Marta Toren, Terry Moore, and Cameron Mitchell.

The picture of the year, in this corner, would be John Huston's *Treasure of the Sierra Madre,* with Humphrey Bogart and Walter Huston. Then let's list Dietrich and Jean Arthur in the Brackett–Wilder *Foreign Affair,* Fonda and Wayne in John Ford's *Fort Apache;* Olivier's *Hamlet;* Huston's *Key Largo;* Orson Welles's *Lady From Shanghai;* Joseph L. Mankiewicz's *A Letter to Three Wives;* Judy Garland and Gene Kelly in Minnelli's *The Pirate;* Wayne and Clift in Howard Hawks's *Red River;* and Clift in Zinnemann's *The Search.* Still others of special note—*Command Decision; A Double Life; Easter Parade; I Remember Mama; Johnny Belinda;* Steinbeck's *The Pearl; The Red Shoes; Sitting Pretty; The Snake Pit; State of the Union; Joan of Arc; Mr. Blandings Builds His Dream House; Paleface; Sorry Wrong Number;* and *The Three Musketeers* could be mentioned. But there were big ones that just didn't come off—Milestone's choppy *Arch of Triumph,* despite Bergman and Boyer . . . Orson Welles's grotesque attempt at *Macbeth* . . . Bette Davis's dreary *Winter Meeting* . . . and, of course, there were those others.

Robert Ryan, Van Heflin's nemesis, has finally tracked him down in *Act of Violence*.

Forgotten Films of 1948

The direction of Fred Zinnemann and the performances of a notable cast made *Act of Violence* gripping in spite of a contrived, implausible story. Robert Ryan had menace as a vengeful ex-GI with Van Heflin excellent as his intended victim. Janet Leigh was a tender leading lady. With Mary Astor, Phyllis Thaxter.

An Act of Murder (also released as *Live Today for Tomorrow*) was bold drama with euthanasia as its theme. Michael Gordon directed and there were particularly eloquent performances by Fredric March and Florence Eldridge. He played a judge who must watch the agony of his incurably ill wife. Others of note—Edmond O'Brien, Stanley Ridges, Geraldine Brooks, and John McIntire. Screenplay by Michael Blankfort and Robert Thoeren.

Another Part of the Forest did not bite as deeply as *The Little Foxes* but neither did Lillian Hellman's play which dealt with the earlier life of the same characters. A new one was Marcus, the patriarch of the family, and, as played by Fredric March, he outdid his progeny in malevolence. Edmond O'Brien, Dan Duryea, and Ann Blyth were the youthful members of the family, all properly evil, with Florence Eldridge pathetic as the mother. Michael Gordon directed.

Fredric March and his real-life wife, Florence Eldridge, portray a tortured couple in *An Act of Murder*.

Bette Davis had one of her few excursions into comedy with *June Bride* and Miss Bette can play comedy with the best of them. Among the best of them, of course, is Robert Montgomery and they made an engaging team in a thin but pleasant little piece about hotshot magazine reporters from the big city disrupting the lives of nice small town people. Young Betty Lynn was among the nicest, an actress whose career never went as far as it should. Bretaigne Windust directed the Ranald Mac-Dougall screenplay.

Joan Fontaine's lovely performance and the quality of a Continental film brought to it by Max Ophuls's direction made *Letter From an Unknown Woman* more special than it should have been. Stefan Zweig's story was sobby romantics from another era. Yet Fontaine made you care about her hopeless love for darkly handsome Louis Jourdan. Screenplay by Howard Koch.

On Our Merry Way (also titled *A Miracle Can Happen*) was tedious and silly in almost every sequence. (It was one of those all-star multiepisode films with Bur-

In the pre–*Little Foxes* era, Ann Blyth is Regina, in *Another Part of the Forest*. Fredric March is the patriarch of the evil clan.

Robert Montgomery and Bette Davis are magazine types from New York, intruding into the small-town domestic life of Tom Tully and Betty Lynn in *June Bride*.

Joan Fontaine's first meeting with Louis Jourdan winds up in sorrow for her in *Letter from an Unknown Woman*.

James Stewart and Henry Fonda are jazz musicians, Burgess Meredith an inquiring reporter, in *On Our Merry Way*.

gess Meredith, Paulette Goddard, Dorothy Lamour, Fred MacMurray, Victor Moore among those badly used.) The exception was one hilarious slapstick session with James Stewart and Henry Fonda as a couple of jazz musicians. But that sequence was the only one written by John O'Hara and directed (without credit) by George Stevens and John Huston. They managed a few minutes of broad fun which is something all the other writers, directors, and stars couldn't even approach.

The Paradine Case ranks on the lowest level of Alfred Hitchcock's work—this kind of courtroom drama doesn't call out the best for his sly talent. Yet he polished it handsomely, aided by the usual glossy David

James Stewart suspects thrill murderers Farley Granger and John Dall in *Rope*.

O. Selznick production values, including an elaborate cast (Gregory Peck, Ann Todd, Charles Coburn, Charles Laughton, Ethel Barrymore, Joan Tetzel, and Leo G. Carroll, along with two handsome newcomers to these shores, Alida Valli and Louis Jourdan).

Hitchcock was more in his element with *Rope*, a thoroughly unpleasant film but a completely fascinating one. Hitchcock worked out some new camera techniques, confining the action to one room and one continuous scene. Farley Granger and John Dall, as thrill murderers, played cat-and-mouse with a surprisingly cast James Stewart, as an effete friend. The film has not been exhibited, even in Hitchcock retrospectives, since its initial release. Arthur Laurents wrote the screenplay from Patrick Hamilton's play.

Eugene O'Neill's gentle, nostalgic comedy, *Ah, Wilderness!* was the basis for an overblown musical, *Summer Holiday.* It didn't work (nor did a similar idea on Broadway, some years later, as *Take Me Along*). The movie had Mickey Rooney—much more Andy Hardy than O'Neill's Richard—along with people like Gloria DeHaven, Selena Royle, Agnes Moorehead, and Frank Morgan. Only Walter Huston was up to the original in characterization. Director Rouben Mamoulian produced some nice special effects (notably in the saloon scene in which Marilyn Maxwell is transformed from a gaudy whore to a soft beauty in Rooney's intoxicated eyes). The songs were undistinguished, intrusive, and made you feel that you were watching a *Meet Me in St. Louis* ripoff without its appeal. Screenplay by Frances Goodrich and Albert Hackett.

Ernst Lubitsch's last movie, *That Lady in Ermine,* must fall somewhere near the bottom of his list but it still had its charms. Lubitsch had done wonders with an ancient operetta (*The Merry Widow*) but, this time, even with a witty script by Samson Raphaelson, the book was plain silly. Betty Grable, hardly the most accomplished comedienne, looked so pretty it really didn't matter and Douglas Fairbanks, Jr., was sufficiently swashbuckling. Cesar Romero carried off comedy honors. And Lubitsch still had the touch.

William Saroyan's *The Time of Your Life* didn't transfer too well to the movie medium in spite of James Cagney's portrayal of the saloon philosher. Blame H. C. Potter's plodding, uncinematic direction and weak casting in some pivotal roles. But Cagney, James Barton, William Bendix, Gale Page, and Broderick Crawford were effectively Saroyanesque. Screenplay by Nathaniel Curtis.

Alida Valli, Gregory Peck, Ethel Barrymore, Charles Coburn, and Ann Todd in *The Paradine Case.*

Mickey Rooney takes his sweetheart (Gloria DeHaven) and his family (Agnes Moorehead, Walter Huston, Selena Royle, and Jackie "Butch" Jenkins) for a ride in the Stanley Steamer in *Summer Holiday.*

Betty Grable and
Douglas Fairbanks, Jr.,
in *That Lady in Ermine*.

Richard Erdman, Paul
Draper, William Ben-
dix, Pedro de Cordoba,
and James Cagney
bring some of Saroyan's
characters to the screen
in *The Time of Your Life*.

If there were a way to separate all the musical numbers of *Words and Music* from the rest of the picture, it would qualify as a "forgotten film to remember." Most of Rodgers and Hart's best songs turned up here, and very effectively performed, too, by Lena Horne, Judy Garland, Gene Kelly, Vera-Ellen, June Allyson, Cyd Charisse, Mel Torme, Betty Garrett, and Perry Como. But best forgotten was the story, purportedly a biography of the composers, directed by Norman Taurog, and featuring one of the most embarrassing performances of all time by Mickey Rooney as Lorenz Hart.

Other Forgotten 1948 Films to Note

Edward G. Robinson was forceful in a watered-down film version of Arthur Miller's play *All My Sons.* . . . Vivien Leigh was dazzling but cold in her version of *Anna Karenina* in which Ralph Richardson captured most of the acting laurels. . . . Jeanne Crain and William Holden were two of the nicest young people you'd want to see—and Edmund Gwenn one of the most lovable old ones—in the pleasant *Apartment for Peggy.* . . . John Farrow directed the tense murder film, *The Big Clock,* with an expert cast (Ray Milland, Charles Laughton, Maureen O'Sullivan, Elsa Lanchester, and George Macready). . . . Richard Conte stood out in a filmization of a real-life melodrama, *Call Northside 777,* but James Stewart, Lee J. Cobb, and Betty Garde scored too, with Henry Hathaway directing in semidocumentary style. . . . Conte was effective again in Robert Siodmak's *Cry of the City* with a menacing Hope Emerson, Shelley Winters, and Victor Mature. . . . William Holden as the psychotic criminal, helped by Lee J. Cobb as the psychiatrist and Nina Foch, made *The Dark Past* a sufficiently gripping remake of *Blind Alley.* . . .

Enchantment was a mild love story but such attractive actors as David Niven, Teresa Wright, Farley Granger, and Evelyn Keyes made it watchable. . . . John Garfield gave one of his stronger performances in Abraham Polonsky's *Force of Evil* . . . A good Western, *Four Faces West* gave Joel McCrea one of his best roles and it was good to see Frances Dee, too. . . . A very human little British movie about small vacation dramas, *Holiday Camp* had a cast that included Flora Robson, Dennis Price, Kathleen Harrison, Jack Warner, and Jimmy Hanley. . . .

A violent Burt Lancaster and a sympathetic Joan Fontaine teamed effectively in *Kiss the Blood Off My Hands.* . . . Although not up to his classic documentaries (*Tabu, Moana, Nanook of the North,* and *Man of Aran*), *Louisiana Story* was an affecting piece about a Cajun boy and the effect on his life of the intrusion of the machine—an oil drilling derrick—into the bayous. . . . Evelyn Keyes had one of her few chances to shine in *The Mating of Millie* and she did even though the film was of the kind more appropriate on TV sitcom. . . . Marius Goring gave an intense performance as a mousy British schoolmaster hysterically jealous of a more popular master (David Farrar) in *Mr. Perrin and Mr. Traill.* . . . *The October Man* was moderate melodrama from an Eric Ambler novel but it had excellent performances by Joan Greenwood, Kay Walsh, Joyce Carey, Adrianne Allen, Catherine Lacey, and particularly, in the title role, by John Mills. . . . *Pitfall* was a tight and suspenseful Dick Powell melodrama with an impressively sinister villian in the comparative newcomer, Raymond Burr. . . .

Loretta Young, with two particularly likable leading men, William Holden and Robert Mitchum, made an appealing film of *Rachel and the Stranger,* from a How-

Rooney and Judy Garland sing "I Wish I Were In Love Again" in *Words and Music.*

ard Fast novel of a bondswoman in the post-Revolutionary War period. . . . Ida Lupino and Richard Widmark gave the routine melodramatics of *Road House* more than routine interest. . . . Robert Montgomery played with elegance the role of a thoroughly despicable Broadway producer in *The Saxon Charm.* . . . Michael Redgrave scored again as the leader of *The Smugglers,* based on a Graham Greene thriller, with Richard Attenborough, Joan Greenwood, and Jean Kent . . . Preston Sturges's *Unfaithfully Yours* didn't hold up but there was Sturges's wit and an amusing portrayal of a jealousy-maddened symphony conductor by Rex Harrison. . . . Only for the performances of Jessica Tandy and Mildred Natwick should the ponderous *A Woman's Vengeance* be listed here. . . . *You Were Meant for Me* was trivial but the 1920s atmosphere and songs were pleasantly nostalgic as were the performances of Jeanne Crain and Dan Dailey. . . .

Chapter Twenty-One

The Movie Year of 1949

The year 1949 begins a black era for Hollywood. Investigating committees continue to hit hard and many careers are cut short because of politically suspect pasts —or, in some cases, by mere rumors of such pasts. You begin to hear words like "blacklist" even though nobody will officially admit that such a list exists.

Television, formerly dismissed as a mere novelty, is now showing signs of becoming a threat to the movie industry. It seems by now as if just about every family has its own set and even the starriest screen names find their theater draws no match for the living room lure of Milton Berle and Arthur Godfrey. And more and more old theatrical movies have been released to the channels.

Yet Hollywood seems to thrive on trouble and it's a good year. Stanley Kramer leads the way for a new generation of independent producers. Other postwar independents had tried. Charles Einfeld's Enterprise, for example, started strongly and thought big—as big as Bergman and Boyer in *Arch of Triumph.* Its failure was Enterprise's end. Liberty Films, with directors like Capra forming their own company, also went under. But Kramer is typical of the young, small outfit that will succeed and help revolutionize the whole major studio setup.

Attention is being paid to a strong list of new players. There are Judy Holliday, Mario Lanza, Tony Curtis, Patricia Neal, Richard Todd, Joan Greenwood, Mel Ferrer, Tom Ewell, David Wayne, Jean Hagen, Ruth Roman, Mercedes McCambridge, James Edwards, John Derek, Jeff Chandler, Valentina Cortesa, Joan Evans, and Sally Forrest.

Personal selections for pictures of the year would be the then unappreciated *The Set Up* with Robert Ryan's powerful performance directed by Robert Wise and Carol Reed's *The Fallen Idol* with Ralph Richardson. And add Cagney's masterpiece, Raoul Walsh's *White Heat.* But there are so many others that are right up there—Hepburn and Tracy in Cukor's *Adam's Rib;* Robert Rossen's *All the King's Men;* Disney's *Cinderella;* Olivia de Havilland, Montgomery Clift and Ralph Richardson in William Wyler's *The Heiress;* Kramer's *Home of the Brave;* the Gene Kelly–Stanley Donen version of the Comden–Green–Bernstein *On the Town;* Maugham's *Quartet;* and John Ford's *She Wore a Yellow Ribbon.* And many others on their heels—*The Barkleys of Broadway; Champion; I Was a Male War Bride; Madame Bovary; My Foolish Heart; Pinky; Samson and Delilah; Sands of Iwo Jima;* and *Twelve O'Clock High.* And there were two so absolutely awful that they live in film history as camp classics, both unhappily by the distinguished King Vidor. They were Bette Davis's *Beyond the Forest* and Gary Cooper's *The Fountainhead.*

Then there were those others to note.

Forgotten Films of 1949

Nunnally Johnson took a James Cain story (previously filmed as a routine comedy *Wife, Husband, and Friend*), worked it over for Paul Douglas, and produced *Everybody Does It*. Douglas had full vent for his rough-house comedy talents as the solid male who discovers he has an operatic voice. The result was frequently hilarious. Celeste Holm, too, was in her best form as his opera-ambitious wife who starts it all. The beauty of Linda Darnell and the performances of Charles Coburn, Lucile Watson, and Millard Mitchell helped. Edmund Goulding directed.

As we now know, the ideal film version of F. Scott Fitzgerald's *The Great Gatsby* may never be made. But there was an interesting attempt in 1949 with a couple of performances—Betty Field as Daisy, and Shelly Winters as Myrtle—which were completely right for Fitzgerald. Nor was there any quarrel with Barry Sullivan, Macdonald Carey, Howard da Silva, Ruth Hussey, Elisha Cook, Jr., and Ed Begley in other roles. Alan Ladd, in the title part, was the right idea but he wasn't up to getting beneath the surface and making it more than just another typical Ladd role. And the script and Elliot Nugent's direction were superficial.

John Patrick's popular war play, *The Hasty Heart,* was transferred to the screen with its blend of quiet humor and touching drama intact. This was primarily due to the performance of Richard Todd, as the dour, aloof little Scot who is thawed out by friendship and the gift of a kilt. Todd gave other good screen performances but never again had a role that would allow him to fulfill the enormous potential he showed here. Screenplay by Ranald MacDougal directed by Vincent Sherman.

He Walked by Night was a taut little melodrama, filmed in actual locations in documentary style. Richard Basehart was compelling as the murderer who leads the Los Angeles Police Department through a fingernail-biting chase. Alfred Werker directed the Bryan Foy production. John C. Higgins and Crane Wilbur wrote the screenplay from Wilbur's original. (Wilbur and Foy were also responsible for *Canon City,* another film in the same genre.)

Clarence Brown, who directed major films from the 1920s into the 1950s, was a consistently underrated craftsman. Yet if he had done nothing else but *Intruder in the Dust,* his name would deserve to go down in the annals of important filmmakers. With Ben Maddow's

Paul Douglas and Celeste Holm in *Everybody Does It.*

Alan Ladd as *The Great Gatsby*. Betty Field is his Daisy.

Richard Todd, as the little Scot, finally feels accepted by his friends in *The Hasty Heart*. Orlando Martins, Ronald Reagan, Patricia Neal, Howard Crawford, Ralph Michael.

Richard Basehart in *He Walked by Night*.

screenplay based on William Faulkner's novel and filmed in Oxford, Mississippi, Brown presented a stunning study of race tensions in a Southern town. It ranked with Lang's *Fury*, Wellman's *Ox Bow Incident*, and LeRoy's *They Won't Forget* as one of the strongest films of lynch madness ever to be put on celluloid. The cast, most of whom never before or since had such dramatic opportunities, was uniformly magnificent—Juano Hernandez, Claude Jarman, Jr., Elizabeth Patterson, Porter Hall, Charles Kemper, David Brian, and Will Geer.

Unlike the sentimentalized *Pinky*, in which a black girl passes for white, *Lost Boundaries* dealt with the same problem but in a considerably more realistic manner. The Louis de Rochemont production was directed by Alfred L. Werker in the style de Rochemont had set for his *March of Time* series. Mel Ferrer headed a cast of good actors largely unfamiliar to movie audiences. They included Beatrice Pearson, Richard Hylton, Susan Douglas, Carleton Carpenter, and the great Canada Lee. Screenplay by Virginia Schaler.

The British were exporting a great number of original and amusing little comedies in the late 1940s and 1950s and *Passport to Pimlico* was one of the best. A middle-class section of London is discovered to rightfully belong to Burgundy. The chaos that results gave the film a chance to poke fun at all manner of solid British values. Margaret Rutherford was exuberant as a local historian

Claude Jarman, Jr., is digging, and Elizabeth Patterson is on the brink in *Intruder in the Dust*.

Beatrice Pearson, Richard Hylton, and Mel Ferrer in *Lost Boundaries*.

Margaret Rutherford, Stanley Holloway, and John Slater in *Passport to Pimlico*.

Donald Thompson, a nonprofessional actor, as *The Quiet One*.

but so were they all, most familiar faces being those of Stanley Holloway, Basil Radford, Naunton Wayne, and Raymond Huntley. Henry Cornelius directed. Screenplay by T. E. B. Clarke.

The story of one young Harlem delinquent—what made him that way and what can be his salvation—was presented straightforwardly and without phony melodramatics in *The Quiet One*. Helen Levitt, Janice Loeb, and Sidney Meyers wrote the screenplay, Meyers directed, and the moving James Agee commentary was narrated by Gary Merrill. Most of the cast—including Donald Thompson, the haunting youngster in the title role—were nonprofessionals but none the less effective for that.

All the elements for making a great movie from John Steinbeck's *The Red Pony* seemed to be present—from Steinbeck's own script to Aaron Copland's score, now a classic of movie music. Why wasn't the picture more moving than, say, *My Friend Flicka*? Lewis Milestone would seem to be (as he had been with *Of Mice and Men*) the ideal director for it nor would you think you could go wrong with a cast including Myrna Loy, Robert Mitchum, Louis Calhern, and young Peter Miles. But the movie was just good—not the moving screen experience it should have been.

One of the least-heralded films of Nicholas Ray—but one of his best—was *They Live by Night*. (This was true also for Robert Altman a couple of decades later when he remade the picture under its original book title, *Thieves Like Us*.) The tender love story of a young fugitive and a drab little girl who gives herself to him featured sensitive performances by Farley Granger and Cathy O'Donnell. Granger had the potential of Montgomery Clift, unrealized because of routine casting in later pictures. Helen Craig, Howard da Silva, and Jay C. Flippen were effective, too. Screenplay by Charles Schnee.

Thieves Highway was a gritty, tough melodrama about the perils in the life of a truck driver. Jules Dassin directed the A. I. Bezzerides script (from his own novel) with the same raw realism, including use of real locales in those still studio-bound days, that he gave us with *Naked City*. Richard Conte's performance was another reason to be puzzled at why the career of this striking actor seemed to go so quickly down the drain. But all the actors were extremely well chosen—Lee J. Cobb, Valentina Cortesa, Joseph Pevney, Jack Oakie, Millard Mitchell, and Morris Carnovsky.

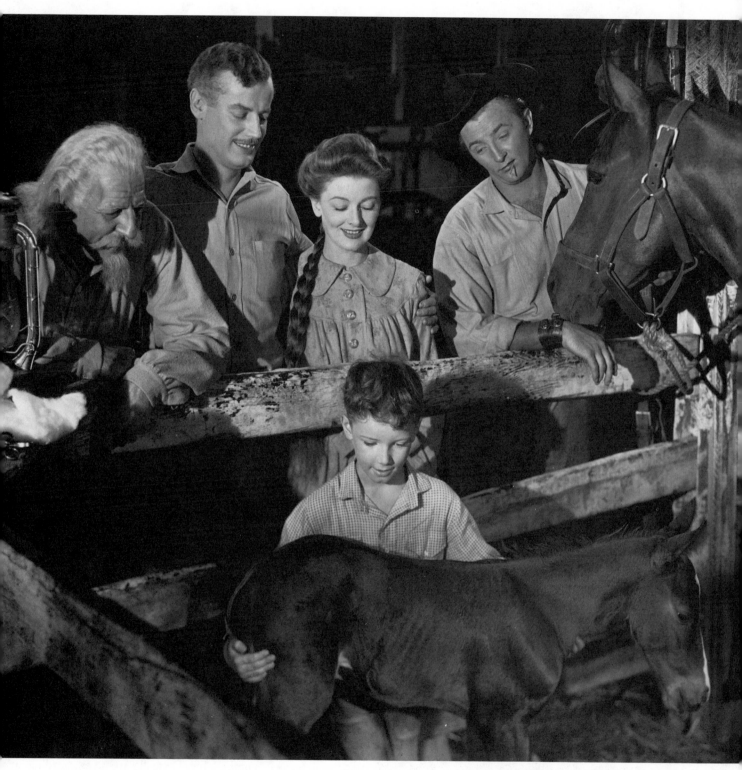

Peter Miles played the boy in Steinbeck's *The Red Pony*. Adults included Louis Calhern, Shepperd Strudwick, Myrna Loy, and Robert Mitchum.

Valentina Cortesa made her American film debut in
Thieves' Highway with Richard Conte.

Farley Granger and Cathy O'Donnell were the
youngsters mixed up with such hardened criminals
as J. C. Flippen and Howard Da Silva in *They Live by
Night*.

Another of those remarkable British comedies, *Tight
Little Island* told the tale of inhabitants of a Hebrides
island and what happens when they are cut off from
their expected whiskey supply. Compton Mackenzie
wrote the original and (with Angus Macphail) the
screenplay while Alexander Mackendrick directed. Joan
Greenwood, Basil Radford, Catherine Lacey, James
Robertson Justice, and John Gregson were just some of
the better-known names in the uniformly fine cast.

An imaginative boy, who makes up stories, actually
sees a murder. But nobody will believe him—except the
murderers themselves who now must dispose of him.
This was the premise of *The Window* , with a suspenseful script by Mel Dinneli based on a Cornell Woolrich story. Young Bobby Driscoll gave an extraordinary
performance as the youngster. (In real life, his was a
tragedy. Involved with drugs from early adolescence, he
died unknown in an abandoned tenement just shortly
out of his teens.) Arthur Kennedy, Barbara Hale, Paul
Stewart, and Ruth Roman were capable in adult roles;
Ted Tetzlaff directed.

Bobby Driscoll has seen a murder involving Ruth Roman, and she knows he has seen it, in *The Window*.

Gordon Jackson, Joan Greenwood, Bruce Seton, and Gabrielle Blunt watch as Wylie Watson disposes of the precious Scotch in *Tight Little Island*.

The rare screen performance by the distinguished Edith Evans made news in *Woman of Dolwyn*. But who was to know that a boy in his movie debut would also make news? His name—Richard Burton. Also present, Anthony James.

The marvelous Edith Evans giving one of her finest performances was reason enough for *Woman of Dolwyn* to be a major movie triumph. It wasn't. It was released without fanfare, lost in the ballyhoo for more pretentious pictures, and almost immediately disappeared. Emlyn Williams wrote the story (about the last days of a Welsh village and of the old lady who fights to save it), directed, and played a particularly unpleasant villain. And it provided the screen debut for an especially likely young actor—a Welsh chap named Richard Burton.

Director William Wellman and screenwriter Lamar Trotti, who had made the classic *The Ox-Bow Incident*, came up with a more conventional Western in *Yellow Sky*. Conventional maybe but exciting, action-filled stuff. A top cast—most notably Gregory Peck, Richard Widmark, Robert Arthur, Anne Baxter, James Barton, Charles Kemper, Henry Morgan, and John Russell— kept it crackling.

Trotti again produced and wrote the screen play (with Will H. Hays, Jr.) for a lively, unsung little Hollywood spoof, *You're My Everything*. This had all kinds of dividends for movie fans. Imagine, if you can, that Clara Bow and a combination William Haines/Buddy Rogers became the parents of Shirley Temple. Something like that was the premise for the movie in which the performances of Dan Dailey, Anne Baxter, Stanley Ridges, Anne Revere, Alan Mowbray, and a bit by Buster Keaton were all to the good.

Other Forgotten 1949 Films to Note

Within a couple of months in mid-1949, we had four pictures about gambling: *Any Number Can Play* had Clark Gable whose chosen profession gave him all kinds of problems, including angina. *The Great Sinner* plunged Gregory Peck into addiction. Barbara Stanwyck dove even deeper into degradation in *The Lady*

A bunch of the boys—John Russell,
Gregory Peck, Henry Morgan,
Robert Arthur—in *Yellow Sky.*

171

Robert Arthur again, more juvenile this time, with flapper Anne Baxter in *You're My Everything*.

Gambles, losing Robert Preston in the bargain. These three were all pretty dreary, although the first two had rather remarkable casts in support of their stars (*Any Number*: Alexis Smith, Frank Morgan, Mary Astor, Marjorie Rambeau, Dorothy Comingore, Wendell Corey, Audrey Totter, Barry Sullivan, Lewis Stone, Darryl Hickman, and Leon Ames; *Great Sinner*: Ava Gardner, Walter Huston, Ethel Barrymore, Melvin Douglas, Frank Morgan, and Agnes Moorehead). None of these names can point to their roles here as any kind of high spot in their careers. Most fun of all was *Sorrowful Jones*, which turned out to be *Little Miss Marker* reworked for Bob Hope. Hope was fun and Lucille Ball a good leading lady for him but Mary Jane Saunders was just a cute moppet—no Shirley Temple by a long shot. . . .

Betty Grable and Preston Sturges seemed like quite a combination but they didn't mix in *The Beautiful Blonde From Bashful Bend* in which he substituted rather crude slapstick for the sly wit of his earlier classics. . . . Max Ophuls's *Caught* was dime novel romantic melodrama but Robert Ryan gave a chilling performance as a mad billionaire (a character seemingly modeled closely on Howard Hughes). . . . *Dancing in the Dark* had William Powell, debonair as ever, in a film that took some amusing jabs at Hollywood but badly misused the Schwartz/Dietz *Band Wagon* score. (A few years later, Astaire, Minnelli and company would see to it that that same score was brilliantly used). . . . Although Deborah Kerr scored as the pathetic wife, *Edward My Son* (in the stage version Robert Morley was brilliant) was sabotaged by the dreadful miscasting of the usually reliable Spencer Tracy and the subsequent softening of his character. . . . Madeleine Carroll was as beautiful as ever in her final film role as Mrs. Erlynne in *The Fan* but Lady Windermere's indiscretions were presented as if it were *East Lynne*, almost completely lacking (except in a brief performance by Martita Hunt) any vestige of Wildean wit. . . . Richard Attenborough gave an affecting performance as a lower-class boy in a British public school in *The Guinea Pig*. . . . *Holiday Affair* might have been almost too saccharine to stomach except that it involved Janet Leigh and Robert Mitchum, their very presence an antidote. . . .

A group of Dublin's Abbey players loaned their considerable talents to Paul Vincent Carroll's delightful *Saints and Sinners*, a film about Irish village life. . . . Flora Robson's pitiable jealousy-wracked countess was the acting highlight of *Saraband* but other good actors (Francoise Rosay, Peter Bull, Joan Greenwood, and Stewart Granger) and the rich atmosphere of Hanoverian England also helped to overcome a ponderous story line. . . . Disney's homey *So Dear to My Heart* had such lovable people as Beulah Bondi and Bobby Driscoll . . . William Powell had a good mystery in *Take One False Step* with Shelley Winters, Marsha Hunt . . . John Ford gathered together a number of his favorite actors (John Wayne, Pedro Armendariz, Ward Bond, Mildred Natwick, Harry Carey, Jr., and Mae Marsh) for a very sentimental, old fashioned, but entertaining Western, *Three Godfathers*. . . . In spite of a cast that included Ingrid Bergman, Joseph Cotten, Michael Wilding, and Cecil Parker, only Margaret Leighton won any laurels in *Under Capricorn*, a curiously lifeless Alfred Hitchcock melodrama. . . . John Garfield, Gilbert Roland, and Pedro Armendariz gave strong performances in John Huston's *We Were Strangers*, but somehow the potentially explosive drama fizzled out. . . . Alan Ladd and Robert Preston were worthy antagonists in a live Western, *Whispering Smith*. . . .

Chapter Twenty-Two

The Movie Year of 1950

The movie box office takes a further dip in 1950 and popcorn sales are sometimes more profitable than admission tickets. Television is now so firmly established that even the ostriches can't brand it just a passing fad. And now, in addition to regular TV programming, movies compete more and more with product made for theaters but now on the channels. You can sit home and see *Stagecoach*, *You Only Live Once*, *Nothing Sacred*, and a batch of British pictures, some of which prove to be not half bad.

A test is made of Phonevision in which new pictures are shown on TV on a "pay as you see" basis. Nothing much comes of it at the time.

The Communist investigations and blacklisting continue. "The Hollywood Ten," directors and screenwriters who have refused to divulge their political affiliations, go to jail. More careers are destroyed.

But there isn't much that's controversial on the screens themselves, other than a couple of final stabs in the antiprejudice cycle. It's much more fun in those bleak days to look into the private lives of ladies like Margo Channing, Norma Desmond, and Billie Dawn.

No newcomer makes a better publicity showing in the fan magazines than does Faith Domergue (aided by the backing of Howard Hughes) but most of them last a lot longer. Among these others are Marlon Brando, Dirk Bogarde, Rock Hudson, Jack Palance, Dean Martin and Jerry Lewis, Dale Robertson, John Barrymore, Jr., Nancy Olson, Lyle Bettger, Jack Webb, Mala Powers, Anne Francis, Richard Egan, Richard Boone, Piper Laurie, Hugh O'Brian, Sidney Poitier, Howard Keel, Robert Wagner, Lex Barker, James Whitmore, Nancy Davis, Phyllis Kirk, and a cuddlesome blonde bit player named Marilyn Monroe.

Let's give personal preference to Joseph L. Mankiewicz's *All About Eve*, with Bette Davis, Anne Baxter, and George Sanders, and to Billy Wilder's *Sunset Boulevard*, with Gloria Swanson and William Holden, as the pictures of the year. Better add Carol Reed's *The Third Man*. But there are many more vying for honors —John Huston's *The Asphalt Jungle*; Cukor's *Born Yesterday*; Gregory Peck in Henry King's *The Gunfighter*; Alec Guiness's *Kind Hearts and Coronets*; and Brando in Zinnemann's *The Men*. Others of particular popularity, merit, or both would include *Annie Get Your Gun*; *Broken Arrow*; *Cyrano de Bergerac*; *Father of the Bride*; *The Flame and the Arrow*; *Harvey*; *King Solomon's Mines*; *The Mudlark, Treasure Island, and Trio*. The Year's big movie letdown was the eagerly awaited, scandal-tinged collaboration of Roberto Rossellini and Ingrid Bergman, *Stromboli*.

There were other pictures of special note even though they may not come immediately to your mind.

Patricia Neal and John Garfield in *The Breaking Point*.

Edmond O'Brien races to beat his own death in *DOA*.

Forgotten Films of 1950

The Michael Curtiz version of Hemingway's *To Have and Have Not* stayed closer to its source than had the Bogart–Bacall movie of a few years earlier. This time, the title was *The Breaking Point* and John Garfield was at his brooding best. Patricia Neal was diamond-hard as one kind of woman and Phyllis Thaxter touching as another. Juano Hernandez scored strongly, too. Screenplay by Ranald MacDougall.

D.O.A. was a "B" picture in every detail except two—but these two counted. The story (by Russell Rouse and Clarence Greene) was a highly intriguing mystery about a dying man searching for the motive and killer in his own murder. And Edmond O'Brien gave a striking performance as this central figure. Rudolph Mate directed.

That Tennessee Williams's shimmering masterpiece, *The Glass Menagerie,* is a forgotten film is a Hollywood black mark. But the neglect is deserved. The unbelievably false performance of Gertrude Lawrence in one of the great roles ever written for an actress effectively destroyed it. Jane Wyman and Kirk Douglas were far from ideally cast but both did as much as possible, unaided by Irving Rapper's static direction, to bring their roles to life. There is a reason for including it here —Arthur Kennedy's sensitive characterization. To this observer, he was the finest of all Toms—including Eddie Dowling's original stage portrayal.

Humphrey Bogart had an unusual role in *In a Lonely Place* but, as a screenwriter who cannot control his rages, he gave one of his most interesting performances. Gloria Grahame, too, was a revelation in her first chance to play something other than the good hearted slut. The Andrew Solt script, based on a novel by Dorothy B. Hughes, was directed by Nicholas Ray to bring out all its dark psychological undertones.

Radio quiz shows were all the rage in 1950—this was before the TV days of "The $64,000 Question." *The Jackpot* was a highly amusing lampoon on the phenomenon, based by Phoebe and Henry Ephron on John McNulty's reportage of the tribulations that befell a real-life jackpot winner. It was all gagged up for the movies and Jimmy Stewart was in his element as the hapless hero deluged with gifts and obligations he couldn't handle. Barbara Hale, Fred Clark, Alan Mowbray, Patricia Medina, and James Gleason contributed. Walter Lang directed.

(RIGHT) A gentleman caller visits in *The Glass Menagerie* (Kirk Douglas, Gertrude Lawrence, Jane Wyman and Arthur Kennedy)

Gloria Grahame and Humphrey Bogart are *In a Lonely Place*.

In *The Jackpot*, Barbara Hale and James Stewart are a couple whose lives are sent into a tailspin when they win the big prize on a radio quiz show.

Beatrice Campbell and Alec Guinness in *Last Holiday*.

Margaret Sullavan's last movie, *No Sad Songs for Me*, with Natalie Wood and Wendell Corey.

You know the one about the repressed little man who goes off on an adventure when he learns he is going to die. It was old stuff when Lionel Barrymore was Kringelein in *Grand Hotel*. But J. B. Priestly's script gave it a few new twists in *Last Holiday* and it had Alec Guinness to play the man with consummate artistry. Henry Cass directed; Kay Walsh and Beatrice Campbell also appeared.

A woman discovers that she is going to die of cancer and sets about to prepare for the end as it will affect her husband and child.

No Sad Songs for Me could have been unbearably grim or hopelessly maudlin. That it was neither was due in part to Howard Koch's honest script but primarily to the luminous performance of Margaret Sullavan in what we didn't know then would be her final screen performance. Viveca Lindfors, Wendell Corey, and Natalie Wood headed the supporting cast; Rudolph Maté directed.

Although it came too far along in the antiprejudice movie cycle to make much of an impact on the box office, *No Way Out*, as written (with Lesser Samuels) and directed by Joseph L. Mankiewicz, was one of the most compelling of them all. This was the conflict between a snarling redneck bigot (Richard Widmark) and a humane black doctor (Sidney Poitier in his first screen role). Both actors gave penetrating performances.

A waterfront killing sets off a search for the murderer, even more frantic when it is discovered that the dead man was infected with pneumonic plague and his murderer may be carrying and spreading the disease. This was *Panic in the Streets* which Elia Kazan directed with mounting excitement. Richard Widmark and Paul Douglas headed the cast and Zero Mostel was superb as a craven stooge. But, in a startling screen debut as the murderer, Jack Palance dominated. Edna and Edward Anhalt, Daniel Fuchs, and Richard Murphy shared writing credits.

Britain's Boulting Brothers developed quite a degree of anxiety in their *Seven Days to Noon* which had Barry Jones as a gentle scientist with an obsession that he must blow up London so that the atomic bomb will be outlawed. John Boulting's direction was worthy of a Hitchcock. Olive Sloane contributed a colorful bit. Screenplay by John Boulting and Frank Harvey.

Richard Widmark, Linda Darnell, and Sidney Poitier in *No Way Out*.

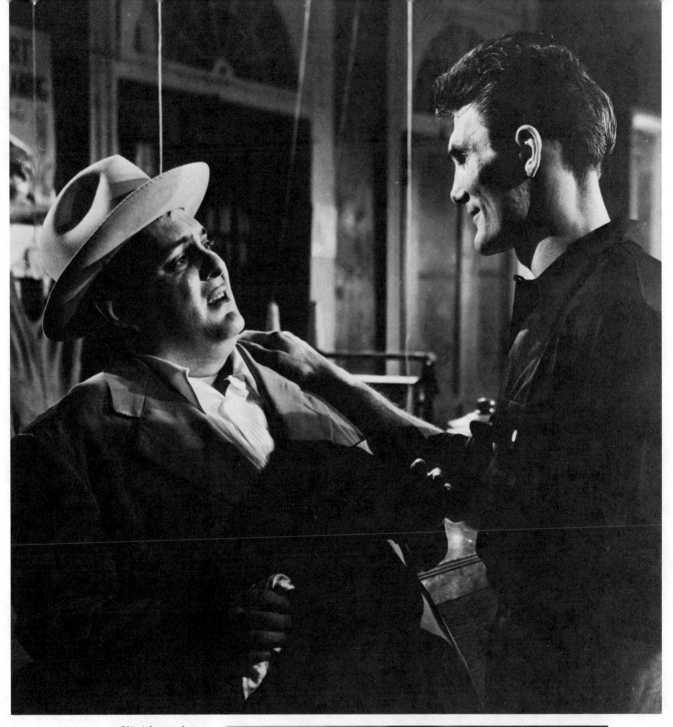

Vivid perform-
ances by two
movie new-
comers, Zero
Mostel and Jack
Palance, high-
lighted Kazan's
*Panic in the
Streets.*

Barry Jones and
Olive Sloane in
*Seven Days to
Noon.*

Marlene Dietrich sings Cole Porter's "The Laziest Gal in Town" in *Stage Fright*.

Alfred Hitchcock promised more suspense than he delivered in *Stage Fright.* It had scattered bits of amusing comedy but very little fright. Jane Wyman, Richard Todd, and Michael Wilding were competent in the leads but Marlene Dietrich took the picture away from them as a cold glamorous villainess. Best, though, were supporting comedy characterizations by Alastair Sim, Joyce Grenfell, and Dame Sybil Thorndike. Screenplay by Whitfield Cook.

Three Came Home, Agnes Newton Keith's own story of her travails as a prisoner of the Japanese during the war, was ably adapted for the screen by Nunnally Johnson. Claudette Colbert played the Keith role with her usual professionalism. But the picture belonged to Sessue Hayakawa, making a return to the Hollywood where he had been a silent screen star. As the Japanese military ruler, he had menace but a strange streak of compassion. Jean Negulesco directed.

Claudette Colbert hides in the jungle in *Three Came Home.*

Ben Johnson, Harry Carey, Jr., and Joanne Dru in *Wagonmaster.*

If John Ford had used one of his stars—John Wayne, say, or Henry Fonda—*Wagonmaster* might not have become one of his few forgotten films. Yet newcomers like Ben Johnson and Harry Carey, Jr., were just right as the leads and Ford's old favorite, Ward Bond, was more than up to his strongest movie role. It was an extremely good Ford Western which has been generally overlooked. Frank Nugent and Patrick Ford wrote the screenplay.

Less characteristic Ford fare was *When Willie Comes Marching Home.* The Mary Loos–Richard Sale script was frankly slanted toward the slapstick side. It was primarily notable for giving to Dan Dailey a rare chance to display his bountiful comic gifts. (Dailey was funny again in another Loos–Sale script, a Western burlesque, *A Ticket to Tomahawk.*)

Terence Rattigan's play *The Winslow Boy* lost little of its tense drama in transit to the screen. Rattigan himself (with Anatole de Grunwald) wrote the screenplay and Anthony Asquith directed with his usual meticulous care. Neil North was the boy unjustly accused of stealing and expelled from school, while Sir Cedric Hardwicke, Marie Lohr, and Margaret Leighton were solid as his parents and sister. But Robert Donat gave the picture its dramatic flair as the lawyer who defends the boy.

Two amusing movies with Dan Dailey: *A Ticket to Tomahawk* with Victor Sen Yung, Connie Gilchrist, and Anne Baxter (and you may recognize the uncredited blond in the background as Marilyn Monroe) . . .

. . . and with Colleen Townsend as his hometown sweetheart in *When Willie Comes Marching Home.*

Other Forgotten 1950 Films to Note

Celia Johnson and Margaret Leighton did everything you would expect of them in Noël Coward's *The Astonished Heart;* the weak link was Coward's strained performance and cliché-filled script. . . . Montgomery Clift is said to have considered *The Big Life* his favorite film —odd choice since it was interesting but not exciting and gave him little of dramatic note. . . . *The Blue Lamp* introduced Dirk Bogarde, striking as a juvenile killer. . . . Clifton Webb did his usual thing with great zest as the father of twelve in *Cheaper by the Dozen*, with Myrna Loy's mother there to keep it charmingly down to earth. . . . *Dial 1119* was a very minor little melodrama—but a compelling one—about a psychotic killer and his hostages. All actors deserved note, especially Marshall Thompson, Richard Rober, Andrea King, Sam Levene, Virginia Field, Leon Ames. . . . Farley Granger had intensity as a priest killer in *Edge of Doom.* . . . Mr. Chips would have been appalled at the goings on in *The Happiest Days of Your Life* but you can just bet that Alastair Sim, Margaret Rutherford, and Joyce Grenfell had a high old time. . . .

Opposing barristers Robert Donat and Francis L. Sullivan in *The Winslow Boy.*

Another study of mob violence was *The Lawless* and, as directed by Joseph Losey, it was one of the better. . . . Louis Calhern's robust portrayal of Oliver Wendell Holmes dominated *The Magnificent Yankee,* with Ann Harding helpful, too. . . . *Mister 880* was all about a lovable old counterfeiter—and Edmund Gwenn lived up to the adjective, with Dorothy McGuire and Burt Lancaster also pleasantly present. . . . Evelyn Keyes gave a warm and charming performance as *Mrs. Mike.* . . . A particularly good, if minor, melodrama was *Mystery Street* with good performances by Ricardo Montalban, Sally Forrest, Jan Sterling, and Elsa Lanchester. . . . There have been stronger studies of the effect of a rape than *Outrage* but Ida Lupino's handling of the theme was bold for its time and Mala Powers was real as the victim. . . . Pushkin's *Queen of Spades* made an eerie film, particularly notable for Edith Evans's stunning performance as the countess. . . . Frank Capra remade his old *Broadway Bill* as *Riding High* and, because of Bing Crosby in the old Warner Baxter role, aided by such people as Raymond Walburn, Clarence Muse,

William Demarest, Ward Bond, Frankie Darro, Percy Kilbride, and even Joe Frisco and Oliver Hardy (many from the original cast), it all worked as well as ever. . . . An extraordinary young actor, John Howard Davies (he would later play Oliver Twist), was the central character in *The Rocking Horse Winner,* a nightmarish but fascinating fantasy. . . . Farley Granger and Cathy O'Donnell, who had teamed so well in *They Live by Night,* did it again in *Side Street* but, although he was particularly effective, the picture was minor crime stuff. . . . *State Secret* was a fast-moving chase melodrama, with comedy, romance, and good performances by Douglas Fairbanks, Jr., Glynis Johns, Jack Hawkins, and Herbert Lom. . . . Jimmy Stewart had his first Western since *Destry* in *Winchester 73;* star and genre worked so well together that you knew he'd be back for more. . . . Kirk Douglas played *Young Man With a Horn* (Harry James actually with the horn) and the music plus performances of Douglas, Juano Hernandez, and Doris Day were enough to compensate for a pretty ordinary story line.

Chapter Twenty-Three

The Movie Year of 1951

In 1951 television continues to grow fat, and the feeling in the movie industry increasingly seems to be that "if you can't lick 'em, join 'em." So the movie companies begin to advertise extensively on the medium and to promote their pictures with hitherto *verboten* TV appearances by stars. Also, many of the motion picture companies form their own television subsidiaries.

There are plenty of big pictures doing outstanding business even with home competition. Upset of the year is the bypassing of *A Place in the Sun* and *A Streetcar Named Desire* by the Academy in favor of *An American in Paris*. This event takes even MGM, producer of *American*, so much by surprise that it takes out a trade ad indicating its astonishment.

Three foreign films run afoul of the censors—the spicy French *La Ronde*, the Rossellini-Magnani *Miracle*, and *Oliver Twist* because Alec Guinness's portrayal of Fagin is deemed offensive to some Jewish groups. All three problems are eventually settled.

Leslie Caron dances to popularity in her first movie role but Grace Kelly appears briefly and without making much of a splash. Other new names in the cast lists belong to Janice Rule, Mitzi Gaynor, Dawn Addams, Julia Adams, Judith Evelyn, Polly Bergen, Carleton Carpenter, Kenneth Tobey, Kevin McCarthy, John Ericson, Pier Angeli, Hildegarde Neff, Danny Thomas, Jeffrey Hunter, Gower and Marge Champion, Sarah Churchill, Anna Maria Alberghetti, Fernando Lamas, Barbara Rush, Ralph Meeker, Beverly Michaels, and Mildred Dunnock.

In spite of the Academy, we'd go along with George Stevens's *A Place in the Sun* with Montgomery Clift, Elizabeth Taylor, and Shelley Winters and Elia Kazan's *Streetcar* (Vivien Leigh–Brando) as the pictures of the year. The Kelly–Minnelli *American* would come close, of course, but so would the Huston–Bogart–Hepburn *African Queen*, and Alfred Hitchcock's *Strangers on a Train*. And Alec Guinness's *Lavender Hill Mob*. Some others, big or good or both, would include *Detective Story*; *Father's Little Dividend*; *The Great Caruso*; *Oliver Twist*; *Quo Vadis*; *The Red Badge of Courage*; *Royal Wedding*; *Show Boat*; and *The Thing*.

But some of the best pictures of the year—far better than a *Show Boat* or *Great Caruso*—are pictures you may not remember.

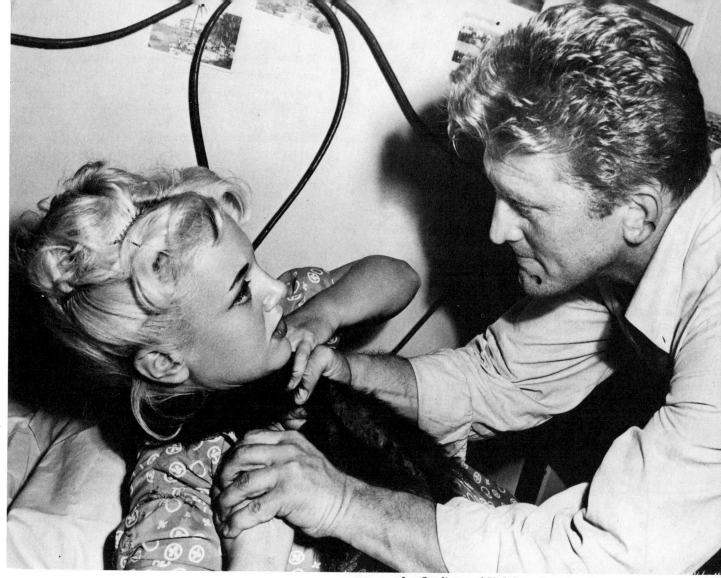

Jan Sterling and Kirk Douglas in *Ace in the Hole* (also known as *The Big Carnival*).

Forgotten Films of 1951

A man trapped in a cave-in becomes the lure for sensation seekers and a nine-day wonder to be used as profitable trade by money-hungry and headline-happy opportunists. *Ace in the Hole* (title later changed to *The Big Carnival*) was director Billy Wilder at his most cynical. (He also scripted with Lesser Samuels and Walter Newman.) Kirk Douglas's performance was admirably in line with Wilder's point of view nor did Jan Sterling try for any sympathy as the sleazy wife of the victim. Bob Arthur, as a cub reporter, was another standout.

Tom Lea's *The Brave Bulls* was brought handsomely to the screen by Robert Rossen. Mel Ferrer was well cast as the unhappy matador and the staging of the bullring scenes had color and flair. Occasionally the private miseries of the bullfighter, when they concerned the vampish Miroslava, seemed straight out of *Blood and Sand*. But mostly the film (aided, too, by Anthony Quinn's supporting performance and the screenplay by John Bright) was realistic and dramatic.

Mel Ferrer in *The Brave Bulls*.

Arthur Kennedy in *Bright Victory*.

One of the most moving moments in film history—Brian Smith makes a gesture of friendship to his despised teacher, Michael Redgrave in *The Browning Version*.

Fred MacMurray, Howard Keel, and Dorothy McGuire in *Callaway Went Thataway*.

By 1951 there had been enough movies about the readjustment to civilian life of disabled veterans that the idea of one more was no cause for joy. But Mark Robson's *Bright Victory* was no pale imitation, it was so superbly acted by Arthur Kennedy as the blinded veteran that it ranked as one of the very finest of all such films. Peggy Dow, who deserted the screen much too soon, was a warm leading woman. Screenplay by Robert Buckner.

The very antithesis of *Mr. Chips* was Andrew Crocker-Harris, the dried-out, unloved schoolmaster of Terence Rattigan's *The Browning Version*. But Michael Redgrave's illuminating performance made his character one of the most pitiful figures in dramatic memory. The film was the work of Anthony Asquith, an always reliable director who has received too little recognition. The cast included such extremely able actors as Nigel Patrick, Jean Kent, Brian Smith, Wilfred Hyde-White, and Ronald Howard. But it is the Redgrave performance that belongs with the absolute greats of screen history.

Callaway Went Thataway was a lighthearted treatment of a theme that would later be handled with bitterness and venom by Elia Kazan and Budd Schulberg in their *Face in the Crowd*. It had to do with hucksters who made an idol out of an unlikely cowpoke for the hero-hungry TV masses. Howard Keel was just right in that part; so were Dorothy McGuire and Fred MacMurray as the exploiters. Norman Panama and Melvyn Frank wrote, directed, and produced.

"Attention must finally be paid to such a man. He's not to be allowed to fall into his grave like an old dog. Attention, attention must be paid," said Arthur Miller concerning Willy Loman in *Death of a Salesman*. Fredric March was one of the best actors in the world. But he was tall, he was handsome, terribly prepossessing, and it's very difficult to believe that he could ever have been anything but *very* well liked or that attention was not constantly paid to him. So he had a couple of strikes on him as Willy Loman, even though his great ability finally forced acceptance in the role. Arthur Miller's great American play was also weakened in Stanley Kramer's screen version by some direction (by Laslo Benedek) that seemed self-consciously arty. But Mildred Dunnock, Kevin McCarthy, and Cameron Mitchell were completely right. And you may diminish *Death of a Salesman*, but you can never entirely take away its terrible power. Forgotten? *Death of a Salesman* never. But the movie—almost completely.

Anatole Litvak went to West Germany to make *Decision Before Dawn* and, except for a couple of token Americans (Richard Basehart and Gary Merrill), he

Oskar Werner and Hildegarde Neff in *Decision Before Dawn*.

filled his cast with excellent German actors. Most notable of these were Hildegarde Neff and a fine young Viennese theater actor, Oskar Werner. The actors and locales added immeasurably to the authenticity of the film, a spy drama with screenplay by Peter Viertel.

There was great outcry against *The Desert Fox* in certain quarters because it depicted Rommel, the German general, in a humane and heroic light. James Mason's vastly sympathetic characterization, along with Nunnally Johnson's script (from Desmond Young's biography) and the direction of Henry Hathaway, combined to forward this interpretation. Ideological considerations aside, they made it an engrossing film. Jessica Tandy, Sir Cedric Hardwicke, Leo G. Carroll, Everett Sloane, George Macready, Richard Boone, and Luther Adler (as Hitler) were actors who added importance.

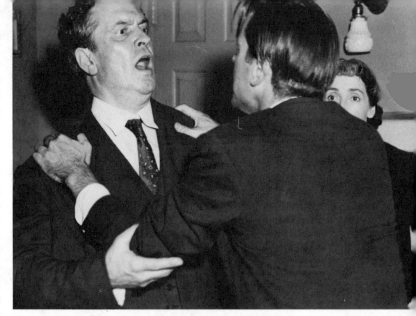

Fredric March, Kevin McCarthy, and Mildred Dunnock as Willie, Biff, and Linda Loman in *Death of a Salesman*.

Selena Royle and
John Garfield in
*He Ran All the
Way.*

James Mason,
Jessica Tandy,
and Richard
Boone in *The Des-
ert Fox.*

William Holden
and Nancy Olsen
in *Force of Evil.*

The name of Ernest Hemingway was never mentioned in the credits of *Force of Arms*. Yet, if it was not a considerably revised remake, one had to believe that author Richard Tregaskis, screenplay writer Orin Jannings, and director Michael Curtiz were considerably influenced by *A Farewell to Arms*. Still, on its own it was an absorbing war–love story, owing most to William Holden and Nancy Olson as the lovers.

Fourteen Hours was a taut, dramatic version of the real-life story of a man on the ledge. John Paxton's screenplay was based on Joel Sayre's reportage of the actual incident, with Henry Hathaway directing in near-newsreel style. Richard Basehart, who has always scored with a good role, had his best as the boy bent on suicide. Paul Douglas, Agnes Moorehead, Barbara Bel Geddes, Howard da Silva, Robert Keith, and Martin Gabel were also in the cast, which included two new faces–Grace Kelly and Jeffrey Hunter—in bits.

John Garfield's last picture, *He Ran All the Way*, cast him as a fleeing murderer terrorizing a family in whose apartment he hides out. Criminals holding shocked hostages have been the basis for many, many plays and movies but Garfield kept the tension high in this one. And so did Shelley Winters, Selena Royle, and Wallace Ford as the family. John Berry directed the screenplay by Hugo Butler and Guy Endore.

Frank Capra's tenure was about at its end when he made *Here Comes the Groom*. While that picture probably didn't hasten the end, it was plain to see that the old Capra magic was about played out. It was a pretty trivial little yarn, mildly amusing, and larded with Capra sentiment, all well enough played by Bing Crosby, Jane Wyman, Franchot Tone, and a couple of kids, Jacky Gencel and Beverly Washburn. But the one surprise of the picture was the hitherto unfailingly elegant Alexis Smith playing broad comedy and having a ball.

Thelma Ritter, whose acerbic presence in a number of small parts had enlivened a good many movies, finally had a couple of her own. Producer Charles Brackett (who also wrote both scripts with Walter Reisch and Richard Breen) is the hero who presented Miss Ritter at the top of the cast in both *The Mating Season* and *The Model and the Marriage Broker*. Mitchell Leisen directed the first in which she played a mother masquerading as a servant in her son's home while George Cukor guided the second (and better) in which her role was a matchmaker, tough but "with heart." Miriam Hopkins, John Lund, and Gene Tierney assisted in the first; the cast for *Marriage Broker* included Jeanne Crain, Zero Mostel, Michael O'Shea, Helen Ford, Nancy Kulp, and Scott Brady.

Richard Basehart climbs to the ledge in *Fourteen Hours*.

Alexis Smith and Bing Crosby in *Here Comes the Groom*.

Two for Thelma Ritter: *The Mating Season* with Gene Tierney . . .

. . . and *The Model and the Marriage Broker* with Michael O'Shea and Helen Ford.

Nobody can be quite as virulent as Bette Davis, particularly when she is playing the woman scorned. So, because of her, *Payment on Demand* became quite a lot more than the rather old hat drama about a wife whose husband leaves her for another woman. You can bet that Bette didn't take it with graceful resignation. Worth mentioning, too, were the lovely young actress Betty Lynn, as a daughter of divorce, and a sharp bit by the one-time Broadway great, Jane Cowl. Bruce Manning wrote and Curtis Bernhardt directed.

Although he did it in his sharpest and wittiest style, Joseph L. Mankiewicz took a number of stiff jabs at the medical profession in *People Will Talk*. Mankiewicz wrote and directed the film, which was an adaptation of a German play, *Dr. Praetorious*, by Curt Goetz. Cary Grant, in one of his most brilliant characterizations, played this most unconventional doctor with Hume Cronyn right up to him as his small-minded antagonist. With Finlay Currie, Jeanne Crain, Walter Slezak, and Katherine Locke.

Joseph Losey dealt with a sordid situation in *The Prowler* but made it a thoroughly fascinating film. Hugo Butler's screenplay (from a story by Robert Thoeren and Hans Wilhelm) concerned an opportunistic cop who meets an unhappy married woman and draws her, uncomprehending, into a vicious scheme. Van Heflin and Evelyn Keyes—two exceptional, but usually unsung actors—were in top form in these roles.

Jean Renoir's camera, in actual locations in India, found amazing and exotic panoramas of life in that country. Visually, his film, *The River*, had seldom been approached. Dramatically, the picture, based on a novel by Rumer Godden, had its ins and outs—the portrait of an adolescent in the throes of her first love quite affectingly played by a youngster named Patricia Walters, although other elements were less dramatically valuable. Nora Swinburne, Esmond Knight, Adrienne Corri, Thomas E. Breen, and Arthur Shields were among the actors in these other roles. But Renoir was the star.

Fred Zinnemann, in *Teresa*, presented a poignant little movie about an American soldier's homecoming with his Italian war bride—home to the tenements of New York. In these roles he cast two highly promising youngsters, John Ericson and Pier Angeli. (Alas, their promise was never to be fulfilled, although she had a couple of moments in succeeding pictures.) The veteran Broadway actress, Patricia Collinge, dominated the supporting cast as a possessive mother. Stewart Stern wrote the screenplay from his (with Alfred Hayes) original story.

Evelyn Keyes and John Maxwell in *The Prowler*. Van Heflin is outside looking in.

(LEFT) Bette Davis and Betty Lynn in *Payment on Demand*.

(BELOW) Thomas E. Breen, Patricia Walters, Adrienne Corri, and Radha in *The River*.

Cary Grant and Jeanne Crain in *People Will Talk*.

Lloyd Bridges, Adele Jergens, Katherine Locke, and
Frank Lovejoy in *Try and Get Me*.

Pier Angeli and John Ericson in *Teresa*.

Still another melodrama of mob violence—but an arresting one—was *Try and Get Me* (also released as *The Sound of Fury*). This had Frank Lovejoy as a weakling, led into crime by a bullying psychopath (Lloyd Bridges). Both actors were effective, as was Richard Carlson, while Katherine Locke had some very touching moments as a plain, shy girl who has an encounter with the criminals. Cyril Endfield directed the Jo Pagano script.

A little black girl disappears. Suspicion points to a white man. The inflammatory situation almost sets off a race riot until the girl is discovered trapped in an abandoned well. Then blacks and whites unite at the frantic attempts at rescue. *The Well* was a low-budget picture with no names in the cast although Richard Rober, Madie Norman, Henry Morgan, and Barry Kelly were up to all demands. It was also much more compelling than many major dramas of social significance. Leo Popkin and Russell Rouse directed with screenplay by Rouse and Clarence Greene.

Another very little picture, *When I Grow Up,* was almost thrown away by its distributors. Yet it was a very moving father–son story with Bobby Driscoll again proving that he was one of the best of all child actors. Robert Preston and Martha Scott were beautifully understanding in the major adult roles. Michael Kanin wrote and directed.

Martha Scott and Robert Preston as concerned parents in *When I Grow Up*.

Ernest Anderson and Maidie Norman as parents of a lost girl, with Richard Rober, in *The Wall*.

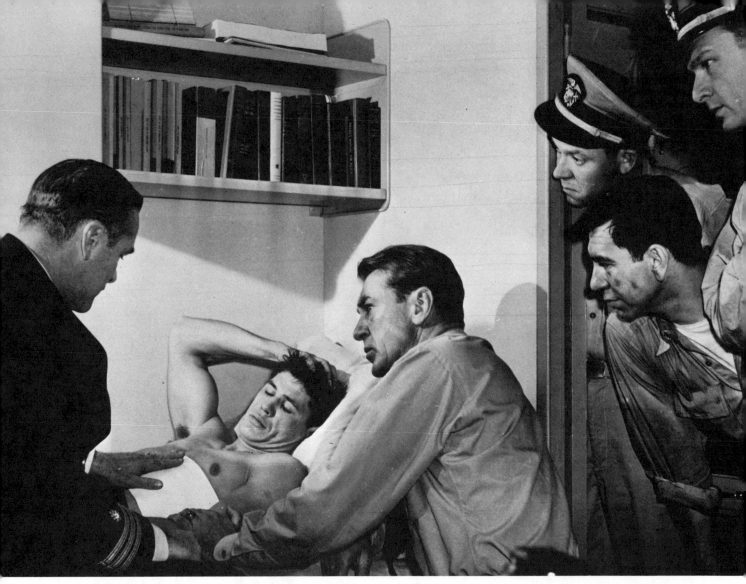

It's Charles Bronson (then known as Buchinski) in bed, Damian O'Flynn the doctor, and navy men Gary Cooper, Richard Erdman, Jack Webb, and Eddie Albert in *You're in the Navy Now* (originally titled *U.S.S. Teakettle*).

Although a movie like *Operation Petticoat* is more renowned, it couldn't even approach the hilarity of *You're in the Navy Now* (also known as *U.S.S. Teakettle*). It was just about the funniest Navy comedy since Laurel and Hardy's *Saps at Sea*. Henry Hathaway directed Richard Murphy's screenplay and lavish comic contributions were dished up by Millard Mitchell, Eddie Albert, Jack Webb, John McIntire, Ray Collins, Jack Warden Richard Erdman, Harvey Lembeck, and Charles Buchinski (who later changed his name to Bronson). Even Gary Cooper, not usually known for such things, joined happily in the fun.

Other Forgotten 1951 Films to Note

Monty Woolley's last major movie role was as a gentleman living up to the title of his movie, *As Young As You Feel,* ably abetted by Thelma Ritter, Constance Bennett, David Wayne, Albert Dekker, and a delectable dish named Marilyn Monroe. . . . James Cagney as a newspaperman who is a reformed alcoholic (he was much more fun when he was drinking) took on the rehabilitation of drunkard Gig Young (an unexpectedly good performance) in *Come Fill the Cup.* . . . Michael Rennie was a visitor from outer space—and not a menacing one—in a quietly effective little science fiction movie, *The Day the Earth Stood Still.* . . . Charles Boyer and Lyle Bettger, as a Jesuit and an agnostic doctor, were imposing antagonists in the film Douglas Sirk fashioned from Emmett Lavery's play, *The First Legion.* . . . Golf is usually neglected by the movies but *Follow the Sun,* a heartwarming film about Ben Hogan's near-fatal accident and comeback on the links, helped make up for the neglect. Glenn Ford was at his best as Hogan; so were Anne Baxter and Dennis O'Keefe. . . . Paul Douglas scored again as an aging has-been who can't forget he once was a football hero in *The Guy Who Came Back.* . . .

The old stage mother plot, transferred to the tennis courts, was the basis for the Ida Lupino directed *Hard, Fast and Beautiful,* with Sally Forrest as the tennis star and Claire Trevor as her grasping ma. . . . Jerome Weidman's *I Can Get It for You Wholesale* lost most of what made the story effective in the book by turning its unscrupulous, ambitious salesman into something for Susan Hayward. . . . Nor was Hayward ideally cast in Henry King's *I'd Climb the Highest Mountain* as the wife of a minister but it was a nice picture of its kind and William Lundigan was well suited to the principal role. . . . Danny Thomas was Gus Kahn—and very effectively—in one of the better movie songwriter biographies, *I'll See You in My Dreams*. . . . Jeff Chandler had the title role in *Iron Man,* a better than average fight film. . . . The life story of *Jim Thorpe, All American* came to films as a very good vehicle for Burt Lancaster. . . .

Kind Lady was a pretty old girl by the time they got around to remaking it in 1951 but Ethel Barrymore and Maurice Evans with a good cast (Angela Lansbury, Betsy Blair, and Keenan Wynn) played the sinister melodramatics as if they were brand new. . . . Joseph Losey and David Wayne did the best they possibly could under the circumstances but a remake of *M* can only remind one, to its disadvantage, of the Fritz Lang–Peter Lorre classic. . . . Who knows what happened in the years it was being cut by Howard Hughes but the Preston Sturges–Harold Lloyd *Mad Wednesday,* after a brilliant beginning (a clip from Lloyd's *Freshman*), degenerated into idiot slapstick. . . . A little boy named William Fox (he grew up to be James Fox of *The Servant* and others) was winning in *The Magnet,* a modest but pleasant British comedy. . . . Gian-Carlo Menotti, using his original star, Marie Powers, along with Anna Maria Alberghetti, brought his *The Medium* to the screen but, in spite of startling moments, it was one more proof that opera and the movie medium don't really mix. . . . Most of the power of Richard Wright's book and play, *Native Son,* was dissipated in the movie version because of lackluster production, direction, and acting—particularly, sad to say, by Wright himself in the role Canada Lee had brought blazingly to the stage. . . . Jimmy Stewart did his Jimmy Stewart thing in *No Highway in the Sky,* reunited with his *Destry* girl, Marlene Dietrich, but without the fireworks of that first one. . . . Danny Kaye pulled out all stops in *On the Riviera* but it was a thrice-told tale (Chevalier and Ameche had preceded Kaye in earlier versions). . . .

Arty and pretentious was *Pandora and the Flying Dutchman* but it rated huzzas for Jack Cardiff's cinematography, particularly as he photographed Ava Gardner, who never looked more gorgeously sexy. . . . Spencer Tracy was in merely standard form in *The People Against O'Hara* but there was a notable bit by William Campbell, who stood out in one or two other films, then just disappeared from the screen. . . . Robert Mitchum and Robert Ryan were such a dynamic combination that *The Racket* was watchable even though the story (based on a 1920s play) was thoroughly shopworn. . . .

Saturday's Hero was still another football exposé but it pulled few punches and was well acted, particularly by John Derek and a gravel-voiced newcomer, Aldo DaRe (his surname was later changed to Ray). . . . That famous old puzzler about the missing man who everybody swears never existed (Hitchcock used a variation in *The Lady Vanishes*) was trotted out again in *So Long at the Fair* but it still had its mystery, with Jean Simmons and Dirk Bogarde attractive as the only two nonconspirators. . . . Ginger Rogers and Doris Day got involved with the Klu Klux Klan in *Storm Warning,* a pale echo of similar but better 1930s movies (like *The Black Legion*), although this featured an interesting villain in snarling Steve Cochran. . . .

Take Care of My Little Girl raked the sorority system over the coals, if you really cared, but the girls (Jeanne Crain, Betty Lynn, Jean Peters, and Mitzi Gaynor) were easy on the eyes. . . . Burt Lancaster was in his element —so was Gilbert Roland—in *Ten Tall Men,* a frequently riotous takeoff on the French Foreign Legion. . . . Jerry Lewis too often overdid the idiot boy routine but *That's My Boy* was one of the funnier Martin–Lewis movies, principally due to the comic abilities of Eddie Mayehoff as a burlesqued "old grad" (although Mayehoff's kind of comedy quickly palled in succeeding appearances). . . . Clouzot's *Le Corbeau,* a grim drama of poison pen panic, was considerably watered down in its American remake, *The Thirteenth Letter,* but it still had its moments along with some good performances, particularly by Charles Boyer, Judith Evelyn, and Francoise Rosay. . . . Cecil Parker was the cast standout in *Tony Draws a Horse* but everybody had a lark in this British comedy—and so did the audiences. . . .

Chapter Twenty-Four

The Movie Year of 1952

Moviegoers wear colored glasses and lions seem to jump right out of the screen in 1952. Three-D is hailed as the savior of the industry. Can TV duplicate this? And there is Cinerama which turns a travelogue into a sensation.

It's commplace now for movies to film in actual locales. And the tendency grows for many stars to refuse all work except abroad for a period of at least eighteen months. This is expected to solve tax problems.

The flurry of dramas with social significance seems to have abated. Old-fashioned Westerns, new-fashioned musicals, and show business themes provide some of the best American movies. France, Italy, and England continue to be big on art house screens and we get a couple of noteworthy ones from Sweden and, surprisingly, Japan.

Shirley Booth is the newcomer—newcomer?!—of the year, but we are also seeing the first major movies made by Richard Burton, Claire Bloom, Jeanmaire, Aldo Ray, John Forsythe, Julie Harris, Sydney Chaplin, Dorothy Dandridge, Rita Moreno, Lori Nelson, Keith Andes, Suzan Ball, Tab Hunter, and Anne Bancroft.

In this corner there was one special picture of the year —Arthur Freed's *Singin' in the Rain,* directed by Gene Kelly and Stanley Donen, written by Bette Comden and Adolph Green, starring Kelly, Donald O'Connor, Debbie Reynolds, and Jean Hagen. But there were others up there, too. Alphabetically, they'd include Minnelli's *The Bad and the Beautiful;* Daniel Mann's *Come Back, Little Sheba;* Mankiewicz's *Five Fingers;* Zinnemann's *High Noon;* Chaplin's *Limelight;* Huston's *Moulin Rouge;* Ford's *The Quiet Man;* and Kazan's *Viva Zapata.* And, because they were very popular or very good or both, let's also list *Affair in Trinidad; The Big Sky; The Greatest Show on Earth; Hans Christian Andersen; Ivanhoe; The Man in the White Suit; My Cousin Rachel; Pat and Mike; Snows of Kilimanjaro; Sudden Fear; Where's Charley?,* and *With a Song in My Heart.*

But there were those that are virtually forgotten today.

Ralph Richardson and Ann Todd in *Breaking the Sound Barrier.*

Forgotten Films of 1952

David Lean's masterly direction—both in the air and on the ground—of Terence Rattigan's *Breaking the Sound Barrier* made it one of the most extraordinary pictures ever filmed of men and airplanes. The drama here was in aviation experimentation but it far outdistanced the usual air action movies. Ralph Richardson gave a strong performance, ably assisted by Nigel Patrick, Ann Todd, John Justin, and Denholm Elliott.

Laurence Olivier's study of the degradation and down-fall of a man was one of his most stunning performances even though *Carrie,* the picture in which it appeared, was a major disappointment. Ruth and Augustus Goetz sentimentalized the Dreiser novel in their screenplay and Jennifer Jones was all sweetness and soap opera sniffles as the title character. William Wyler's direction was his usual professional job. Miriam Hopkins and Eddie Albert were effective in supporting roles.

Clash by Night was never one of Clifford Odets's best plays but it had some strong and steamy moments. The film version, as adapted by Alfred Hayes and directed by Fritz Lang, inherited both the play's weaknesses and its strengths. The characters of the triangle could not have been better cast for the screen with Barbara Stanwyck and Paul Douglas in top form and Robert Ryan particularly explosive as the lover. J. Carrol Naish was effective, too, and in a secondary role Marilyn Monroe took another step up the ladder from cheesecake.

Alan Paton's saga of Africa, *Cry, the Beloved Country,* came to the screen in Zoltan Korda's production as an always impressive, frequently deeply moving motion picture. The distinguished Canada Lee had his one completely worthy screen role; there were fine performances by Charles Carson, Sidney Poitier, Joyce Carey. The picture presented an Africa never before seen on movie screens.

Television was still "the enemy" to Hollywood in 1952. *Dreamboat,* therefore, was an amusing comedy which directed its mild satiric shafts at the tube. The satire was helped by Clifton Webb's acid delivery. As a former silent screen idol who resents his old movies being dredged up as TV fare, he had opportunities for the kind of sharp comedy that was his forte. With Ginger Rogers as his one-time leading lady, the film had takeoffs on some styles of silent movie epics. Claude Binyon wrote and directed.

Except for a couple of imports, anthology films, which combined two or more short stories to make a feature, never found much favor in the United States. *Face to Face* was no exception yet both the short features had quality. *The Secret Sharer,* directed by John Brahm with a screenplay by Aeneas Mackenzie from a Joseph Conrad story, starred James Mason. But the joy was in

Laurence Olivier on Skid Row in *Carrie.*

Robert Ryan and Barbara Stanwyck in *Clash by Night.*

(ABOVE) Sidney Poitier and Canada Lee in *Cry the Beloved Country*.

(BELOW LEFT) Clifton Webb and Ginger Rogers portraying silent-screen stars in *Dream Boat*.

Robert Mitchum in *The Lusty Men*.

The sheriff and his bride (Robert Preston and Marjorie Steele) run into the town bad man (Minor Watson) in *The Bride Comes to Yellow Sky* segment of *Face to Face*.

the second segment, *The Bride Comes to Yellow Sky,* directed by Bretaigne Windust and with a rich and funny screenplay by James Agee from a Stephen Crane story. This had Robert Preston absolutely wonderful as an unconventional Western hero while the usually staid Minor Watson had the time of his life as a drunken rapscallion. Majorie Steele, the leading lady was the real-life wife of the producer, millionaire Huntington Hartford, but she was bright enough to be accepted as more than the wife of the boss.

Anthony Asquith assembled just about the best possible cast for Oscar Wilde's *The Importance of Being Earnest* and just put it on the screen without too much worry about whether or not it was cinematic. It wasn't, but the Wilde quips and epigrams came through loud and clear. How could they miss when Lady Bracknell was Dame Edith Evans and the rest of the cast included Michael Redgrave, Joan Greenwood, Margaret Rutherford, Dorothy Tutin, Michael Denison, and Miles Malleson?

Life on the rodeo circuit has become a not-uncommon subject for movies but Nicholas Ray brought us one of the earliest—and still one of the best—in *The Lusty*

Men. Except for the casting of Susan Hayward as a cowpoke's wife (although she did her best to be unglamorous), Ray kept it all as unHollywood as possible. Arthur Kennedy and Robert Mitchum were particularly realistic as rodeo cowboys. Horace McCoy and David Dortort wrote the screenplay.

Judy Holliday had a new kind of role in *The Marrying Kind,* a Garson Kanin–Ruth Gordon script directed by George Cukor. Here she was still our Judy, delectably dizzy and happily teamed with likable, rasp-voiced Aldo Ray. Their romantic and marriage problems were loaded with laughs. But they had their unhappy moments, and Miss Judy was terribly touching in these sequences, too.

Fred Zinnemann did a brave thing in his filmization of Carson McCullers's *The Member of the Wedding*—he recast the three principals in the roles that had brought them glory on Broadway. He also—except for a brief episode, taken by screenwriters Edna and Edward Anhalt from the McCullers book—stuck faithfully to the play. But lack of real dramatic incident made the film too sketchy frequently. Ethel Waters and Brandon De-Wilde were every bit as affecting on screen as they had

The extraordinary actors of *The Importance of Being Earnest*—Dame Edith Evans, Dorothy Tutin, Joan Greenwood, Michael Redgrave, Michael Denison, Margaret Rutherford, and Aubrey Mather.

been on stage. But, though no fault could ever be found in the acting of Julie Harris as the tormented child, the sad truth is that the pitiless camera revealed her as very definitely an adult. All of her artistry couldn't change that.

The Narrow Margin was a true sleeper, made on a lower-than "B" budget with no names of any box-office appeal. Yet it was a train thriller, full of suspense and worthy of comparison to, if not really up to the level of, the similar films of Hitchcock and Carol Reed. It lifted Richard Fleischer several notches in importance as a director but, strangely, did nothing at all for anybody else involved—not screenwriter Earl Felton, not Charles McGraw, who returned to playing the secondary heavies he always played competently, not Marie Windsor or anyone else in the cast.

One of those atmospheric chase pictures the British do so well was *The Stranger in Between*. This presented Dirk Bogarde, extremely effective as a fleeing murderer, and pitted him against the small boy who is his hostage. Jon Whiteley was completely winning in this part. Charles Crichton directed, Jack Whittingham wrote the screenplay, and Kay Walsh gave a notable supporting performance.

Julie Harris, Ethel Waters, and Brandon DeWilde in *Member of the Wedding*.

Judy Holliday and Aldo Ray in *The Marrying Kind*.

Charles McGraw and Marie Windsor in *The Narrow Margin*.

Dirk Bogarde and Jon Whiteley in *The Stranger in Between*.

Other Forgotten 1952 Pictures to Note

In Ben Hecht's *Actors and Sin*, even such good actors as Marsha Hunt, Edward G. Robinson, and Dan O'Herlihy couldn't save the tedious *Actor's Blood*, which was the dramatic half of the two-story film, but *Woman of Sin* was a merry movie takeoff with Eddie Albert in top form. . . . Joseph Losey managed some moody atmosphere in *The Big Night* and cast some interesting actors (Philip Bourneuf, Dorothy Comingore, and Joan Lorring). . . . An excellent film about jockeys, *Boots Malone,* had an even better than his usual good performance by William Holden, along with two capable kids, Stanley Clements and Johnny Stewart. . . . The W. Somerset Maugham short story anthologies (*Quartet, Trio*) were wearing thin by the time of *Encore* but there were good performances in rather second-rate tales by Kay Walsh, Nigel Patrick, and Glynis Johns. . . . Two of the Broadway hits transferred to the screen by Producer Stanley Kramer did not travel at all well. *The Fourposter* miscast Rex Harrison and Lilli Palmer (although, of course, they were elegant) in what became on screen much too much of a gimmick. *The Happy Time*, in spite of good actors (Charles Boyer, Marsha Hunt, Louis Jourdan, Bobby Driscoll, and Kurt Kasznar), reminded viewers of TV situation comedy with a French–Canadian accent. . . . Keenan Wynn's heartbreaking performance as a punch-drunk ex-fighter deserved a better showcase than *Holiday for Sinners*. . . . Dorothy McGuire's poignant performance made more than was there out of *Invitation* but couldn't keep it from being soap opera. . . .

Robert Arthur, one of the more likable juveniles of the 1950s, teamed well with Bing Crosby in a father–son movie, *Just for You*, but the story line was contrived. . . . Robert Donat gave his usual meticulous performance in a biography of William Friese-Greene, a British film pioneer, *The Magic Box*. . . . Howard Hawks went back to his *Bringing Up Baby* kind of screwball comedy for *Monkey Business*. Cary Grant, Ginger Rogers, and Marilyn Monroe were amusing although the joke ran out of mirth. . . . John Beal, Gilbert Roland, Millard Mitchell, and Henry Morgan made the most of good roles in a different kind of prison picture, *My Six Convicts*. . . . Robert Ryan gave his usual taut performance as a sadistic cop in a Nicholas Ray melodrama, *On Dangerous Ground*, in which Ida Lupino and Ward Bond were also effective. . . . All of Carol Reed's artistry and the performances of Trevor Howard, Robert Morley, Wendy Hiller, and Ralph Richardson couldn't make *Outcast of the Islands* any more than that chestnut about the Britisher going to rack and ruin in the tropics. . . . It was the cameo performances of able actors (Bette Davis, Shelley Winters, Evelyn Varden, Beatrice Straight and, particularly, Keenan Wynn) that made *Phone Call From a Stranger* work, not the contrived story. . . . Dan Dailey showed up well as a comedian in the 1950s (even though his films were not always first-rate) with one of his better jobs being Dizzy Dean in *The Pride of St. Louis*. . . . *The Promoter* didn't have the sly wit of many of the Alec Guinness films of the period but Guinness and Glynis Johns made the most of fewer opportunities. . . .

MGM tried to make their own latter-day Douglas Fairbanks/Errol Flynn by remaking old swashbucklers with Stewart Granger. *Scaramouche* was best (he later would do *The Prisoner of Zenda* and *Beau Brummel*), with a worthy antagonist in Mel Ferrer and such lovely ladies as Janet Leigh and Eleanor Parker. But the time was past . . . Joseph Cotten and Teresa Wright had a good little suspense story in *The Steel Trap* about a fleeing bankrobber who changes his mind and must return the money before the vault opens. . . . Walt Disney brought out the old legend in *The Story of Robin Hood*, handled it with care and made a fine movie but one that never achieved anything close to the popularity of Errol Flynn and Douglas Fairbanks versions. Perhaps Richard Todd, a better actor but not the usual type, was the reason. . . . *We're Not Married* brightly told stories of several couples who learn their marriages are not legal. All actors (Victor Moore, Fred Allen, Ginger Rogers, Marilyn Monroe, David Wayne, Eve Arden, Paul Douglas, Mitzi Gaynor, Louis Calhern, and Eddie Bracken) are given at least a brief chance to do their things. . . .

Chapter Twenty-Five

The Movie Year of 1953

Moviegoers are still wearing colored glasses in 1953 although there are beginning to be signs of rebellion. A couple of pictures, produced in 3-D, are eventually released only in conventional dimensions. Cinerama still has long lines waiting at the few theaters able to handle the process.

The big news is CinemaScope, the anamorphic lens process espoused by 20th Century-Fox. Neither 3-D nor Cinerama, CinemaScope has elements of both and is heralded as "The miracle you see without glasses." Darryl F. Zanuck films *The Robe* in CinemaScope and the combination of the new process with the proven appeal of Biblical drama makes for box-office figures even more spectacular than the film. Other new processes are announced but none makes any lasting dent.

By now, drive-in theaters, a stepchild when they started, have become an important element in exhibition. No longer dismissed as "passion pits," the drive-ins are becoming more impressive establishments and are showing top films at the same time as regular runs.

Censorship hits again against pictures like *The Moon Is Blue, The French Line, The Captain's Paradise* under fire by the Legion of Decency, the Production Code,

local censorship boards—or by all of them. *Moon,* for instance, has dared to use the word "v-i-r-g-i-n."

Audrey Hepburn is the bright new star of the year and others are showing up for the first time with some prominence—Harry Belafonte, Nicole Maurey, Ernest Borgnine, Maggie McNamara, George Nader, Kenneth More, Merv Griffin, and Rosemary Clooney. And if you see Italian movies, you'll glimpse a willowy beauty named Sophia Loren.

Let's call Minnelli's *The Band Wagon* and Wyler's *Roman Holiday* our favorite movies of the year. Certainly they were the most fun. But two other toppers would be Fred Zinnemann's *From Here to Eternity* and George Stevens's *Shane*. Other movies of the year would include the Marilyn Monroe duo, *How to Marry a Millionaire* (with Lauren Bacall and Betty Grable) and *Gentlemen Prefer Blondes* (with Jane Russell); Mankiewicz's *Julius Caesar*; and Billy Wilder's *Stalag 17*. Some others that were popular included *Calamity Jane; House of Wax; Kiss Me Kate; Knights of the Round Table; Lili;* and Disney's *Peter Pan*.

And there were those others, not perhaps as easy to remember.

Jean Simmons and a new young actor, Anthony
Perkins, in *The Actress*.

Forgotten Films of 1953

Ruth Gordon's *Years Ago* was an affectionate memoir
of her own girlhood and it made a lovely Broadway
vehicle for Fredric March, Florence Eldridge, and Patricia Kirkland. Spencer Tracy, Teresa Wright, and Jean
Simmons filled these roles in the movie version, retitled
The Actress, and you couldn't ask for anything more.
(But you did get more—Ruth Gordon's script which
added some effective touches to her play; George Cukor's experienced directorial touch; and Anthony Perkins's amusing movie debut.)

Jean Simmons had another title role but her *Angel Face*
was as far away as you could imagine from her happy
little "actress." In Otto Preminger's strange melodrama
(screenplay by Frank Nugent and Oscar Millard), Simmons's angelic countenance was only a facade for a
vicious neurotic—or worse. Robert Mitchum, Barbara
O'Neill, Herbert Marshall, and Mona Freeman were
among the victims of the mixed-up girl.

John Gay's *The Beggar's Opera* was brought to the
screen with impeccable credentials—directed by Peter
Brook, screen play by Denis Cannan from the Christo-
pher Fry adaptation, and with a cast headed by Sir
Laurence Olivier as Macheath. There were also Dorothy
Tutin, Stanley Holloway, George Devine, Mary Clare,
Hugh Griffith, Athene Seyler, and Daphne Anderson.
But to a world that had taken up the Brecht/Weill *Three
Penny Opera*, this seemed a pallid thing. It sank to box-
office depths and has not been seen or heard about since
its original release.

Fritz Lang wasn't a director to flinch from violence and,
in *The Big Heat*, he portrayed more than an audience
usually saw in those pre-Peckinpah days. Sydney
Boehm's script dealt with corruption—in the police department, as well as the underworld—and Glenn Ford
had one of his best roles as a detective seeking it out.
This is the one with that famous scene in which a thug-
gish Lee Marvin hurled a cup of scalding coffee in the
face of Gloria Grahame as one of those not-too-bright
tough broads she played so well.

Not quite in a class with his classic comedies—which
may explain why it is among the least remembered—
was Alec Guinness's *The Captain's Paradise*. But Guinness was, as always, an absolute delight as the skipper
with a wife in every port (his boat sails between Gibral-
tar and Morocco). In his merry double life, Celia Johnson made a fine sensible helpmate on one end of the

Robert Mitchum and Jean Simmons in *Angel Face*.

journey, with Yvonne DeCarlo as a livelier companion on the other. Alec Coppel and Nicholas Phipps wrote the screenplay directed by Anthony Kimmins.

Nicholas Monserrat's *The Cruel Sea* formed the basis, in Eric Ambler's adaptation, for sea–war drama, done with the usual skill of the British for such subjects. England has sent us so many of them that this had a familiar quality, but it was a particularly good example of the genre. Charles Frend directed; Jack Hawkins gave his strongest performance.

Not one of Alfred Hitchcock's more suspenseful films was *I Confess*; not one of Montgomery Clift's better roles either. Yet the film had its moments and so did the Clift performance as a priest, bound by the seal of confessional, who is suspected of a murder but cannot tell the real culprit because of that confession. George Ta-

Laurence Olivier and Daphne Anderson in *The Beggar's Opera*.

Alec Guinness with his "other" wife, Yvonne DeCarlo, in *The Captain's Paradise*.

Jack Hawkins in *The Cruel Sea*.

Montgomery Clift in *I Confess*.

(RIGHT) Lee Marvin gets rough with Gloria Grahame in *The Big Heat*.

bori and William Archibald wrote the screenplay; Anne Baxter, Karl Malden, Dolly Haas, and Brian Aherne were in the cast.

Certainly one of the least pretentious pictures of any year but certainly also one of the most enjoyable was *Little Fugitive*. Simply the chronicle of a day and a night in the life of one pint-sized resident of Brooklyn, the movie was filmed by Ray Ashley, Morris Engel, and Ruth Orkin. Richie Andrusco was quite as natural and believable as any youngster picked directly from the streets—which is exactly where he had been found.

Elia Kazan directed and Fredric March starred in *Man on a Tightrope*, a taut drama of members of a small carnival attempting to escape from behind the Iron Curtain. Kazan cast with his usual finesse—Gloria Grahame, Cameron Mitchell, Adolphe Menjou, and Richard Boone down to interesting bit players like Paul Hartman, Pat Henning, and Dorothea Wieck. Robert E. Sherwood wrote the screenplay.

Five excellent actors brought a great deal of tension to *The Naked Spur*, an effective Western directed by Anthony Mann. James Stewart was more than the conventional Western hero and Robert Ryan very much more than the cold-blooded villian. But so was Janet Leigh, as anything but the usual western leading lady. Millard Mitchell and Ralph Meeker scored, too. Sam Rolfe and Harold Jack Bloom wrote the script.

The Star was a fairly obvious script (by Katherine Albert and Dale Eunson) about a washed-up glamour girl and it was directed without much inspiration by Stuart Heisler. What it did have was Bette Davis playing the has-been movie actress with no holds barred. Davis didn't let down for a minute in an uncompromising characterization and to watch her tear into her role was more than enough.

The Stooge foreshadowed what would actually happen to Dean Martin and Jerry Lewis. In the movie, the team broke up. But then the Martin character flopped as a single with Jerry handily arriving to team again and hit again. That's not quite the way it happened in real life, is it? The movie had a little more substance than the usual Martin–Lewis slapstick outing with Jerry attempting some of the pathos behind the clowning that caused his admirers to drag out the adjective "Chaplinesque." Dean, too, had some characterization as the entertainer whose success goes to his head. Norman Taurog directed; Fred Finkelhoffe and Martin Rackin wrote the script.

Richie Andrusco observes the action on the beach in *Little Fugitive*.

Fredric March, Cameron Mitchell, and Terry Moore in *Man on a Tightrope*.

Dean Martin on stage, Jerry Lewis in the box, in *The Stooge*.

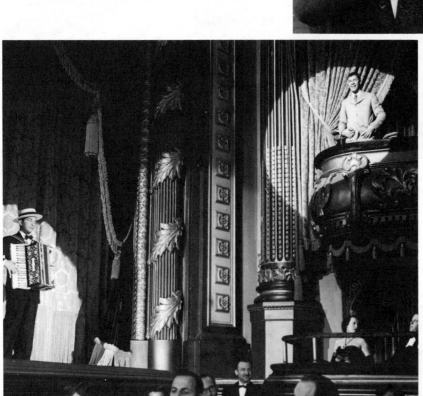

Janet Leigh, Ralph Meeker, and Robert Ryan in *The Naked Spur*.

206

Other Forgotten 1953 Films to Note

Dorothy Dandridge and Harry Belafonte were the sympathetic adults but a youngster named Philip Hepburn had the focal role in *Bright Road,* a quiet but sometimes touching drama of the problems of a small black boy.... Less dramatic than Arthur Penn's *Miracle Worker* of almost a decade later, *Crash of Silence* (also known as *The Story of Mandy*) was still engrossing in its semi-documentary treatment of the education of a congenitally deaf child.... It was a joy to watch Robert Morley and Margaret Rutherford, each complementing the other's special comedy style, but their vehicle, *Curtain Up,* was feeble.... Richard Burton made more of his role than he was given but *The Desert Rats* was routine movie battle fare that couldn't approach its impressive *Desert Fox* predecessor.... *Gilbert and Sullivan,* in spite of the casting of Robert Morley and Maurice Evans in the title roles, was tedious as biographical drama but excerpts from their operettas, brightly presented, were more than enough to compensate.... *Give a Girl a Break* was lightweight but fun with well-staged musical numbers featuring people like Debbie Reynolds, Bob Fosse, and Gower and Marge Champion....

Ida Lupino directed *The Hitch-Hiker* as a straightforward little thriller which benefited considerably from the performances of Edmond O'Brien, Frank Lovejoy and, especially, William Talman, as the psychopath who hitches a ride with them.... Bing Crosby had one of his rare serious roles, as a father in search of a son (Christian Fourcade) he doesn't know, in *Little Boy Lost*.... James Mason, Claire Bloom, and Hildegarde

Neff in a Carol Reed-directed movie promised more than *The Man Between* delivered—blame a muddled story ... John Mills had one of his best roles in *Mr. Denning Drives North,* a good tight little suspense drama from Britain ... Samuel Fuller's lurid little melodrama, *Pickup on South Street,* with Richard Widmark, Jean Peters, and Thelma Ritter, has its admirers.... Dick Powell, in his directorial debut, got some excitement out of shopworn situations in *Split Second* but the film's main value was in uncovering unexpected acting potential of Alexis Smith, hitherto thought of mostly as just a chilly beauty.... Richard Todd was a swashbuckling hero and Glynis Johns his lady fair in a brace of handsome costume dramas, *The Sword and the Rose* and *Rob Roy,* both produced in Britain by Disney.... Dan Dailey wasted yet another good performance in another flimsy vehicle, *Taxi*.... *Titanic,* about the maiden voyage of a doomed ship, was interesting rather than particularly dramatic, but had some impressive names among the crew and passengers (Clifton Webb, Barbara Stanwyck, Richard Basehart, Robert Wagner, Thelma Ritter, Brian Aherne, and Allyn Joslyn).... Joan Crawford sang, danced, and showed her legs like old times in *Torch Song* but it took blind pianist Michael Wilding to soften her into "a woman." ... Jean Simmons was a very lovely *Young Bess* in a lavish historical drama, the good cast of which also included Deborah Kerr, Stewart Granger, Rex Thompson, Kay Walsh, Robert Arthur, Leo G. Carroll, and Charles Laughton briefly repeating his Henry VIII....

Sterling Hayden and Bette Davis in *The Star.*

Chapter Twenty-Six

The Movie Year of 1954

In 1954 3-D with glasses is all washed up but most pictures of any pretension are being made in Cinema-Scope or Paramount's new VistaVision. Even so, some of the top movies of the year are plain old black-and-white on the regulation screen.

Movie fans had paid scant attention when the U.S. Supreme Court agreed with the Justice Department's Anti-Trust Division that exhibition be "divorced" from production and distribution. But, as film historian Stuart Byron has written, "The decision was—is—*the* seminal event in the history of the film business." And now the results are obvious. The "consent decrees" have separated the major studios from the theatre chains they owned. The changes in theatre exhibition are the direct result. Before the end of the fifties the studio system will have changed, too—no more planned annual program of pictures (so many "A's," a corresponding slate of "B's") to be sold to theatres in a block. And soon the big studios as we have known them will have changed radically, even to eliminating their lists of contract players.

Walt Disney, of all people, runs afoul of the censors when, in *The Vanishing Prairie,* a buffalo gives birth to a calf. The New York State Censor Board is aghast but the head of that organization eventually reverses the decision, made during his absence, to ban the film.

Some of the new faces on the screen belong to Jack Lemmon, Eva Marie Saint, Rod Steiger, Kim Novak, Paul Newman, Laurence Harvey, Brenda de Banzie, May Wynn, Robert Francis, Eartha Kitt, Maria Schell. And a new production company, American International, takes its first faltering steps.

The Brando–Kazan–Schulberg *On the Waterfront* is far in front of other English-language pictures of the year. But the Judy Garland–James Mason–George Cukor *A Star Is Born,* and Alfred Hitchock's *Rear Window,* are high in the running, too. Others of special note would include (alphabetically) *Bad Day at Black Rock; The Barefoot Contessa; Beat the Devil; Carmen Jones; The Country Girl; Dial M for Murder; Executive Suite; Genevieve; Romeo and Juliet; Sabrina; Seven Brides for Seven Brothers;* and *The Wild One.* And some mention should go to *Broken Lance; The Caine Mutiny; The Glenn Miller Story; The High and the Mighty; Johnny Guitar; Magnificent Obsession; There's No Business Like Show Business; Three Coins in the Fountain; 20,000 Leagues Under the Sea;* and *White Christmas.*

Then there were the others. . . .

Forgotten Films of 1954

Using the Daniel Defoe classic as a starting point, Luis Buñuel went far beyond the expected and usual adventure story in his *Adventures of Robinson Crusoe.* With the valuable assistance of an excellent actor, Dan O'Herlihy, it became a serious study of the effects of human isolation. Buñuel, with Philip Roll, also wrote the screenplay.

His Andy Hardy and Judy Garland days far behind him, Mickey Rooney had been popping up in some grade "B" movies. *Drive a Crooked Road* was one of these but one which gave Mickey a chance to use his extraordinary talents to develop a real characterization. He played a misfit, befriended by sharpies (Kevin McCarthy, Jack Kelly, and Dianne Foster) who are out to use him. It was the kind of performance that, in a more important movie made in his palmier days, would have been nominated for awards. Richard Quine directed the Blake Edwards screenplay.

Charles Laughton hammed it up to a fare-thee-well as the tyrant of his family in *Hobson's Choice* but it all worked for robust humor. Brenda de Banzie and John Mills, much more restrained, were just as right, as Laughton's spunky daughter and the humble little shop assistant who eventually challenges the old man. David Lean directed with full appreciation of the thick Lancashire atmosphere. Lean, Norman Spencer, and Wynyard Browne adapted Harold Brighouse's play for films.

The Holly and the Ivy brought out some of the finest British actors (Celia Johnson, Margaret Leighton, and Ralph Richardson heading the cast) in a tranquil film with emotions boiling beneath the surface as far-flung members of one family reunite for a holiday party. That family reunion story is an old chestnut but actors like these made it fresh. Anatole de Grunwald wrote and produced; George More O'Ferrall was credited as director.

Garson Kanin as writer and George Cukor as director launched the movie career of Judy Holliday in *Adam's Rib,* let her repeat her Broadway triumph in *Born Yesterday,* and gave her a chance to vary her roles a little with *The Marrying Kind.* Their fourth time out was *It Should Happen to You,* another joyous treat for Judy lovers. They never worked together again. Although Judy remained a marvel, it was never quite the same. *It Should Happen* also introduced one of the most likely lads to come along for quite a time. He was Jack Lemmon who kept on going strong.

Crusoe and Friday as seen by Buñuel: Dan O'Herlihy and James Fernandez in *The Adventures of Robinson Crusoe.*

Mickey Rooney under the influence of Kevin McCarthy and Jack Kelly in *Drive a Crooked Road.*

Judy Holliday becomes a celebrity in *It Should Happen To You*. Really becoming a celebrity with this movie was the lad at her right, Jack Lemmon.

Charles Laughton and Brenda de Banzie in *Hobson's Choice*.

Two lonely little Nova Scotia boys, Jon Whitely and Vincent Winter, denied a pet, find a "babby," the seeming answer to their prayers. It's a girl—but Jon calls her Edward after the King. Vincent sticks resolutely to the name he had already chosen, "Rover." *The Little Kidnappers* was one of those completely entrancing pictures about children that the British do so appealingly. Duncan Macrae, Jean Anderson, Theodore Bikel, and Adrienne Corri were the adults; Philip Leacock directed Neil Paterson's screenplay.

Rene Clement's *Monsieur Ripois* had a checkered American career. Released here first as *That Frenchman,* the title was switched to *Lovers, Happy Lovers* but, under any name, it seemed to be too much for the censors. Later, very radically revised, it emerged as *Lover Boy,* but, by this time, the whole ironic point had disappeared in the editing. The New York Film Festival,

Celia Johnson, Ralph Richardson, and John Gregson in *The Holly and the Ivy.*

A wet kiss for Joan Greenwood and Gerard Philipe in *Monsieur Ripois.*

(ABOVE) James Hayter as Mr. Pickwick and James Donald as Mr. Winkle in *The Pickwick Papers*.

Jon Whiteley, Vincent Winter, and the "babby" they find in *The Little Kidnappers*.

eleven years later, restored it to its original condition and presented it as a retrospective under the new title of *Knave of Hearts* but that was the end of it. Shame, too. It was the one English language picture for Gerard Philipe who was brilliant as the deceptively boyish, compulsive seducer. Some of his victims were Joan Greenwood, Margaret Johnson, Germaine Montero, Valerie Hobson, and Natasha Parry.

Noel Langley, as faithfully as possible, brought *The Pickwick Papers* to film and, for the most part, it was a treat for Dickens addicts. But sometimes what is charming on the printed page turns silly and slapstick on film even when played by the best actors. And it had the best actors you could imagine for the roles—James Hayter as Mr. Pickwick, Nigel Patrick as Mr. Jingle, Kathleen Harrison, Joyce Grenfell, Hermione Gingold, Hermione Baddeley, James Donald, Harry Fowler, and Donald Wolfit, to mention a few.

Alexis Smith, who had been repressed all these years as just a beautiful leading woman, had begun to break out of that mold in recent pictures like *Here Comes the Groom* and *Split Second*. But, in a modest British melodrama, *The Sleeping Tiger,* she finally had a chance to play with all stops out, particularly in her scenes with the most electric young British actor of the period, Dirk Bogarde. Unfortunately their picture disappeared quickly and was no real help to either career. Victor Hanbury directed the Derek Frey script.

William Wellman gave us a movie classic with his filming of a Walter Van Tilburg Clark novel, *The Ox-Bow Incident.* Another Wellman–Clark collaboration (screenplay by A. I. Bezzerides) was much less successful in every way. *Track of the Cat* was stark and unpleasant, overloaded with symbolism. But there were strong compensations—the use of color, for instance, was unusual and effective, and some of the performances were notable. Beulah Bondi dominated the film as the harsh, bitter matriarch and Tab Hunter revealed unsuspected sensitivity as one of her sons. Robert Mitchum, Teresa Wright, Diana Lynn, and William Hopper had their moments, too.

Other Forgotten 1954 Films to Note

There was a strong scent of detergent from *About Mrs. Leslie* but Shirley Booth and Robert Ryan almost made it seem real. . . . Stewart Granger played *Beau Brummell* well enough but its high points were the performances of Peter Ustinov and Robert Morley, the look of

Alexis Smith and Dirk Bogarde in *The Sleeping Tiger.*

Tab Hunter and Beulah Bondi in *Track of the Cat.*

the Regency costumes and settings and, above all, the beauty of Elizabeth Taylor. . . . If blonde beauty was your bent, you couldn't beat Janet Leigh in her costume spectacles, *The Black Shield of Falworth* and *Prince Valiant.* The latter, based on the comic strip, turned out to be much more fun and with an excellent cast, headed by James Mason and Robert Wagner. . . . The Lerner and Loewe Broadway delight, *Brigadoon,* still had some charms on screen but, in spite of the should-be-surefire team of Vincente Minnelli, Gene Kelly, and Cyd Charisse, the movie seemed curiously lifeless. . . . Sigmund Romberg's story in *Deep in My Heart* was just as dreary as most composers' biographies but, if you liked Romberg music, a lot of it was well presented by a full supply of talents who ranged from Ann Miller to Helen Traubel. . . . Alec Guinness was just what you hoped he'd be as G. K. Chesterton's Father Brown, *The Detective,* but the story line was pretty tame. . . . Graham Greene's *The Heart of the Matter* seemed curiously placid and undramatic in spite of good performances by Trevor Howard, Maria Schell, Elizabeth Allen, Peter Finch, and Denholm Elliott. . . . Alexander Mackendrick, who made *Tight Little Island,* gave us another amusing picture about the Scots in *High and Dry,* this time with a blowhard American anatagonist as played by Paul Douglas. . . .

Danny Kaye was in his best form in years in *Knock on Wood* which gave him plenty of opportunity to do all the things he does best. . . . Unlike the movie in which Judy Holliday and Jack Lemmon first appeared together, *It Should Happen to You, Phffft* was broad and mostly unfunny marital farce—but Judy and Jack held their own. . . . *Riot in Cell Block 11* was a good tough prison melodrama, as directed by Don Siegel and played by a realistic cast of lesser-known actors (Neville Brand, Emile Meyer, Frank Faylen, among others). . . . *Rogue Cop* was good melodrama of its type with Robert Taylor, in the title role, pitted against George Raft, with Janet Leigh, Robert Ellenstein, Steve Forrest, Anne Francis also present. . . . Frank Sinatra gave an unexpectedly effective performance in *Suddenly* as a would-be Presidential assassin, which makes it obvious why it is seldom revived or shown on TV any more. . . . John Ford is supposed to have considered *The Sun Shines Bright* as his favorite film. We must confess a preference for the earlier Ford version of the same story, *Judge Priest* with Will Rogers—and even that is far from our favorite Ford. . . . Giant ants were the title characters in *Them,* a good, scary science fiction thriller. . . .

Chapter Twenty-Seven

The Movie Year of 1955

In 1955 the major movie honors go to a little picture, *Marty*, made in black-and-white for a regulation screen. But more and more big pictures are being made to take advantage of the values of CinemaScope and VistaVision. Todd A-O is the new process, introduced with *Oklahoma!* More similar to Cinerama than any other process, Todd A-O doesn't really draw its biggest attention until the second picture in the process, *Around the World in 80 Days*, comes out a year later.

TV has continued to furnish heavy competition and that is increasing as most movie companies plan to turn over their libraries to the channels. RKO and the majority of independents have already done so.

James Dean is the new star of the year but, before 1955 is over, a tragic accident has claimed his life. Others new to films in 1955 would include Shirley MacLaine, Joanne Woodward, Jo Van Fleet, Shirley Jones, Marisa Pavan, Peggy Lee, Sal Mineo, Richard Kiley, Dana Wynter, Dolores Grey, John-Kerr, Susan Strasberg, Jack Lord, and Joan Collins.

Let's list the movies of the year as Kazan's *East of Eden*, Delbert Mann's and Paddy Chayefsky's *Marty* and Nicholas Ray's *Rebel Without a Cause*. Others of special note would include *Blackboard Jungle; I'll Cry Tomorrow; Love Me or Leave Me; The Man With the Golden Arm; Mister Roberts; Oklahoma!; Picnic; The Rose Tattoo; The Seven Year Itch; Summertime;* and *To Catch a Thief*. But not such "big ones" as *Battle Cry; Guys and Dolls;* and *Love Is a Many Splendored Thing*.

There were, of course, the others. . .

Everett Sloane and Jack Palance in *The Big Knife*.

Forgotten Films of 1955

It wasn't easy to be very sympathetic to the premise of Clifford Odets's *The Big Knife*. His movie star protagonist seemed hardly worth saving, especially when he

seemed to have so little interest in saving himself. Yet, as directed by Robert Aldrich, and given searching performances by its cast—Rod Steiger, Ida Lupino, Wendell Corey, Shelley Winters, Jean Hagen, Everett Sloane and, especially, Jack Palance—it was pungent drama, even when you couldn't go all the way with it emotionally. James Poe wrote the screen adaptation.

Basically, Terence Rattigan's *The Deep Blue Sea* was fairly shallow romantic drama—the wife who leaves her kind and patient husband to live with an immature and selfish lover. But Rattigan wrote it with style and the somewhat hackneyed characters were superbly realized by excellent actors. Vivien Leigh gave one of her best, if least appreciated, performances and Kenneth More has never been finer than as the irresponsible lover. Notable, too, were Eric Portman, Emlyn Williams, Moira Lister, Arthur Hill, and the firm direction of Anatole Litvak.

Kenneth More tries to elude Vivien Leigh in *The Deep Blue Sea.*

Yvonne Mitchell and Michel Ray in *The Divided Heart.*

The Divided Heart was a British film dealing with the conflict in a custody fight for a young boy. The participants were a German couple who have raised him, believing him to be a war orphan, and the real mother who has finally returned from a prison camp. Jack Whittingham's screenplay and the performances of Yvonne Mitchell, Cornell Borchers, Michel Ray, and Armin Dahlen presented all of these characters with such compassion that a final decision could not be less than agonizing. Charles Crichton directed.

Like *Men in White* and all those other studies of the dedicated young medical men, *Doctor in the House* dealt with the youthful group who would become doctors. Unlike these others, it never had a serious thought. It was a merry affair with such normally solid citizens as Dirk Bogarde, Kenneth More, Donald Houston, Donald Sinden, and James Robertson Justice completely in the madcap spirit of it all. Its success spawned

Three boys and a bear—Dirk Bogarde, Donald Sinden, and Kenneth More in *Doctor in the House*.

Julie Harris as Sally Bowles in *I Am a Camera*.

Eleanor Parker as opera star Marjorie Lawrence with Glenn Ford in *Interrupted Melody.*

Dan Dailey, Gene Kelly, and Michael Kidd in *It's Always Fair Weather.*

several more *Doctor* movies—none with the fresh fun of this first. Richard Gordon adapted his own novel, Nicholas Phipps did the screen play, and Ralph Thomas directed.

Julie Harris repeated her Sally Bowles stage role in the film version of *I Am a Camera* and her performance was still very definitely something special to experience. But Henry Cornelius's direction and John Collier's script (from the John Van Druten play and Christopher Isherwood stories) made the movie a jumble of styles, seldom either funny or moving. The rest of the cast—Laurence Harvey, Anton Diffring, Shelley Winters, and Ron Randell—brought little of note to it. But there was still that Julie Harris performance.

One forgets what a good actress the attractive Eleanor Parker could be. Hollywood so seldom took advantage of her considerable talents. But, in *Interrupted Melody,* as Marjorie Lawrence the Australian opera star who overcame polio, she had every opportunity and seized

Robert Mitchum menaces Shelley Winters in *Night of the Hunter*.

Jack Webb carries the unconscious Peggy Lee in *Pete Kelly's Blues*.

each one. She, of course, did not do her own singing—there was the glorious Eileen Farrell to handle that—but, with the aid of Glenn Ford, she made a fine and inspirational movie that avoided the obvious pitfalls of maudlin sentimentality. William Ludwig and Sonya Levien wrote the screenplay; Curtis Bernhardt directed.

Most of the same talents who made *Singin' in the Rain* (producer Arthur Freed, directors Gene Kelly and Stanley Donen, stars Kelly and Cyd Charisse, writers Betty Comden and Adolph Green) reassembled for *It's Always Fair Weather*. It may not have had the magic of *Singin'*—what did?—but it was every inch a joy in its story of a civilian reunion of three servicemen buddies. There were plenty of barbs hurled at that upstart, television. Kelly, Dan Dailey, and Dolores Gray contributed particularly bright performances with Charisse and Michael Kidd around to aid mightily in the musical sequences. Yet it came at the end of the movie musical cycle, didn't do well at the box office, and is almost never remembered when the best musicals of the 1950s are recalled. Yet it belonged right up there with them.

Jack Hawkins and Alec Guinness in *The Prisoner.*

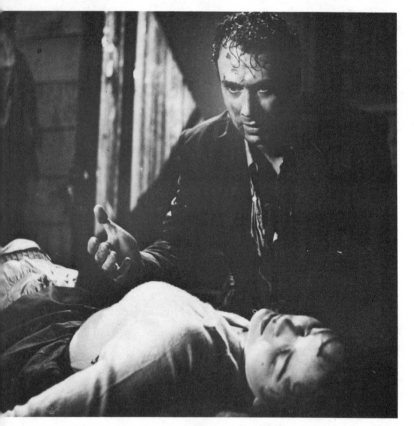

Richard Kiley and Kathryn Grant in *The Phenix City Story.*

James Agee wrote a brilliant screenplay from Davis Grubb's novel, *The Night of the Hunter,* and some excellent actors, under the direction of Charles Laughton, brought it to the screen as a darkly haunting melodrama of nightmare horror. Robert Mitchum was the personification of sinister evil as pitted against two children (Billy Chapin and Sally Ann Bruce) and a kind old lady (Lillian Gish). Shelley Winters had a marvelous vignette. Perhaps Laughton's direction was occasionally too self-consciously arty but it superbly maintained suspense.

What was right about *Pete Kelley's Blues?* Peggy Lee singing and, in a couple of brief dramatic moments, breaking your heart, Janet Leigh as a bewitching flapper, and Ella Fitzgerald being Ella Fitzgerald. Also, actors like Lee Marvin and Edmond O'Brien. And some good jazz. What was wrong? Richard L. Breen's script tailored to making the whole thing a vehicle for Jack Webb and Webb's direction which allowed actor Webb to get away with the same monotone, clichéd performance.

Certainly no actor could have been more convincingly cast as the great Edwin Booth than Richard Burton and it was when Burton played Booth as actor that *Prince of Players* came most excitingly alive. But the acting scenes were fragmentary—a snippet of *Hamlet* with Eva LeGallienne as the queen, a bit of *King Lear* with Raymond Massey as Junius Brutus Booth, and such. John Derek's John Wilkes Booth was flamboyant, too. But, except for such theatrical flashes, the script of Moss Hart and the direction of Philip Dunne left Burton often with long, placid plot and no theatrical excitement at all.

A sharp film, done in semidocumentary style by director Phil Karlson from a script by Crane Wilbur and Dan Mainwaring, was *The Phenix City Story.* Its story of crime and corruption in a town alive with vice came right from the headlines. John McIntire, Richard Kiley, and Edward Andrews headed a good cast of actors chosen for their rightness, not their "name value."

Alec Guinness is remembered from the 1950s for all manner of gentle comedy performances, almost not at all for the stunning dramatic characterization that may

Richard Burton as Edwin Booth, with Maggi McNamara, in *Prince of Players.*

June Allyson and José Ferrer in *The Shrike*.

be his screen masterpiece. In *The Prisoner*, a drama of ideologies proved as nerve-racking as any Hitchcock chase, as a brilliant and polished inquisitor attempts to brainwash a political prisoner, who is an honored cardinal of the Church. Almost entirely one long dialogue, this duel of wits was so forcefully projected by two of our most distinguished actors—Jack Hawkins was as striking as the interrogator—that the film never seemed static, never flagged in dramatic momentum. Peter Glenville directed Bridget Boland's screen play.

June Allyson was still the nice wife next door in *The Shrike* and any deeper implications in the character eluded her. And there were compromises which diluted the drama of the play. Jose Ferrer's agonized stage performance was somewhat weakened on screen but only because the story itself was weakened. For the most part it remained strong stuff. Ferrer directed the film as he had Joseph Kramm's play, adapted for films by Ketti Frings.

Other Forgotten 1955 Films to Remember

Robert Searle's *Belles of St. Trinian's* were as horren-

dous a bunch of moppets as you would care to meet in the film based on their adventures, but the adults, toothy Joyce Grenfell and especially Alastair Sim, as the headmistress, provided the real comedy. . . . Vincente Minnelli gathered together an impressive group of players (Lauren Bacall, Charles Boyer, Gloria Grahame, John Kerr, Susan Strasberg, Richard Widmark, and Lillian Gish) to play the patients and the sometimes even more neurotic staff of a psychiatric clinic in the film version of William Gibson's *The Cobweb*. . . . A pleasant country movie, *Count Three and Pray* gave Van Heflin another good role and, more importantly, introduced a marvelously scrappy tomboy, Joanne Woodward. . . . David Niven and Margaret Leighton were impressive in Anthony Asquith's excellent courtroom drama, *Court Martial*. . . . Also from Britain, four good, if not exceptional, melodramas, each starring the exceptional Michael Redgrave—*The Dam Busters* (with Richard Todd); *The Green Scarf* (Ann Todd and Leo Genn); *The Night My Number Came Up* (Alexander Knox and Denholm Elliott); *The Sea Shall Not Have Them* (Dirk Bogarde and Nigel Patrick). . . . The Evelyn Nesbit–Stanford White–Harry K. Thaw scandal was unbelievably brought to the screen in *The Girl in the Red Velvet Swing* but the art directors (Lyle R. Wheeler and Maurice Ransford) deserved a nod and so did most of the cast (Farley Granger, Cornelia Otis Skinner, Glenda Farrell, Luther Adler, Frances Fuller, and especially a lush Joan Collins in the title role). . . . *House of Bamboo* had a routine gangland story line but director Samuel Fuller gave it excitement and made full use of its Tokyo locales while Robert Ryan contributed another of his icy villain characterizations. . . . Although there were some good performances (notably by Irene Kane and Felice Orlandi), *Killer's Kiss* seemed primitive, yet with something a little special about it. (You'd soon know that there was always something special about a Stanley Kubrick movie.) . . . Robert Aldrich's *Kiss Me Deadly* is one of the best, if least known examples of 1950s film *noir* with a cast including Ralph Meeker, Albert Dekker, Juano Hernandez, Paul Stewart, Cloris Leachman, Wesley Addy, Gaby Rodgers, Jack Lambert, and Jack Elam. . . . John Ford dealt with two of the subjects dearest to his heart—the Irish and the Army—in *The Long Gray Line* with Tyrone Power heading a cast of such Ford familiars as Maureen O'Hara, Ward Bond, and Donald Crisp. . . .

Richard Todd's deeply human characterization (with

assist from Jean Peters) was the principal reason that *A Man Called Peter* was affecting religious drama. . . . Another of these James Stewart/Anthony Mann Westerns but a pretty good representative of the type was *The Man From Laramie* which had some other good actors (Arthur Kennedy, Aline MacMahon, Donald Crisp, and Alex Nicol) in support. . . . Too bad John Justin was so uncharismatic in the title role of *The Man Who Loved Redheads*. There was an amusing Terence Rattigan script and bright bits by Gladys Cooper, Roland Culver, Denholm Elliott, and Moira Shearer in four different roles. . . . William Campbell (what ever happened to him?) stole King Vidor's *Man Without a Star* right out from under the noses of veterans Kirk Douglas, Claire Trevor, Jeanne Crain, and Richard Boone. . . . We resented the Jule Styne/Leo Robin version of *My Sister Eileen* because it meant we'd never have a film version of the Bernstein/Comden and Green *Wonderful Town* but still had to give high marks to Betty Garrett, Jack Lemmon, Bob Fosse, and an adorable Janet Leigh as Eileen. . . . It certainly wasn't what you'd expect as the ideal movie *Othello* but leave it to Orson Welles to make it fascinating. . . . Charlton Heston got a long way from the Bible in *The Private War of Major Benson*, which was enjoyable even though it got a little over-cute at times. . . .

Tight Spot, a tight little Phil Karlson melodrama, brought Ginger Rogers happily back to the kind of Roxie Hart characters she once was able to play. She managed it well, with good support by Brian Keith, Edward G. Robinson, Eve McVeagh, Katherine Anderson, and Lorne Green. . . . Arthur Kennedy's vivid portrayal of an unscrupulous defense attorney was the most impressive element in *Trial*. . . . There was almost no suspense and very little real humor, in spite of Alfred Hitchcock, in *The Trouble With Harry* but it was a pleasure to welcome Shirley MacLaine to movies. . . . Richard Fleischer mixed up three bank robbers (Lee Marvin, J. Carrol Naish, and Stephen McNally) with some unpleasant residents of a Peyton Place-type small town (Richard Egan, Sylvia Sidney, and Victor Mature) for a lurid and far-fetched *Violent Saturday*. . . . Bette Davis was again every inch *The Virgin Queen* and Richard Todd's Raleigh was a much more worthy antagonist than had been Errol Flynn's Essex whom Good Queen Bette loved fifteen-odd years earlier. . . .

Chapter Twenty Eight

The Movie Year of 1956

The year 1956 is filled with big ones. Not just big screens, but epic pictures—each attempting to outdo its predecessor in length, expense, and sheer magnitude. There are George Stevens's *Giant*, King Vidor's *War and Peace*, and Cecil B. DeMille's *The Ten Commandments*. Don't forget *The King and I*, *Carousel*, *Anastasia*, *Richard III*, *Moby Dick*, and *Alexander the Great*. But the biggest hit of all is Mike Todd's *Around the World in 80 Days*, not just because of length, stars, and spectacle but because it is, first and foremost, an entertainment with more fun than the circus.

TV continues to be even more of a threat when it uses ammunition provided by Hollywood itself. For now almost all movie companies have sold their old product to the channels. When there's a choice between catching, say, Bette Davis in *Dark Victory* in your living room and going out to see Bette in *Storm Center*, chances are you'll stay home. Also, most studios now have TV subsidiaries and, in some cases, these are more active than their parents.

The art theaters are booming, not only with imports, but as showcases for some specialized product from the majors. With a *Lust for Life*, such handling pays off but not even art house treatment can save a *Gaby* or an *Invitation to the Dance*.

Location shooting has reached its peak and it's a rare spot on the globe which doesn't know what it is to have an entire movie company move in. All but a very few of the major movies of the year have been shot, at least in part, outside of Hollywood.

Yul Brynner, in his first movie year, has three hits and wins an Oscar. Carroll Baker gets more publicity attention than any of the rest of the year's newcomers, but others becoming familiar for the first time include Cliff Robertson, Eli Wallach, Anita Ekberg, Eileen Heckart, William Smithers, Don Murray, Hope Lange, Earl Holliman, Stephen Boyd, John Cassavetes, Victoria Shaw, Bill Travers, and the elderly Katie Johnson.

Our own particular favorite movies of the year are not what you would call big ones. They are John Ford's *The Searchers* and Stanley Kubrick's *The Killing*. But there are also Kazan's *Baby Doll*; Marilyn Monroe in Joshua Logan's *Bus Stop*; Gary Cooper in Wyler's *Friendly Persuasion*; Don Siegel's *Invasion of the Body Snatchers*; Hitchcock's new version of *The Man Who Knew Too Much*; and Douglas Sirk's *Written on the Wind*. And we would include *Forbidden Planet*; *High Society*; *The Lady Killers*; *The Rainmaker*; *The Solid Gold Cadillac*; *Somebody Up There Likes Me*; *The Swan*; *Tea and Sympathy*; *Teahouse of the August Moon*; and *Trapeze*.

And then there were those other worthy contenders which don't leap as quickly to the memory. . . .

Forgotten Films of 1956

A war film in which the principal antagonists were American army officers—dealing not with the Flagg–Quirt sort of buddy bickering but with a deep-rooted personal war—was Robert Aldrich's *Attack!* James Poe wrote an explosive screen play based on Norman Brooks's play, *Fragile Fox.* Jack Palance was a fierce avenger; Eddie Albert gave dimension to the unexpected role of a craven captain. Notable, too—Lee Marvin, William Smithers, Richard Jaeckel, and Buddy Ebsen.

An intriguing, if somewhat far-fetched story by Douglas Morrow had a lawyer framing himself for murder in order to test the law. This was *Beyond a Reasonable Doubt,* which Fritz Lang directed straightforwardly and in which Dana Andrews played the pivotal character. A good cast (Joan Fontaine, Philip Bourneuf, Sidney Blackmer, and Shepperd Strudwick) supported.

George Cukor brought John Masters's novel, *Bhowani Junction* (screenplay by Sonya Levien and Ivan Moffet) to turbulent life on the screen. Filmed in Pakistan, it dealt with political problems in India with Ava Gardner, still in the period of her greatest beauty, as an Anglo-Indian of divided loyalties.

The Nicholas Ray cultists give *Bigger Than Life* high marks although it was pretty well dismissed by critics and audiences of its time. Based by Cyril Hume and Richard Maibaum on a *New Yorker* article by Berton Roueche, it detailed the unpredictable effects of the drug cortisone on a man whose illness demands it. Although the picture veered from seeming too clinical to going too melodramatically overboard, there was a frighteningly real performance of the victim by James Mason. With Barbara Rush and Walter Matthau.

Mickey Rooney's virtuouso and seemingly extemporaneous crap game sequence in *The Bold and the Brave* was one of those scenes that stay with you even if you may have forgotten the movie in which they appeared. That was no great loss in what was basically a movie made up of shameless borrowings from earlier and better films. Wendell Corey, Nicole Maurey, and Don Taylor were capable but it was Rooney who counted. Lewis R. Foster directed the Robert Lewin screen play.

In *The Catered Affair,* Paddy Chayefsky wrote (with Gore Vidal doing the screenplay) of Irish-Americans in the Bronx. And although they can be many things, it was not easy to accept Bette Davis and Ernest Borgnine

Eddie Albert and William Smithers in *Attack!*

The district attorney (Philip Bourneuf) questions Dana Andrews in *Beyond a Reasonable Doubt.*

(ABOVE) Stanley Adams and Wright King flank Mickey Rooney in the crap-game scene in *The Bold and the Brave*.

Walter Matthau, Christopher Olsen, Barbara Rush, James Mason in *Bigger Than Life*.

Ava Gardner in *Bhowani Junction*.

as Irish or Bronx. And Barry Fitzgerald seemed still in the old country. Still Davis has such command that she eventually made you believe her as Aggie Hurley, not just as Bette Davis trying something new. Debbie Reynolds, out of her usual cutie-pie element, was real, there was a good bit by Joan Camden, and such others as Ray Stricklyn, Dorothy Stickney, Madge Kennedy, and Rod Taylor helped. Richard Brooks directed.

If you were lucky, you saw *Come Next Spring* on the lower half of a double bill, a position to which it was doomed. It was a very simple little movie but had great

feeling and rated a better fate. Steve Cochran and Ann Sheridan reveal unexpected insight in roles unusual for them while Sherry Jackson and Richard Eyer were more than mere movie children. R. G. Springsteen and Montgomery Pittman directed and wrote respectively.

Al Morgan's stinging attack on hypocrisy in the radio industry, *The Great Man*, was brought honestly and effectively to the screen. Morgan wrote the screen play with Jose Ferrer, who also directed and played the principal role of an investigative reporter who uncovers the deception that hides the fact that a beloved personality

Debbie Reynolds, Ernest Borgnine, and Bette Davis in
The Catered Affair.

of the airwaves is really a cold-blooded heel. Julie London, Dean Jagger, Jim Backus, and particularly Keenan Wynn and Ed Wynn gave strong support.

Budd Schulberg's *The Harder They Fall* made good movie exposé of an unsavory side of the prizefight racket as brought to the screen by director Mark Robson and screenwriter Philip Yordan. Rod Steiger gave one of his snarling performances as an unscrupulous promoter, Mike Lane was the giant, childlike South American prizefighter who is used, and Jan Sterling played a disillusioned wife. Humphrey Bogart, in his last film role, had the nominal lead.

Gregory Peck had a role that fitted him well in *The Man in the Gray Flannel Suit*, Nunnally Johnson's film version of the popular Sloan Wilson novel about the men who move between their Madison Avenue offices and suburban homes. Other roles were cast as carefully with Fredric March, Ann Harding, Marisa Pavan, Keenan Wynn, and Lee J. Cobb most notable. Jennifer Jones overdid the neuroticism of the wife.

José Ferrer and Ed Wynn in *The Great Man.*

An outstanding television drama of the 1950s was Rod Serling's *Patterns,* an engrossing study of big business and of personal conflicts in the executive suites. Brought to the big screen with Fielder Cook again directing Serling's screenplay and most of the original television cast —Van Heflin was a replacement and a good one—it remained as compelling as the original. Everett Sloane, Ed Begley, Elizabeth Wilson, and Beatrice Straight repeated their heralded television performances.

Another Rod Serling television drama less impressively brought to the screen was *The Rack* but it had an intensely affecting performance by Paul Newman as an Army officer accused of collaborating with the enemy. Otherwise it was fairly regulation courtroom drama. Wendell Corey, Edmond O'Brien, Walter Pidgeon, Anne Francis, Lee Marvin, and Cloris Leachman had supporting roles; Stewart Stern wrote the screenplay, Arnold Laven directed.

While the City Sleeps was a good newspaper/murder melodrama made better by the direction of Fritz Lang and the performances of a good cast. The latter included Dana Andrews, Sally Forrest, Ida Lupino, George Sanders, Vincent Price, Rhonda Fleming, Thomas Mitchell, Howard Duff, and John Barrymore, Jr. Casey Robinson wrote the screenplay.

Humphrey Bogart, Nehemiah Persoff, and Rod Steiger in *The Harder They Fall.*

The Man in the Gray Flannel Suit (Gregory Peck) at the office with executives Fredric March, Arthur O'Connell, and Henry Daniell.

Sherry Jackson, Richard Eyer, Steve Cochran, and Ann Sheridan in *Come Next Spring.*

Other Forgotten 1956 Pictures to Note

That murdering child came to the screen in *The Bad Seed* but, in spite of a fairly faithful transcription and a cast including most of the original stage players (Nancy Kelly, Eileen Heckart, Henry Jones, and Patty McCormack), it had lost a lot of its horror. . . . Danny Kaye was *The Court Jester* in a broad and funny take-off on movies of medieval romance and derring-do with Glynis Johns, Angela Lansbury, Mildred Natwick, Basil Rathbone, and Cecil Parker. . . . Reginald Rose's movie version of his TV play, *Crime in the Streets,* was better than standard juvenile delinquency melodrama, as directed by Don Siegel, and particularly because of John Cassavetes, Mark Rydell, Sal Mineo, and Ray Stricklyn as principal young punks. . . . Carol Reed's *A Kid for Two Farthings* had nice touches all the way through but couldn't sustain its charm, although Celia Johnson brought her special gifts to a role too slight. . . . Ira Levin's novel about a psycopathic killer (Robert Wagner), *A Kiss Before Dying,* lost most of its suspense in screen form but is notable for the performance of Joanne Woodward as a pathetic victim. . . . *Lease of Life* was a quiet little drama with an intensely moving performance by Robert Donat as a dying vicar, and fine work, too, by Kay Walsh. . . . A good wartime spy thriller, based on an actual case, was *The Man Who Never Was* with Clifton Webb, Stephen Boyd. . . . *Nightmare* was rather ingenious suspense melodrama with a particularly effective performance by Kevin McCarthy. . . . George Orwell's *1984* came to the screen as a mildly scary, futuristic melodrama, with good performances by Edmond O'Brien, Michael Redgrave, and Jan Sterling. . . . *The Proud and the Profane* was a conventional wartime love story, given more importance by the performances of its stars, William Holden and Deborah Kerr. . . . Peter Finch and Kay Kendall amusingly parodied British television talk shows in *Simon and Laura.* . . . Bette Davis gave another strong performance as a librarian fighting prejudice in *Storm Center.* . . . Bob Hope had one of his more solid comedy roles as the ghost writer for a famous and unpleasant cartoonist (George Sanders) in *That Certain Feeling.* . . . *Wee Geordie* was Bill Travers and he was just fine as a weakling who becomes a muscle man in a nice little movie which also had the benefit of Alastair Sim. . . .

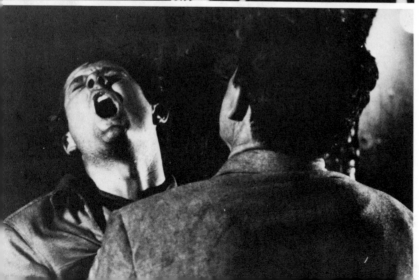

(TOP) Van Heflin and Ed Begley in *Patterns.*

(CENTER) Paul Newman and Lee Marvin in *The Rack.*

(LEFT) Dana Andrews collars John Barrymore, Jr., in *White the City Sleeps.*

Chapter Twenty-Nine

The Movie Year of 1957

The movie box office continues to dip in 1957. Big hits seem bigger than ever before. Everybody goes to see them. But when they stay away, they stay away in droves. And they're staying away from many really fine films. The studios are hurting and one major, RKO radio, gives up the struggle and folds.

It's a year, too, in which many of the old guard—writers, directors and actors—seem tired in contrast to the vitality of comparative youngsters. Certain youthful TV-trained directors bring a fresh approach to the screen in some comparatively minor budget movies whose originality is a prime selling point. Few of these, it must be admitted, do as well at the box office as more conventional, expensive product. Even so, they've started something.

Some censorship bars are let down and the screen finds material in such hitherto tabu subjects as impotence, nymphomania, miscegenation and drug addiction. Pat Boone and Elvis Presley transfer to films with Boone doing well enough. But Elvis, still sending the rock-and-roll set, is savaged by the critics. (It will be that way through his whole movie career but it's a career that lasts long after clean-cut Pat has given up.) Sophia Loren and Kay Kendall are particularly welcome imports. Others, making their first big push this year, are Tony Randall, Anthony Franciosa, James MacArthur, Ernie Kovacs, Inger Stevens, Mary LaRoche, Red Buttons, Carol Haney, Robert Ivers, Georgiann John-son, Carmen Sevilla, Hal March, Norma Moore, Kay Thompson, Taina Elg, Leora Dana, Bobby Sherwood, Heather Sears, Jayne Mansfield, Patricia Owens, Dolores Michaels, Augusta Dabney, James Daly, John Raitt, Dina Merrill, Robert Evans, Pat Hingle, Andy Griffith, and Suzy Parker. There is a lot of promise there but surprisingly few will make it. Movie studios are no longer pushing their contract players as they once did. And, before too long, there will be no more contract players at all.

We'll pick three as the pictures of the year—Sidney Lumet's *Twelve Angry Men* with Henry Fonda heading a perfect cast, Stanley Kubrick's *Paths of Glory*, and David Lean's *Bridge on the River Kwai*. Better add Stanley Donen's *Funny Face*, with Astaire and Audrey Hepburn, for sheer joy. Others of very special note could include *Designing Woman; A Hatful of Rain; The Incredible Shrinking Man; Love in the Afternoon; Sayonara; Sweet Smell of Success;* and *Witness for the Prosecution.* And a nod to a number of others for varied reasons including, in some cases, their popularity—*An Affair to Remember; The Brave One; A Farewell to Arms; Gunfight at the OK Corral; Pajama Game; Pal Joey; Peyton Place; The Prince and the Showgirl; Raintree County; Silk Stockings;* and *The Spirit of St. Louis.*

But then there were the others you may no longer remember.

E. G. Marshall, Philip Abbott, Don Murray, and Jack Warden in *Bachelor Party.*

Forgotten Films of 1957

Bachelor Party, like all of Paddy Chayefsky's work, had the wonderful comedy of recognition, the almost unbearable pathos of frustration, and immediate identification for a big percentage of its audience. Delbert Mann again (he had also directed *Marty*) caught the full flavor of Chayefsky characters. It was one of those pictures in which every single member of a cast—Don Murray, Jack Warden, E. G. Marshall, Philip Abbott, Carolyn Jones, and the rest—was so completely right that he or she seemed not to be acting at all.

Martin Ritt's first movie directorial job was *Edge of the City,* adapted from his own television play by Robert Alan Aurthur. Though vaguely reminiscent of *On the Waterfront,* it was something very different for the screen. Primarily it was a story of friendship. That the friendship was between a white boy and a black was all the more compelling because no attempt was made to point at the picture's bravery in handling such a relationship. Sidney Poitier played with lusty vitality with John Cassavetes giving intensity to his role. Other worthy performances by Jack Warden, Ruby Dee, and Kathleen Maguire.

With sure, telling strokes, Director Elia Kazan and Writer Budd Schulberg ripped into the fabric of fame for

Jack Warden, Sidney Poitier, and John Cassavetes in *Edge of the City.*

Andy Griffith is lionized by TV moguls, with his sharp PR man, Anthony Franciosa, at his side, in *Face in the Crowd.*

232

the devastating discussion of mob hysteria in the worship of a public idol. But *A Face in the Crowd* built to a striking peak, then tapered off to an unsatisfying ending. Andy Griffith was frightening as the superstar; such comparative newcomers as Anthony Franciosa, Lee Remick, Walter Matthau, and Kay Medford scored as did veterans Patricia Neal and Paul McGrath.

Fear Strikes Out covered the mental crackup of Red Sox centerfielder Jim Piersall. This was handled without sensationalism by director Robert Mulligan with Anthony Perkins in a tortured performance as Piersall. Karl Malden was strong, too, as his demanding father. Ted Berkman and Raphael Blau wrote the screen play.

Put a nun on a deserted island with a marine. Chances are it will become objectionably sexy or else veer to the other extreme becoming sloppily spiritual. But not with writer/director John Huston keeping the situation well in hand. *Heaven Knows, Mr. Allison* was an appealing, intimate movie with Deborah Kerr lovely as the nun and Robert Mitchum giving one of his top performances. John Lee Mahin co-authored the screen play.

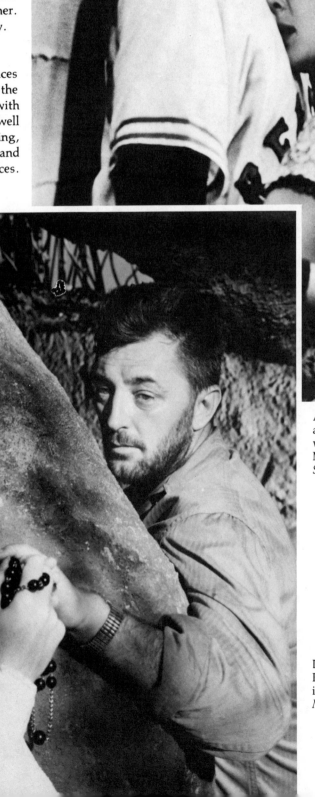

Anthony Perkins, as Jim Pearsall, with Norma Moore in *Fear Strikes Out.*

Deborah Kerr and Robert Mitchum in *Heaven Knows, Mr. Allison.*

233

Kay Kendall finally got that full-length movie role to give her a chance to repeat what she had done so brilliantly but briefly in *Genevieve. Les Girls* was the movie that gave her the part. Deftly directed by George Cukor, it had a *Rashomon* kind of plot in which the events are seen through different eyes. It also had such eyefuls as Mitzi Gaynor and Taina Elg, with Gene Kelly doing all the things he knows how to do better than anyone. John Patrick wrote the screenplay and there was a Cole Porter score—not his best perhaps but any Porter score is special.

There may have been more than a touch of melodrama in *No Down Payment* and its four young couples living in a housing development may have been overboard on problems. But, as directed by Martin Ritt and played by an extremely good group of actors, it had dramatic urgency in its study of a phase of contemporary life. Tony Randall as a pathetic phony and Joanne Woodward as a mistreated wife may have had the acting edge but it's difficult to see how any of the actors—also including Sheree North, Cameron Mitchell, Pat Hingle, Jeffrey Hunter, Barbara Rush, and Patricia Owens—could have been improved. Script by Philip Yordan.

The Smallest Show on Earth was the title of what must have been one of the smallest movies of its time. But it was big in amusement in its look at some of the employees and patrons of a decrepit British movie theatre. Bill Travers and Virginia McKenna played the new owners coping with every misfortune that could occur. Among their principal trials were their cashier, projectionist, and doorman but they were our pleasures as played by Margaret Rutherford, Peter Sellers, and Bernard Miles. Basil Dearden directed the William Rose and John Eldridge screenplay.

The Spanish Gardener, A. J. Cronin's study of the relationships among a lonely boy, his possessive father, and the peasant gardener who gives the boy warmth and understanding, came to the screen as a minor but moving little drama. It had fine performances by Dirk Bogarde in the title role, Michael Hordern as the father, and Jon Whiteley as the boy. Lesley Storm and John Bryan wrote the screenplay. Philip Leacock directed.

Darryl F. Zanuck obviously spared no expense in bringing Ernest Hemingway's *The Sun Also Rises* to the screen. Peter Viertel's screen play remained close to its source and Henry King put the characters on a big, splashy canvas that effectively recreated the Paris and Spain of the 1920s. The cast—Tyrone Power, Ava Gardner, Mel Ferrer, Errol Flynn, and Eddie Albert—might have been ideal as members of Hemingway's lost

(LEFT) Gene Kelly surrounded by *Les Girls* (Kay Kendall the sobbing one, Mitzi Gaynor, and Taina Elg).

Repentant Tony Randall returns home after a spree to wife Sheree North and son Charles Herbert in *No Down Payment*.

Jon Whiteley and Dirk Bogarde in *The Spanish Gardener*.

(ABOVE) Virginia McKenna and Bill Travers (with Leslie Phillips) meet the run-down staff (Peter Sellers, Bernard Miles, and Margaret Rutherford) of the run-down cinema they will operate in *The Smallest Show on Earth*.

A sympathetic railroad conductor helps John Beal, who is having a heart attack, in *That Night*.

generation if they had played the roles some dozen years earlier. (Newer faces Robert Evans and Juliette Greco were more convincing in support.) But the main problem with *The Sun Also Rises* is that it seemed to have been filmed some twenty-five years too late.

John Beal, one of the most underrated of fine actors, gave a vivid performance as an advertising executive stricken with a heart attack in *That Night*. The New York-made film (produced by Himan and Mende Brown; directed by John Newland; written by Robert Wallace and Jack Rowles; featuring actors like Augusta Dabney, Rosemary Murphy, Jan Miner, and Shepperd Strudwick) sometimes looked like a television drama (it had been adapted from one) but its lack of movie slickness was an asset. And the unsparing anguish of Beal's performance can't be forgotten by the very few who saw it.

Hemingway's "lost generation" characters in *The Sun Also Rises* as played by Ava Gardner, Tyrone Power, Mel Ferrer, Eddie Albert, Errol Flynn.

Don't confuse *This Could Be the Night* with *That Night* even though they played theatres at approximately the same time. *This Could Be . . .* was an amiable fairy tale in the Capra–Runyon mold which had to do with Jean Simmons as Riding Hood in the den of such likable wolves as Anthony Franciosa (his movie debut) and Paul Douglas. Julie Wilson, Joan Blondell, and Neile Adams were around, too. Robert Wise directed the Isobel Lennart screenplay.

Time Limit, an engrossing Broadway play by Henry Denker and Ralph Berkey, was intelligently adapted to the screen by Denker. Intelligent, too, was the film's direction by Karl Malden, and the performances of the entire cast. There were Richard Widmark (who also co-produced the film), as the judge advocate, and Richard Basehart, as an Army major accused of treason in Korea

Martin Balsam, Rip Torn, and Richard Widmark in *Time Limit*.

Anthony Perkins and Henry Fonda in *The Tin Star*.

Jean Simmons and Anthony Franciosa in *This Could Be the Night*.

—estimable antagonists as characters and as actors. But notable too were others—Rip Torn, Martin Balsam, Carl Benton Reid, Dolores Michaels, June Lockhart, and Yale Wexler.

Although *The Tin Star* may not have had the sweep of, say, *My Darling Clementine*, it gave Henry Fonda another characterization in which he could be just as courageous and just as laconic. This time he also tutored youthful Anthony Perkins in the business of being a fearless western sheriff. They made a likable combination. Dudley Nichols wrote the screenplay with Anthony Mann directing.

Frank Tashlin, who wrote, directed, and produced *Will Success Spoil Rock Hunter?* for films, threw away virtually everything that was in George Axelrod's Broadway play except the title and Jayne Mansfield. The latter's spectacular equipment was used to the same effect in the movie and she played virtually the same role but just about everything else was redone for the film. Now it was a takeoff on television and advertising and you could almost forgive Tashlin for sacrificing the original play premise because he gave Tony Randall a chance to show off all of his special talents as a frantic ad man. That was enough for complete merriment.

Alfred Hitchcock tried something different in *The Wrong Man*—almost documentary drama in its picturization of a well-known true case. But there was no chance for the Hitchcock trademark of suspense where the ending was already a matter of record. Even so, it was engrossing drama with an honest, untheatrical characterization by Henry Fonda and notable work as well by Vera Miles and Anthony Quayle. Screenplay by Maxwell Anderson and Angus McPhail.

An extremely youthful group—producer Stuart Millar, director John Frankenheimer, writer Robert Dozier, and actor James MacArthur—joined to make their first movie. In *The Young Stranger*, they came up with an extremely good little one—the story of a misunderstood boy who is, praise be, neither a *Rebel Without a Cause* nor yet a *Blackboard Jungle* delinquent. Young MacArthur was the kind of youngster to whom any audience could relate, rare in that era's treatment of youth.

Other Forgotten 1957 Films to Remember

Mickey Rooney gave another offbeat performance as a psychopathic killer in Don Siegel's *Baby Face Nelson*. . . . *Full of Life* was hardly typical Judy Holiday fare in

Tony Randall and Jayne Mansfield cut a rug in *Will Success Spoil Rock Hunter?*

Henry Fonda in the paddy wagon in *The Wrong Man*.

James MacArthur as *The Young Stranger*. Kim Hunter is his mother.

its treatment of pregnancy and mixed marriage but Judy remained winning even against the sometimes comic, more often too heavy, caricature of an Italian father-in-law by Salvatore Baccaloni. . . . Alastair Sim was again in top form—this time as an unlikely assassin—in a modest little British comedy, *The Green Man*. . . . *Island in the Sun* was considered courageous at the time because it flirted with miscegenation but the chief rewards were pictorial—the lush Caribbean scenery and the physical attractiveness of such cast members as Harry Belafonte, Dorothy Dandridge, Joan Fontaine, Joan Collins, James Mason, Patricia Owens, and Stephen Boyd. . . . Speaking of something special to see, we had Suzy Parker in *Kiss Them for Me* but the picture was one long servicemen-on-leave cliché which even Cary Grant couldn't help. . . . Such actors as Buster Keaton and Jeanne Eagels were savaged by movie biographies; Lon Chaney fared better in *Man of a Thousand Faces*, particularly because he had the advantage of a dynamic characterization by James Cagney. . . . Nunnally Johnson's screen version of *Oh Men! Oh Women!* retained much of the merriment of Edward Chodorov's stage spoof of psychoanalysis, particularly in the giddy goings-on of Tony Randall and Dan Dailey to whom David Niven played suave straight man. . . . Lionel Rogosin's *On the Bowery* was straightforward camera reportage of life on Skid Row, more akin to magazine pictorial journalism than to motion picture drama. . . . *Operation Mad Ball* was military comedy, lots of tomfoolery, played to the hilt by such maniacs as Jack Lemmon, Ernie Kovacs, and Mickey Rooney. . . . *Reach for the Sky* was a standard inspirational biography of an amputee RAF hero but it had something special going for it—Kenneth More's performance. . . . John Ford was always happy involved with the Irish and, in *Rising of the Moon*, he indulged himself by presenting three inconsequential but entertaining stories from the Emerald Isle. . . . Robert Ruark's *Something of Value* was brought to the screen by Richard Brooks as an effective drama of the Mau Mau uprising with excellent performances by Rock Hudson and Sidney Poitier as boyhood friends who wind up on opposite sides of the bloody events. . . . No longer an indictment of the military school system, Calder Willingham's *End As a Man,* brought to the screen as *The Strange One,* had more to do with some very strange ones brought incongruously together, although Ben Gazzara retained his glittering magnetism as the evil Jocko DeParis. . . . *The Tall T* was one of those lively Budd Boetticher Westerns with Randolph Scott and Maureen O'Sullivan. . . .

Director Douglas Sirk and actors Rock Hudson, Dorothy Malone and Robert Stack, who had scored with *Written on the Wind*, reteamed for *Tarnished Angels,* based on an obscure William Faulkner novel, with much less satisfactory results. . . . Although the story line of *3:10 to Yuma* was too close to that of *High Noon* to put the movie on the top shelf of Westerns, it had its excitements and was well played by Van Heflin, Glenn Ford, and Richard Jaeckel . . . George Cukor's *Wild Is the Wind*, based on the Italian film, *Furia,* and also owing plenty to *They Knew What They Wanted*, merged Anna Magnani, Anthony Franciosa, and Anthony Quinn in a steamy but old-fashioned triangle drama. . . . *Woman in a Dressing Gown* was kitchen sink drama, British style, with Yvonne Mitchell pathetic as a slob of a wife and Anthony Quayle believable as the husband who can't take it any more. . . .

Chapter Thirty

The Movie Year of 1958

Things are about the same in 1958. The studios are talking about getting even chummier with television. There's conversation about selling blocks of post-1948 movies, very recent ones, for exhibition on the tube and even exhibiting current hits on some sort of pay TV. Neither happens—yet.

Another movie company bites the dust—Republic. (What, no more Vera Hruba Ralston?) Studio contract lists are almost a thing of the past. Most major stars are long since free of their contracts and work independently. Contract lists are mostly made of young hopefuls.

Among the personalities who are getting first attention in 1958, there is nothing to indicate that Sean Connery, Steve McQueen, Clint Eastwood, and James Garner will be any more valuable movie acquisitions than, say, William Shatner, Al (David) Hedison, Clint Kimbrough, or Felice Orlandi. Others whose movie debuts or first major roles come in 1958 include Bradford Dillman, May Britt, Troy Donahue, Sandra Dee, Suzanne Pleshette, Peter Falk, James Franciscus, Tuesday Weld, Dorothy Provine, Tom Tryon, Natalie Trundy, Tommy Sands, John Saxon, Evelyn Rudie, John Gavin, Will Hutchins, Steve Ihnat, Tina Louise, France Nuyen, Patty Duke, Gary Crosby, Linda Cristal, Joanna Barnes, James Drury, Christine Carrere, and Darren McGavin. Melina Mercouri does her first film in the English language and so does Maximillian Schell. Some imports from the theatre, TV, or nightclub worlds who try their movie wings but go back to greener fields elsewhere are Irene Worth, Paul Anka, Elaine Aiken, Toni Arden, Phyllis Newman, Peggy Cass, Barrie Chase, Jill Corey, Della Reese, Mort Sahl, Joan Copeland, George Gobel, Buddy Hackett, Betty Lou Holland, Dorothy Tutin, Kim Stanley, and Jean Stapleton. But Maureen Stapleton, Susan Strasberg, Eileen Heckart, Christopher Plummer, and Elizabeth Wilson will do more regular movie work even though they never desert the theatre.

To this corner, Orson Welles's *Touch of Evil* and Hitchcock's *Vertigo* are probably the best films of a not too exciting year. And the Lerner–Loewe–Minnelli *Gigi* turns out to be just about the last triumph of the golden era of original movie musicals. Other movies to note would include *Cat on a Hot Tin Roof; Separate Tables; Some Came Running;* and *The Young Lions,* while to be mentioned for their quality and/or popularity would be *Auntie Mame; Damn Yankees; The Defiant Ones; The Fly; I Want to Live; The Last Hurrah; The Old Man and the Sea;* and *South Pacific.*

Then there were those others—the virtually forgotten good films of 1958.

Forgotten Films of 1958

They laughed when Marilyn Monroe insisted she wanted to play Grushenka in *The Brothers Karamazov.* But Maria Schell, imported for the occasion, didn't satisfy them either. Schell, with a mocking smile, played it in cooly enigmatic style that hardly fit the Monroe concept. There was really no way a filmization of Dostoevski's immense classic could succeed. The purists would resent any condensation; the ordinary theatergoer would find it sprawling and overlong. Still Richard Brooks's screenplay and direction of a well-chosen cast (Yul Brynner, Richard Basehart, Lee J. Cobb, Claire Bloom, Albert Salmi, William Shatner, and Judith Evelyn) did probably the best job possible. An ideal screen version may have to wait for a PBS-TV series.

Speaking of Marilyn Monroe, she may have been a superficial inspiration for the character of the miserable movie actress created by Paddy Chayefsky in *The Goddess.* But, particularly as played by Kim Stanley, any

Maria Schell as Grushenka, Yul Brynner, one of *The Brothers Karamazov*, glowers.

Kim Stanley breaks down at the funeral of her mother in *The Goddess*. With her are Elizabeth Wilson and Joan Linville.

Robert Ryan and Jack Lord in *God's Little Acre*. Do the legs belong to Tina Louise (probably) or Fay Spain?

resemblances to Monroe or any other known star was unimportant. The Stanley character was very much a real, original, full-bodied characterization, not just a pale cinematic reflection of real-life Judys and Marilyns. Stanley, one of the most extraordinary actresses of our time, was surrounded by other fine actors—notably Betty Lou Holland, but also Elizabeth Wilson, Lloyd Bridges, Steve Hill, Joan Copeland, Patty Duke, and others. John Cromwell directed.

Screenwriter Philip Yordan, director Anthony Mann and a top cast managed to do with *God's Little Acre* what John Ford and Nunnally Johnson couldn't pull off in *Tobacco Road*—bring Erskine Caldwell's colorful Georgia rednecks to the screen as believable people, not just figures out of an Al Capp cartoon. The ribald humor, the stark tragedy, the animal sex—all of the elements that made the book an all-time best-seller—were present in the picture. The remarkable Robert Ryan (was he ever given proper credit as a great American actor?) headed a cast composed of players who normally are given short shrift in any discussion of real actors. Yet it is difficult to conceive of others who would so perfectly fit their roles as did Aldo Ray, Tina Louise, Buddy Hackett, Fay Spain, Rex Ingram, Jack Lord, Helen Westcott, Vic Morrow, Michael Landon, and Lance Fuller.

Forget every other movie about an artist you have ever seen. They all pale before Alec Guinness's amazing portrayal of Gulley Jimson in *The Horse's Mouth,* the film adapted by Guinness himself from the Joyce Cary novel. The mad, dedicated Gulley may be the masterpiece characterization in the entire gallery of notable Guinness. Honors, too, to director Ronald Neame and to Kay Walsh heading an excellent supporting cast (Renée Houston, Mike Morgan, Michael Gough, and Robert Coote).

Marvelous actors can do a lot for even an inferior script. *Hot Spell* could have been trivial family drama. That it succeeded in being, for the most part, poignantly touching is primarily due to the actors who played under Daniel Mann's direction. Shirley Booth was a pitiful woman trying to hold on to her family. Anthony Quinn made an unlikable husband real and understandable. Their children were given depth by Shirley MacLaine, Clint Kimbrough, and Earl Holliman. Eileen Heckart's talents made something special of what could have been a silly and superfluous comedy scene. (Screenplay by James Poe.)

Michael Gough and Alec Guinness in *The Horse's Mouth.*

Shirley MacLaine and Shirley Booth in *Hot Spell*.

Cyd Charisse and Robert Taylor discover a suicide in *Party Girl*.

Henry Fonda, Susan Strasberg, Joan Greenwood, and Christopher Plummer in *Stage Struck*.

Gary Cooper and Suzy Parker as the girl with whom he falls in love in *Ten North Frederick.*

Partisans of director Nicholas Ray have raised *Party Girl* to the status of a cult film. It was a good, fast gangster film, a throwback to another era. In another era, it would have been just one more example of an okay but not especially noteworthy film of its type. It did give Cyd Charisse one of her rare chances to prove that she could have been more than a luscious dancing girl with incredible legs. Robert Taylor, Lee J. Cobb, and John Ireland played standard roles in standard style. George Wells wrote the screenplay.

The basic story line of Zoe Akins's *Morning Glory* had been done so often that a new version, *Stage Struck,* in 1958 seemed a thrice-told tale, even with Ruth and Augustus Goetz's intelligent script. Nor could all the talents of Susan Strasberg erase the memory of Katharine Hepburn who had made the lead role her own some twenty-five years earlier. Still the picture gave us a first chance to witness Sidney Lumet's love affair with New York and the theater. No director has a better eye. And a distinguished cast—Henry Fonda, Christopher Plummer, Joan Greenwood, and Herbert Marshall—brought quality to their roles and to the picture.

Although John O'Hara's big book was watered down to what became primarily another May-December romance of an aging lawyer with family problems and a much younger model, *Ten North Frederick* remained an interesting film, primarily because of the actors. Gary Cooper played away from his usual strong, silent image and Suzy Parker brought more than her cover girl looks to her role. Geraldine Fitzgerald, in her first screen role in years, came back as a strong character actress. Ray Stricklyn and Diane Varsi were the difficult children. Screenplay and direction by Philip Dunne.

Other Forgotten 1958 Films to Remember

Nicholas Ray's *Bitter Victory* teamed Richard Burton and Curt Jurgens in a strong personal drama played against the background of the African campaign in World War II. . . . *The Bravados* was a well-made Western with Gregory Peck, more steely than ever, as a man, bent on revenge, tracking down killers. . . . Glenn Ford was a straightforward Western leading man in both *Cowboy* and *Sheepman* but other cast members gave both pictures unexpected amusing touches—Jack Lemmon in the first; Shirley MacLaine, Mickey Shaughnessy, and Edgar Buchanan in *Sheepman* . . . *The Doctor's Dilemma* did not translate to the screen as well as some other Shaw plays; still there were the formidable presences of actors like Dirk Bogarde, Robert Morley, Alastair Sim, Felix Aylmer, and Leslie Caron. . . . *Home Before Dark* may have resembled the book length novel you'd read in a woman's magazine but Jean Simmons's performance made her character wrenching. . . . Two flimsy plays—Norman Krasna's *Kind Sir* and William Douglas Home's *The Reluctant Debutante*—made much more satisfactory movies because of the direction and casting. Krasna also did his screenplay, retitled *Indiscreet* for director Stanley Donen and stars Cary Grant and Ingrid Bergman. Home adapted his play with Vincente Minnelli directing; Rex Harrison, Kay Kendall, Angela Lansbury to star. . . .

Sophia Loren and William Holden, aided by Trevor Howard, played out a rather murky wartime love story, directed by Carol Reed, in *The Key.* . . . It wasn't a success—audiences want Billy the Kid played straight —but Paul Newman, director Arthur Penn, writers Gore Vidal and Leslie Stevens made an interesting try with the decidedly offbeat *The Left Handed Gun.* . . . Thornton Wilder's *The Matchmaker* was transferred to the screen in style by Joseph Anthony with just the right actors—Shirley Booth, Paul Ford, Anthony Perkins, Robert Morse, and Shirley MacLaine—in the roles. . . . *A Night to Remember* recreated the disaster of the Titanic in a well-made film. . . . Although Audie Murphy was badly miscast and Graham Greene's anti-American venom was diluted, *The Quiet American* was still superior screenfare, due largely to the writing and direction of Joseph L. Mankiewicz and a brilliant performance by Michael Redgrave. . . . Max Shulman's *Mad* magazine type of comedy writing didn't travel too well to the screen in *Rally Round the Flag, Boys!* but it did give Joan Collins a chance to be unexpectedly very funny— she always was sexy—but without equal opportunities for Paul Newman and Joanne Woodward. . . . Clark Gable and Doris Day made a surprisingly effective team as a hard-bitten newspaper editor and a journalism professor in an amusing movie, *Teacher's Pet.* . . . *The Truth About Woman* was reminiscent, to its detriment, of one of those Ernst Lubitsch comedies but the cast (Laurence Harvey, Julie Harris, Eva Gabor, Mai Zetterling, Diane Cilento, and others) gave it style. . . .

Chapter Thirty-One

The Movie Year of 1959

By 1959 most of the really big stars who dominated our screens in the 1930s, 1940s, and 1950s are gone and a new breed is taking over. Women's movies—the kind that carried Davis and Crawford, Garbo, Stanwyck, and the rest through the years—are almost a thing of the past. Among women, Elizabeth Taylor is potent. So, of course, are Marilyn Monroe, Audrey Hepburn, Joanne Woodward, Shirley MacLaine, a few others. But the great days of the girls are coming to an end.

The movie world as we knew it has changed—from production to distribution—and all of the changes that will show up in the 1960s are already evident in 1959.

George C. Scott is the only new movie name who shows immediate screen excitement (in *Anatomy of a Murder*) although some of the others will establish themselves. They include James Coburn and Annette Funicello as well as Shirley Knight, Maggie Smith, Colleen Dewhurst, Cicely Tyson, Margaret Phillips, Harry Millard, Millie Perkins, Diane Baker, Donna Ander-

son, Constance Towers, Julie Newmar, Strother Martin, Bethel Leslie, Zohra Lampert, Anne Jackson, Haya Harareet, Warren Berlinger, Ina Balin, Fabian, Barbara Eden, Michael Callan, and, from television where you watched them grow up, David and Ricky Nelson.

Let's list pictures of the year alphabetically—Otto Preminger's *Anatomy of a Murder;* William Wyler's *Ben Hur;* Richard Fleischer's *Compulsion;* George Stevens's *The Diary of Anne Frank;* Sidney Lumets *The Fugitive Kind;* Alfred Hitchcock's *North by Northwest;* Fred Zinnemann's *The Nun's Story;* Jack Clayton's *Room at the Top;* and add Douglas Sirk's *Imitation of Life;* Michael Gordon's *Pillow Talk;* Preminger's *Porgy and Bess;* Hawks's *Rio Bravo;* Martin Ritt's *The Sound and the Fury;* Joseph L. Mankiewicz's *Suddenly Last Summer;* and maybe best of all—certainly the most fun —Billy Wilder's *Some Like It Hot.*

And there were some good ones you probably don't remember.

Forgotten Films of 1959

John Ford had two pictures released in 1959—both, for him, quite minor items but, because they were Ford, to be noted. The more successful was the more unusual. This was *Gideon of Scotland Yard,* made in London and merely detailing one day in the life and work of a Scotland Yard inspector. Jack Hawkins was just right for such a role and the script, by T. E. B. Clarke, had plenty of understated humor and some mild suspense. *The Horse Soldiers* was closer to what you'd expect from Ford—another cavalry action picture starring, of course, John Wayne with William Holden as a likely antagonist. The screen play by John Lee Mahin and Martin Rackin was routine but Ford could always pull out some entertainment when he was dealing with men and horses in battle.

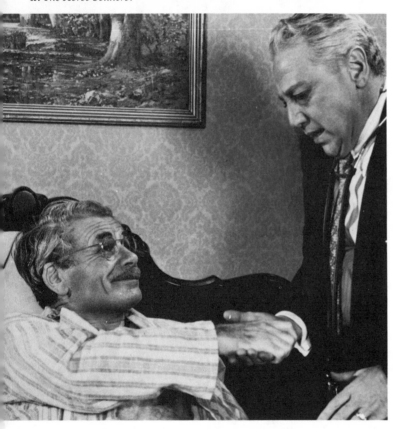

John Wayne, William Holden, and Constance Towers in *The Horse Soldiers.*

Paul Muni and Luther Adler in *The Last Angry Man.*

After many years away from the screen, Paul Muni returned in a picture that turned out to be his final film performance, *The Last Angry Man.* Gerald Green's screenplay, based on his own novel as adapted by Richard Murphy, gave Muni the role of an aged doctor still maintaining his individuality in changing times. Muni, who was always most watchable when he played without restraint, did exactly that. But Luther Adler matched his performance as a more worldly associate. Other good actors—David Wayne, Billy Dee Williams, Joby Baker, Joanna Moore, Nancy R. Pollock, Claudia McNeil, and Godfrey Cambridge—contributed, too. Daniel Mann directed.

Dore Schary couldn't have found better actors—Montgomery Clift, Robert Ryan, Myrna Loy, Maureen Stapleton, and Frank Maxwell—to play the tortured principal characters in the film he produced and scripted from Nathaniel West's *Miss Lonelyhearts* but somehow the agonized drama of West's novels does not really survive in transition to the screen. (That would be true again with his *Day of the Locust.*) Vincent J. Donehue directed the film retitled *Lonelyhearts.*

Romain Gary's novel, *Colors of the Day,* provided the source but *The Man Who Understood Women* was really a Nunnally Johnson creation—he wrote, directed, and produced. For the better part, it was a sharp and witty study of a Hollywood "genius" and his wife whom he has molded into a famous star. Although it eventually disintegrated into rather muddled melodrama, that doesn't explain why it was generally passed over at the time of release and why it is barely remembered now. Henry Fonda played expertly against type

in, for him, a rare flamboyant role. Leslie Caron was winning, with Cesare Danova and Myron McCormick standing out, too. But today it's as if it had never been made. It is never revived even in a festival of Fonda films, barely mentioned even in a discussion of his entire career.

The Mating Game is overlooked in any history of comedy movies but it was just about as funny as a movie could get. William Roberts's screenplay, based on a novel by H. E. Bates, was a variation on the joke about the traveling salesman (here a tax collector) and the farmer's daughter. That old pro, director George Marshall, knew just how to keep it rolling merrily along. Debbie Reynolds always had her own special pert appeal; here she had all the pizzazz of a Lombard as well. Paul Douglas, Fred Clark, and Una Merkel did the things they did best. But the real joy was Tony Randall —in another era a performance like his would have enshrined him with Hollywood's comedy greats. But, as the 1960s approached, nobody was paying much attention to movie comedy—even when it was as hilarious as in *The Mating Game*.

Of course, nobody can write about the everyday lives of ordinary people with more insight and compassion than

You wouldn't know from Leslie Caron's expression but Henry Fonda is *The Man Who Understood Women*.

Paddy Chayefsky. *Middle of the Night,* his sad little love story of a middle-aged Jewish garment manufacturer and a disillusioned young divorcee, worked on Broadway, as played by Edward G. Robinson and Gena Rowlands. Chayefsky himself wrote the screenplay and Delbert Mann, his principal movie collaborator (*Marty, Bachelor Party*) again directed. Supporting actors (like Lee Grant, Martin Balsam, Joan Copeland, Glenda Farrell, Edith Meiser, and Lee Phillips) were well cast. But then there were those two leads. Nobody was more physically imposing, even in his later years, than Fredric March but the very fact of his being Fredric March made him all wrong for this part. And Kim Novak was totally out of it in a role that required some emotional depth.

Odds Against Tomorrow vividly explored the conflict between two bankrobbers—one black, one a vicious bigot. Nobody could play that latter character as well as Robert Ryan. Nobody could be more attractive than Harry Belafonte. So they gave an extra dramatic dimension to a tough crime drama, as written by John O. Killens and William P. McGivern and directed by Robert Wise. Ed Begley, Shelley Winters, and Gloria Grahame were prominent, too.

Fredric March and Kim Novak in *Middle of the Night*.

Race relations were again an issue in *Sapphire,* a tense British murder mystery. Janet Green's screenplay, directed by Basil Dearden, was provocative. Good actors —Nigel Patrick, Yvonne Mitchell, Michael Craig, Paul Massie, Earl Cameron, Gordon Heath, and Bernard Miles—played assorted investigators and suspects.

Clifford Odets wrote and directed a strong, realistic courtroom drama in *The Story on Page One.* Although Rita Hayworth and Gig Young were cast as adulterous lovers on trial for the murder of her husband, their characters were drab, never glamourized. Anthony Franciosa can be an electric actor when he gets the right character to play. He had it here as attorney for the defense. Other good actors, notably Mildred Dunnock, Sanford Meisner, and Hugh Griffith, had their innings, too.

There was nothing in the credits (screenplay by Walter Bernstein from a story by Robert Lowry) to prove it but there was every reason for those with sharp movie memories to presume that *That Kind of Woman* was an updated version of *Shopworn Angel.* The latter (filmed in

Robert Ryan and Harry Belafonte in *Odds Against Tomorrow*.

1929 and remade in 1938) had to do with a kept woman (Nancy Carroll in the first; Margaret Sullavan in the remake) who sacrificed her wealthy protector (Paul Lukas; Walter Pidgeon) when she is touched by and then falls in love with a naive World War I soldier (Gary Cooper; James Stewart). The story line this time was the same except that the period was World War II; the woman, as played by a luscious Sophia Loren, was an international playgirl rather than a chorus cutie. It was considered smart to put down Tab Hunter, but he was capable of sensitive performances. This was one of them. George Sanders, Barbara Nichols, Jack Warden, and Keenan Wynn contributed, too, and Director Sidney Lumet again lovingly used New York locations. The critics sat down pretty hard on this. But the director and actors made it work well.

Warlock had all the elements of the best Westerns but it was more than just a Western. Robert Alan Aurthur's screenplay, based on Oakley Hall's novel, did not stint on conventional action but it also had some strong psychological twists. Henry Fonda again played a cool, nerveless marshal—"the fastest gun in the West"—but there was much more to his characterization in relationship to the Anthony Quinn character, a hanger-on who lives in the reflection of the marshal's glory, with hints of latent homosexuality. These two kept it out of the conventional rut but there was good work, too, by Richard Widmark, Dorothy Malone, Dolores Michaels, and a number of old timers—Richard Arlen, Wallace Ford, Tom Drake, De Forrest Kelley, Regis Toomey, and others. Edward Dmytryk directed.

Other Forgotten 1959 Movies to Remember

Anthony Franciosa was very believable as an actor trying to get a break and there were other interesting people (Shirley MacLaine, Dean Martin, Joan Blackman, and Carolyn Jones) on hand but *Career* generally explored territory that was all too familiar. . . . Laurence Olivier's General Burgoyne was a brilliant performance, but a short one; otherwise George Bernard Shaw's *The Devil's Disciple* was curiously flat on screen with Burt Lancaster and Kirk Douglas unexciting in the leads. . . . Audrey Hepburn was just the actress to play the "bird girl" in *Green Mansions* but the strange mysticism of the W. H. Hudson novel lacked poetry in its adaptation to the screen. . . . Dirk Bogarde was notable in a moderately interesting courtroom drama, *Libel.* . . .

Somehow *The Scapegoat* didn't come close to living up to its potential (a Gore Vidal adaptation of a Daphne Du Murier best seller with Alec Guinness in a dual role and other actors like Bette Davis, Irene Worth, Nicole Maurey, and Pamela Brown) but, with that line-up, it had its moments. . . . The actors were the reasons for

Tony Randall and Debbie Reynolds in *The Mating Game.*

Olga Lindo and Paul Massie in *Sapphire.*

mentioning both *A Summer Place* and *This Earth Is Mine,* not their routine stories—Dorothy McGuire, Arthur Kennedy, Richard Egan, Constance Ford, and a lovely bit by Beulah Bondi in the first; McGuire again, Claude Rains, Jean Simmons, Rock Hudson in the second. . . . And again it was the actors—Paul Newman, Alexis Smith, Barbara Rush, Billie Burke, Brian Keith, John Williams, and particularly Robert Vaughn—who counted most in *The Young Philadelphians.* . . .

That's George Sanders being embraced by Sophia Loren in *That Kind of Woman*. Tab Hunter and buddies Keenan Wynn and Jack Warden aren't happy about it.

Anthony Franciosa defends Rita Hayworth and Gig Young in *The Story on Page One*. Biff Elliot is at the left.

Henry Fonda in the classic shoot-out in *Warlock*.

Chapter Thirty Two

The 1960s and 1970s

And then the 1960s. And the 1970s.

The movie studios have lost their contract players. Jane Fonda, say, works in a Warners picture today, but tomorrow it will be Columbia. And then 20th Century-Fox. But work she does. And work. And work.

She is one of the few women in American movies with the same star magic as those ladies of the past. Streisand has it—when she can get around to making a film. Faye Dunaway occasionally. There are European actresses like Liv Ullmann, Glenda Jackson, Vanessa Redgrave, Julie Christie, a few others. But not Raquel, not Dyan, not Jacqueline or Jennifer.

On the other hand, the actors flourish. We have "the buddies." There is a period when men don't have leading ladies—just some feminine types hovering vaguely in the background. It's Newman and Redford, Redford and Hoffman, Hoffman and Voight or McQueen, McQueen and back to Newman again. Not to forget Beatty and Nicholson. Nicholson and Brando, Brando and Pacino, Pacino and Hackman, Hackman and Beatty (but maybe that doesn't count—we seem to remember a Dunaway in there, too). And don't forget Fonda and Hopper, Fonda and Stewart—different Fondas, different kinds of buddies.

Among women, there is still impact from some holdovers from the 1950s—Elizabeth Taylor, Shirley MacLaine, Audrey Hepburn, and Joanne Woodward are examples. But of actresses beginning their careers in the 1960s, only those few mentioned earlier have real voltage. Actresses who, in another generation, might have become major film names—Jessica Walter is an example—give up and defect to television.

But then, in the late 1970s, movies for women begin to come back. Actresses new to this decade—like Diane Keaton, Jill Clayburgh, Ellen Burstyn, and Sally Field—score while Shirley MacLaine and Anne Bancroft regain some of their glory. Meryl Streep and Jane Alexander, both already stage names, are on their way to equal screen prominence. Jane Fonda lives up to the prediction

once made by Pauline Kael—that she would become the Bette Davis of the 1970s.

"Going to the movies" is a whole new thing. The magnificent movie cathedrals are gone—turned into parking lots or perhaps gutted and converted into three or four small "cinemas" where there once was one. Huge percentages of what were the moviegoing public now stay home and do their moviegoing on television where the best pictures show up on Home Box Office within a matter of months and are presented free (even if edited and with plenty of breaks for commercials) a year or two later. It beats standing in line to pay your $4 or $5 per movie.

By the 1970s, there is almost complete freedom about what can be seen on the screen. The hardcore porno films have moved from stag parties and smokers and are available in side street theaters in almost any moderate size city. Some of them—*Deep Throat* is the best example—have even become rather chic.

But there seem to be no holds barred in even the output of the major movie studios. By the end of the 1960s and the beginning of the 1970s, movies like *Who's Afraid of Virginia Woolf?* and *Midnight Cowboy* are daringly flirting with "X" ratings. But soon, there is no stir at all even at the realistic serviceman language in Jack Nicholson's *The Last Detail* or such explicit sex scenes as that between Julie Christie and Donald Sutherland in *Don't Look Now.* The violence of the Arthur Penn/Warren Beatty *Bonnie and Clyde* causes some shocked editorials but, before long, there are Sam Peckinpah, Charles Bronson's *Death Wish,* and worse.

By the end of the 1970s, we're completely accustomed to blood, gore, and sex in all its variations. So what else is new?

Fifty years have passed since the movies began talking in earnest. There have been roller coaster ups-and-downs. And every time they tell us that depression or inflation, radio or television, miniature golf or canasta has finally licked Hollywood, the motion picture industry springs back more healthy than ever with the kind of entertainment that you can find nowhere else—not on your 21-inch screen, not within the confines of a theatre proscenium, not in the splashiest aquacade ever dreamed up by Billy Rose.

It's hard to find "forgotten films" of the 1960s and 1970s. If they were good enough to be considered, they survive in regular television showings or in the hundreds of revival theatres that have sprung up. Those you don't remember are generally not worth remembering.

Pictures like Michael Ritchie's *Smile* or Jonathan Demme's *Citizen's Band* may have made a disappointing theater showing but every true buff knows about them. Sidney Lumet's remarkable *The Offense* is withdrawn after bad box-office reaction. That also happens with films like Arthur Penn's *Mickey One*, John Frankenheimer's *Seconds*, and Joseph Losey's *The Go Between*. But critics write about them and they show up on TV. Hal Ashby's *Harold and Maude* is an example of a picture that might have been forgotten but has become a cult film. The same is happening for others—Harold Prince's *Something for Everyone*, for example. The ultimate in cults are such as *The Night of the Living Dead* and, particularly, *The Rocky Horror Picture Show*, which have won their own immortality on Saturday midnights.

But there are still those films which are in danger of becoming, in another decade or two, what those in the body of this book have already become—movies you may not remember that are too worthy to forget. The following lists a few of them in alphabetical order, with a parenthetical nod to the participants most involved in making them movies that should remain in the lists of worthwhile films of screen history.

The Abominable Dr. Phibes: Directed by Robert Fuest, written by James Whiten and William Goldstein, with Vincent Price and Virginia North.

Accident: Directed by Joseph Losey, screenplay by Harold Pinter, with Dirk Bogarde, Stanley Baker, Michael York, Vivien Merchant, and Delphine Seyrig.

All Fall Down: Directed by John Frankenheimer, screenplay by William Inge from James Leo Herlihy's original, with Warren Beatty, Eva Marie Saint, Brandon de Wilde, Angela Lansbury, and Karl Malden.

All The Way Home: Directed by Alex Segal, written by James Agee, Tad Mosel, and Philip Reisman, Jr., with Robert Preston, Jean Simmons, Aline MacMahon, and Pat Hingle.

America, America: Written, produced, and directed by Elia Kazan.

Badlands: Written and directed by Terrence Malick, with Martin Sheen, Sissy Spacek, and Warren Oates.

The Ballad of Cable Hogue: Directed by Sam Peckinpah, screenplay by John Crawford and Edmund Penney, with Jason Robards, Stella Stevens, David Warner, and Strother Martin.

A Big Hand for the Little Lady: Directed by Fielder Cook, screenplay by Sidney Carroll, with Henry Fonda, Joanne Woodward, Jason Robards, Kevin McCarthy, and Burgess Meredith.

Billy Budd: Directed and written (with DeWitt Bodeen) by Peter Ustinov, with Robert Ryan, Terence Stamp, Peter Ustinov, Melvyn Douglas, and John Neville.

The Bliss of Mrs. Blossom: Written by Alec Coppel, Josef Shaftel, and Denis Norden, with Shirley MacLaine, James Booth, and Richard Attenborough.

Blume in Love: Written, directed, and produced by Paul Mazursky, with George Segal, Susan Anspach, Kris Kristofferson, and Marsha Mason.

Child's Play: Directed by Sidney Lumet, screenplay by Leon Prochnik from Robert Marasco play, with Robert Preston, James Mason, Beau Bridges, and David Rounds.

The Comic: Directed and written (with Aaron Ruben) by Carl Reiner, with Dick Van Dyke, Mickey Rooney, Michele Lee, and Cornel Wilde.

The Conversation: Written and directed by Francis Ford Coppola, with Gene Hackman, John Cazale, Cindy Williams, and Frederic Forrest.

A Day in the Death of Joe Egg: Directed by Peter Medak, written by Peter Nichols with Alan Bates and Janet Suzman.

Desperate Characters: Written and directed by Frank D. Gilroy, with Shirley MacLaine, Kenneth Mars, Sada Thompson, and Gerald O'Laughlin.

The Downhill Racer: Directed by Michael Ritchie, screenplay by James Salter, with Robert Redford and Gene Hackman.

The Effect of Gamma Rays on the Man-in-the-Moon Marigolds: Directed by Paul Newman, screenplay by Alvin Sargent based on play by Paul Zindel, with Joanne Woodward, Nell Potts, and Roberta Wallach.

End of the Road: Directed by Aram Avakian, screenplay by Dennis McGuire, Terry Southern, and Avakian from John Barth novel, with Stacy Keach, Harris Yulin, Dorothy Tristan, and James Earl Jones.

Entertaining Mr. Sloane: Directed by Douglas Hickox, screenplay by Clive Exton from play by Joe Orton, with Peter McEnery, Beryl Reed, Harry Andrews, and Alan Webb.

The Family Way: Directed by John and Roy Boulting, written by Bill Naughton, with John Mills, Marjorie Rhodes, Hywel Bennett, and Hayley Mills.

Fat City: Directed by John Huston, written by Leonard Gardner, with Stacy Keach, Jeff Bridges, Susan Tyrrell, and Candy Clark.

The Grasshopper: Directed by Jerry Paris, screenplay by Jerry Belson and Garry Marshall, with Jacqueline Bisset and Jim Brown.

The Green Carnation: Directed and written by Ken Hughes, with Peter Finch, Yvonne Mitchell, Nigel Patrick, John Fraser, Lionel Jeffries, James Mason, and James Booth.

Happy Ending: Produced, written, and directed by Richard Brooks, with Jean Simmons, John Forsythe, Teresa Wright, Lloyd Bridges, and Shirley Jones.

Hard Times: Directed by Walter Hill, screenplay by Hill, Bryan Gindorff, and Bruce Henstell, with Charles Bronson, James Coburn, Strother Martin, and Jill Ireland.

The Heart Is a Lonely Hunter: Directed by Robert Ellis Miller, screenplay by Thomas Ryan from Carson McCullers's novel, with Alan Arkin, Sondra Locke, Stacy Keach, Cicely Tyson, Chuck McCann, and Percy Rodriguez.

Hearts of the West: Directed by Howard Zieff, screenplay by Bob Thompson, with Jeff Bridges, Andy Griffith, Blythe Danner, Alan Arkin, and Donald Pleasance.

The Honeymoon Killers: Written and directed by Leonard Kastle. With Shirley Stoler, Tony Lo Bianco, and Doris Roberts.

The Iceman Cometh: Play by Eugene O'Neill directed by John Frankenheimer, with Robert Ryan, Fredric March, Jeff Bridges, Bradford Dillman, George Voskovec, and Moses Gunn.

Junior Bonner: Directed by Sam Peckinpah, with Robert Preston, Ida Lupino, Ben Johnson, Steve McQueen, and Joe Don Baker.

A Kind of Loving: Directed by John Schlesinger, screenplay by Willis Hall and Keith Waterhouse, with Alan Bates and June Ritchie.

King and Country: Directed by Joseph Losey, screenplay by Evan Jones, with Dirk Bogarde and Tom Courtenay.

King of Marvin Gardens: Directed by Bob Rafelson, screenplay by Jacob Brackman, with Jack Nicholson, Bruce Dern, and Ellen Burstyn.

The L-Shaped Room: Directed and screenplay by Bryan Forbes, with Leslie Caron, Brock Peters, Cicely Courtneidge, Emlyn Williams, Tom Bell, and Kay Walsh.

The Last American Hero: Directed by Lamont Johnson, written by William Roberts, with Jeff Bridges, Geraldine Fitzgerald, Gary Busey, Art Lund, and Valerie Perrine.

Law and Disorder: Directed by Ivan Passer, screenplay by Passer, William Richert, and Kenneth Harris Feldman, with Carroll O'Connor and Ernest Borgnine.

Lilith: Directed by Robert Rossen, screenplay by Rossen, with Warren Beatty, Jean Seberg, Peter Fonda, Kim Hunter, Anne Meachum, Jessica Walter, and Gene Hackman.

Lord Love a Duck: Directed and written (with Al Hine and Larry H. Johnson) by George Axelrod, with Roddy McDowall, Tuesday Weld, Ruth Gordon, and Lola Albright.

Loves of Isadora: Directed by Karel Reisz, screenplay by Melvyn Bragg and Clive Exton, with Vanessa Redgrave, James Fox, and Jason Robards.

Loving: Directed by Irvin Kershner, screenplay by Don Devlin, with George Segal, Eva Marie Saint, Keenan Wynn, and Sterling Hayden.

Madigan: Directed by Don Siegel, written by Henry Simoun, Abraham Polonsky, and Richard Dougherty, with Henry Fonda, Richard Widmark, Steve Ihnat, Sheree North, Harry Guardino, James Whitmore, and Don Stroud.

Medium Cool: Directed and written by Haskell Wexler, with Robert Forster, Verna Bloom, and Peter Bonerz.

A New Leaf: Directed, written, and starring Elaine May, with Walter Matthau, Jack Weston, George Rose, James Coco, and Doris Roberts.

No Love for Johnnie: Directed by Ralph Thomas, screenplay by Nicholas Phipps, with Peter Finch, Stanley Holloway, Donald Pleasance, Mary Peach, and Billie Whitelaw.

Payday: Directed by Daryl Duke, written by Don Carpenter, with Rip Torn.

Petulia: Directed by Richard Lester, written by Lawrence B. Marcus, with Julie Christie, George C. Scott, Richard Chamberlain, Shirley Knight, and Arthur Hill.

Play It As It Lays: Directed by Frank Perry, written by Joan Didion, John Gregory Dunne, with Tuesday Weld, Anthony Perkins, Tammy Grimes, Adam Roarke, and Ruth Ford.

Pretty Poison: Directed by Noel Black, screenplay by Lorenzo Semple, Jr., with Anthony Perkins and Tuesday Weld.

The Private Life of Sherlock Holmes: Directed and written (with I. A. L. Diamond) by Billy Wilder, with Robert Stephens, Colin Blakely, and Genevieve Page.

The Pumpkin Eater: Directed by Jack Clayton, written by Harold Pinter and Penelope Mortimer, with Anne Bancroft, Peter Finch, James Mason, Cedric Hardwicke, Alan Webb, and Maggie Smith.

The Rain People: Written and directed by Francis Ford Coppola, with Shirley Knight, James Caan, and Robert Duvall.

Requiem for a Heavyweight: Directed by Ralph Nelson, screenplay by Rod Serling, with Anthony Quinn, Mickey Rooney, Jackie Gleason, and Julie Harris.

The Rounders: Directed and written by Burt Kennedy, with Henry Fonda, Glenn Ford.

Seance on a Wet Afternoon: Written and directed by Bryan Forbes, with Kim Stanley and Richard Attenborough.

Secret Ceremony: Directed by Joseph Losey, screenplay by George Tobori, with Elizabeth Taylor, Mia Farrow, Peggy Ashcroft, Pamela Brown, and Robert Mitchum.

7 Women: Directed by John Ford, with Anne Bancroft, Margaret Leighton, Flora Robson, Betty Field, Mildred Dunnock, Sue Lyon, Anna Lee, and Eddie Albert.

Sisters: Written (with Louisa Rosa) and directed by Brian De Palma, with Margot Kidder, Jennifer Salt, and Charles Durning.

Sometimes a Great Notion: Directed by Paul Newman, adapted from Ken Kesey novel by John Gay, with Newman, Henry Fonda, Richard Jaeckel, Lee Remick, and Michael Sarrazin.

Thieves Like Us: Directed by Robert Altman, adapted from Edward Anderson novel by Altman, Calder Willingham, and Joan Tewkesbury, with Shelley Duvall, Keith Carradine, John Schuck, Bert Remsen, and Louise Fletcher.

This Sporting Life: Directed by Lindsay Anderson, written by David Storey, with Richard Harris, Rachel Roberts, Alan Badel, and Colin Blakely.

Tomorrow: Directed by Joseph Anthony, written by Horton Foote from a William Faulkner story, with Robert Duvall.

Two Weeks In Another Town: Directed by Vincente Minnelli; written by Irwin Shaw, Charles Schnes; with Kirk Douglas, Edward G. Robinson, Cyd Charisse, Claire Trevor, and George Hamilton.

Victim: Directed by Basil Dearden, screenplay by Janet Green and John McCormick, with Dirk Bogarde, Peter McEnery, Dennis Price, and Sylvia Sims.

Wanda: Written, directed, and starring Barbara Loden, with Michael Higgins.

What's the Matter with Helen? Directed by Curtis Harrington, written by Henry Farrell, with Debbie Reynolds, Shelley Winters, Dennis Weaver, Michael McLiammoir, and Agnes Moorehead.

The Whisperers: Written (with Robert Nicolson) and directed by Bryan Forbes, with Dame Edith Evans, Eric Portman, and Nanette Newman.

Wild River: Directed by Elia Kazan, written by Paul Osborn, William Bradford Huie, and Bordon Deal, with Montgomery Clift, Lee Remick, and Jo Van Fleet.

Zandy's Bride: Directed by Jan Troell, screenplay by Marc Norman, with Liv Ullmann, Gene Hackman, and Eileen Heckart.

And come to think of it, a good many of these have already joined the lists of Forgotten Films to Remember.